Women and Documentary Film in Contemporary Iran

Women and Documentary Film in Contemporary Iran

Reframing Reality

Najmeh Moradiyan-Rizi

EDINBURGH
University Press

Edinburgh University Press is one of the leading university presses in the UK. We publish academic books and journals in our selected subject areas across the humanities and social sciences, combining cutting-edge scholarship with high editorial and production values to produce academic works of lasting importance. For more information visit our website: edinburghuniversitypress.com

Grateful acknowledgement is made to the sources listed in the List of Illustrations for permission to reproduce material previously published elsewhere. Every effort has been made to trace the copyright holders, but if any have been inadvertently overlooked, the publisher will be pleased to make the necessary arrangements at the first opportunity.

Edinburgh University Press Ltd
13 Infirmary Street
Edinburgh EH1 1LT

First published in hardback by Edinburgh University Press 2025

Typeset in Monotype Ehrhardt
by Cheshire Typesetting Ltd, Cuddington, Cheshire,
and printed and bound in Great Britain

A CIP record for this book is available from the British Library

ISBN 978 1 3995 2570 1 (hardback)
ISBN 978 1 3995 2571 8 (paperback)
ISBN 978 1 3995 2573 2 (webready PDF)
ISBN 978 1 3995 2572 5 (epub)

Contents

List of Figures

Acknowledgments

This book is the result of more than a decade of thinking, researching, and writing about women and/in Iranian cinema. While my interest in documentary film studies goes back to my undergraduate years in Iran when I was a Cinema student at the Tehran University of Art, the seed for this project was first planted when I was a Ph.D. student in the Department of Film and Media Studies at the University of Kansas. The bulk of the research for this book was conducted at Kansas for my Ph.D. dissertation, and I am forever grateful for a truly supportive and inspiring community that made my Ph.D. education in general, and the writing of the dissertation in particular, such an amazing and life-changing experience. My sincere gratitude goes to my Ph.D. dissertation committee members—Dr. Tamara Falicov, Dr. Nasrin Rahimieh, Dr. Ayesha Hardison, Dr. Joshua Miner, and Professor Robert Hurst—who all showed much support and enthusiasm for my project and offered invaluable insights regarding my dissertation.

At Old Dominion University in Virginia, I had generous support from faculty in the Department of Communication and Theatre Arts, Department of Women's and Gender Studies, Department of World Languages and Cultures, Department of Philosophy and Religious Studies, and the Institute for the Humanities. The research and writing for the final chapter of the book (Chapter 5) were made possible by a Summer Research Fellowship Program Grant from the Office of Research at the Old Dominion University, for which I am very grateful. I am also grateful to Kris King, the curator of the Naro Video at ODU Perry Library, for making sure the quality of the images used in the book meets the publisher's requirements.

My deepest thanks go to my interviewees—Mina Keshavarz, Azadeh Bizargiti, Rakhshan Banietemad, Shirin Barghnavard, Mahnaz Afzali, Nahid Rezaei, Mahvash Sheikholeslami, and Katayoon Shahabi—who graciously accepted to participate in this project and generously shared their experiences and knowledge with me and my readers. I am beyond grateful to Mojtaba Mirtahmasb, who was my main interlocutor and connected me to most of my interviewees. My thanks also go to the staff of the Documentary and Experimental Film Center (DEFC), especially Mrs. Shirin Naderi, as well as the staff of the Iranian Documentary Filmmakers Association (IRDFA), who all patiently took time to answer some inquiries and requests regarding my research.

An earlier version of Chapter 1 was published in *The I.B. Tauris Handbook of Iranian Cinema* (2024), co-edited by Michelle Langford, Maryam Ghorbankarimi, and Zahra Khosroshahi. I am grateful to the editors, Bloomsbury Publishing, and its imprint I.B. Tauris for granting me permission to use the chapter here. At Edinburgh University Press, Gillian Leslie has been a pleasure to work with. She was very supportive and enthusiastic about the project from its beginning and this in turn encouraged me to finish the manuscript in a timely manner. Publishing with Edinburgh University Press is a dream come true, and I thank Nicola Ramsey for making me feel part of the EUP family since the first time we met in 2015 (at the Middle East Studies Association (MESA) annual conference in Denver, Colorado).

Last but not least, my deepest appreciation and recognition go to my kind parents, Manizheh and Amin, whose unwavering love and support and myriad sacrifices made it possible for me to cross continents and pursue my education. Thank you for everything, and this is for you!

Introduction

On September 16, 2022, the death of a twenty-two-year-old Iranian Kurdish woman, Mahsa (Zhina) Amini, at the hands of Iran's notorious morality police for what they deemed her lack of a proper hijab, required for women by the Islamic Republic, sent shockwaves across the country and led to massive anti-government protests that came to be globally known as the Woman, Life, Freedom movement. While the movement has initiated groundbreaking forms of activism through which Iranian women advocate for their agency, bodily autonomy, and freedom, it is also rooted within a long and rich history of feminist activism in the country that has in part showcased itself through the arts, including women's documentary filmmaking.[1] Given the direct connection between documentary and social reality, Iranian women's documentaries have served as a powerful tool for voicing women's perspectives and demands in order to enhance gender equality. As feminist film scholars Kristin Lené Hole and Dijana Jelača aptly observe, "Women documenting their lives in the non-Western world face a struggle on several fronts—they are both critiquing representations of the nation that have excluded women and sexual, religious, and racial minorities, while also forging their own distinct feminist visions that are not subsumed by Western feminist narratives."[2] Discussing the imperatives of such documentary activism within an Iranian context, this study investigates the documentary practices of Iranian women, mostly active in independent documentary production since the late 1990s, in order to highlight a significant revival in documentary film practices in contemporary Iran in terms of both the expansion of the medium's infrastructure and the increasing presence of women documentarians. Drawing on in-depth email interviews, which I conducted over a period of one year with eight leading Iranian women documentary filmmakers and producers—Mina Keshavarz (born in 1984), Azadeh Bizargiti (born in 1979), Shirin Barghnavard (born in 1976), Mahnaz Afzali (born in 1963), Nahid Rezaei (born in 1963), Mahvash Sheikholeslami (born in 1946), Rakhshan

Banietemad (born in 1954), and Katayoon Shahabi (born in 1963)—this study locates a "gendered turn" in contemporary Iranian documentary that depicts itself in both the infrastructures of the practice and the aesthetics and subjects of the documentaries themselves. I contend that the unprecedented and significant rise in Iranian women's involvement in the documentary field since the late 1990s points to broader sociocultural, gender, political, and technological transformations simultaneously occurring in the country. And as such, this "gendered turn" requires an urgent and closer investigation of the state of contemporary Iranian documentary. The interviews are not intended to provide an exhaustive survey of the documentary field in Iran, or to offer a homogenous and fixed perspective on the conditions of documentary practice for all women documentarians working in the country. Rather, to avoid abstract discussions and generalizations in my arguments, the interviews with these selected individuals whose documentary activities this study particularly engages with aim to provide first-hand, micro-level perspectives and experiences regarding Iranian documentary context, thus allowing my readings to go deeper into the fabric of Iran's documentary film culture.

By merging three main (inter)disciplinary areas of documentary film studies, women's and gender studies, and Iranian studies, this study offers, for the first time, a closer and deeper look at Iranian women's documentary practices in relation to the larger context of Iranian society in terms of its gender politics and the broader field of transnational documentary in terms of its production and circulation practices. The volume therefore examines how contemporary women documentarians in Iran have engaged with gender politics and sociocultural and technological changes in recent decades to produce a dynamic new range of documentary modes in regard to production, financing, distribution, and exhibition as well as forms and themes, while at the same time emphasizing the significance of the documentary medium itself for documenting and progressing women's issues.

On May 23, 1997, Mohammad Khatami, a reformist clergy and the former Minister of Culture and Islamic Guidance (1982–1986 and 1989–1992), was swept to victory by the support from Iranian youth and women beginning a period of sociopolitical, economic, and artistic transformations known as the Reform Era (1997–2005). As women's rights scholars Homa Hoodfar and Shadi Sadr observe:

> [U]nder President Rafsanjani (1989–97) many legal reforms were introduced … such as the revision of the law on divorce, women being reinstated as judges in family courts, the introduction of the Office of Women's Affairs, and so on. After the

> election of President Khatami (1997–2005) Iran witnessed the birth of a modern civil society and the expansion of political organisations, including many women's organisations whose *raison d'être* was to advance women's causes and keep gender justice at the centre of public discourse.[3]

This foregrounding of gender issues and the sociopolitical openness in the discursive landscape widened the cinematic space in which not only were the censorship criteria to some extent relaxed,[4] but also, as film and media scholar Hamid Naficy argues, the "documentary filmmakers [were allowed] to emerge from [Iran-Iraq] war wariness and dystopic inertia by producing critical and innovative films."[5] Significantly, while the negotiations for the establishment of the Iranian Documentary Filmmakers Association (IRDFA)—*Anjoman-e mostanadsazan-e sinemay-e Iran*—the first domestic documentarians' guild within the House of Cinema (*Khaneh Sinema*), which is the Iranian alliance of motion picture guilds,[6] began in 1996, it was some months after the election of President Khatami and the changes that occurred in the Ministry of Culture and Islamic Guidance (MCIG) by the appointments of Ataollah Mohajerani as the new Minister, and Seifollah Dad as the new Deputy Minister for Cinematic Affairs, that the IRDFA finally materialized.[7] The establishment of the IRDFA in the House of Cinema in the late 1990s (on January 25, 1998), therefore, marks a significant chapter in the history of Iranian cinema as it became "the first society that pushed for the recognition of the rights of documentary filmmakers, not only those working in the public sector but also those in the commercial and independent sectors."[8] This recognition of documentary and documentary practice at this time, as this book argues, also finds another significance, which is entangled with the rise of both women documentarians and the documentaries produced on women's lives and gender issues in Iran.

The initiation of the so-called Reform Era is thus concomitant with a new breath of change that energized both the documentary cinema and the women's movement.[9] The strong presence of women in the sociocultural and political spheres at this time occurred simultaneously with the rise of women documentarians who turned their cameras to women's lives to foreground their voices and subjectivities. In order to bring these advances in gender and documentary contexts into dialogue with each other and to shed light on the less-studied contributions of Iranian women to documentary cinema in the last decades as well as on the importance of this medium for documenting, advocating, and progressing women's issues in contemporary Iran, this study's goal is two-fold: to "reframe" the discussions on Iranian cinema and its related gender issues, which have been predominantly centered on fiction cinema, by focusing instead on Iranian documentary, and to "reframe" the debates in feminist film studies and documentary film studies, particularly in regard to the notions of realism and authenticity in cross-cultural encounters, which have been understood from a dominantly Eurocentric perspective, by providing instead an account of the complexity of such encounters in regard to Iranian women's lives and the documentary practices associated with them. In this regard, postcolonial studies scholar Lindsey Moore argues that "while productive theoretical debates have taken place recently on the subject of relatively valorized forms of women's agency in diverse cultural contexts, ... a certain fascination remains with images of 'other' women as cultural victims."[10] It is in this context that Moore further suggests that "once subjected to a cross-cultural viewing dynamic, Iranian women on screen continue to signify ethnographically as the 'always already known.'"[11] Therefore, challenging the reductive perception that identifies Iranian women as "cultural victims" is crucial to this study as it unsettles the fixity of truth and verisimilitude associated with realism in both fiction and documentary films by introducing various documentary strategies that Iranian women deploy to perform their agency and subjectivity. The result is a colorful tapestry of artistic visions and commitments that offers audiences and critics across the world a nuanced glimpse of Iranian society and its gender dynamics.

The Iranian documentary cinema, in fact, has never been separated from the complex matrix of Iranian society and politics, and given the interconnected relationship between documentary and sociocultural and political contexts, the consideration of gender issues in regard to this medium is a vital category of analysis. As documentary film scholar Belinda Smaill aptly argues:

> [Documentary] is overwhelmingly the genre to be taken up for advocacy purposes and as a tool within grassroots movements—the documentary genre is crucially tied to the politicization of women's experience. In comparison with fiction feature film, more women work as directors or in key roles in documentary production, making it critical to women's representation in the industry in many parts of the world. Despite this, documentary directors achieve a more modest public profile than their counterparts in fiction. Moreover, documentary has been under-theorized in scholarly approaches to media and cinema.[12]

This "under-theorization" of documentary in general, and women's roles and gender issues in documentary in particular, explicitly shows itself in scholarship on Iranian cinema. The existing works in English either discuss documentary from a historical perspective providing a broad overview of the medium in an Iranian cinematic context (Tahaminejad 2017; Naficy 2011 and 2012; Naficy 1981), or offer comparative or case studies of selected documentary films (Merás 2018; Akhavan 2015; Rahimieh 2009).[13] While the consideration and analyses of gender tropes often come to the fore in the latter category, the main point of the arguments in these works occurs through textual and representational readings. The contextual aspects such as production, distribution, and exhibition, if they are discussed at all, are mostly relegated to the background serving as a foundation for textual analyses or a limited framework for discussing some individual films.

More recently, emerging English-language scholarship showcases an increase in the scholarly and academic attention to the documentary film in Iran (Gharabaghi 2018; Atwood 2016; Sadegh-Vaziri 2015).[14] Yet, in these as well as Persian-language texts on Iranian documentary cinema (Tahaminejad 2011; Emami 2006; Dehghanpour 2003),[15] gender and women's studies still do not constitute the central framework of analysis, and while gender issues are sporadically mentioned in some of these works, in others, they are mostly overlooked. In her 2015 doctoral dissertation, "Iranian Documentary Film Culture: Cinema, Society, and Power 1997–2014" (Philadelphia: Temple University), documentary scholar and filmmaker Persheng Sadegh-Vaziri offers valuable insights into the context of independent documentary filmmaking in Iran between 1997 and 2014, focusing on independent documentarians' films, their working conditions, and their interactions with each other and with the state institutions. While Sadegh-Vaziri points to the significant and increasing presence of Iranian women documentarians and their films, these readings form only some parts of the overall framework, which mainly concentrates on the ways in which independent documentarians navigate various power structures within local and global settings to perform their agency. I draw from Sadegh-Vaziri's valuable insights in my reading of power structures in documentary filmmaking in Iran and within a transnational setting. Yet, I center my study on the ways in which Iranian women documentarians explore these structures to emphasize that the politics of gender is an essential and inevitable factor in regard to these structural and artistic practices.[16]

While discourses on women, gender, and sexuality in Iranian cinema have generated a considerable amount of scholarship, the majority of these works directly link these issues to fiction cinema, thus overlooking documentary (Mottahedeh 2008; Talattof 2011; Naficy 2000; Naficy 1994; Kheshti 2009).[17] For instance, Negar Mottahedeh's influential book, *Displaced Allegories: Post-Revolutionary Iranian Cinema*

(Duke University Press, 2008), engages with feminist film theory in its reading of the politics and aesthetics of post-revolutionary Iranian films and their relation to gender issues. The scope of the book, however, is focused not only on Iranian fiction cinema, but on the works of a few male filmmakers including Bahram Beyzaie, Abbas Kiarostami, and Mohsen Makhmalbaf. In fact, Iranian fiction cinema dominates documentary in various ways: through its dominion over the domestic market in terms of production, distribution, and exhibition; its widely celebrated art-house films within international venues and film festival circuits; and its occupation of the majority of scholarly and critical debates in academia. As such, this study seeks to "reframe" discourses on Iranian cinema and its intersections with women's and gender studies by focusing on the documentary medium. Post-revolutionary Iranian documentary has been in part influenced by cinematic policies and procedures governing post-revolutionary fiction cinema. At the same time, some filmmakers have been active within both cinemas. Yet, I argue that the understanding and reading of the state of post-revolutionary documentary and its achievements through the prism of fiction films—especially since the 1990s, a time that Iranian fiction cinema (also known as the New Iranian Cinema) was celebrated at the international film festivals[18]—prevent us from a thorough comprehension of complexities and specificities pertinent to the documentary medium. In this regard, Hamid Naficy aptly observes, "Postrevolutionary fiction cinema benefited from the continuity of technical personnel and the reinstatement of new-wave directors; postrevolutionary documentary cinema did not rely so much on experienced directors for its revival. … The resurgence of the documentary awaited new filmmakers, including women, and a generational change in the 1990s."[19] As such, while I may allude to the possible convergences and divergences of Iranian documentary cinema with/from Iranian fiction cinema, my foremost goal here is to highlight Iranian women documentarians' works and their activities using the framework of documentary film studies. Examining the state of documentary cinema from a gendered perspective also allows me to advance the existing scholarship on Iranian documentary cinema and to expand our knowledge on this medium based on the experiences and practices of some women documentarians working within national and/or transnational settings.

In 2016, *Film Monthly*, the foremost cinematic magazine in Iran, dedicated a special issue to two decades of Iranian documentary cinema from 1996 to 2016. Rare in its scope and indispensable in its discussions, the issue analyzes the contemporary state of documentary film in Iran over these two decades. The volume's introductory article by Pirooz Kalantari, titled "Chera in bist sal?" ("Why These Twenty Years?"), briefly encapsulates the significance of this periodization, which he refers to as the era of "contemporary Iranian documentary cinema."[20] Some of the characteristics of this period, as Kalantari writes, are:

> The breakaway from the cinematographic era of film negative and the entry to the digital era; the decrease in price of, and the easy access to, documentary-making equipment; the emergence of a new generation, born or raised during the revolutionary years, in the artistic scene, ... and particularly in documentary production; the end of television's monopoly in documentary production and the incredible increase in [the number of] documentary films by over 1000 documentaries per year; the breakaway from the centralization of filmmaking in the capital [Tehran] and [the spread of] filmmaking all over Iran ...; the entry to the virtual world and the connection and interaction with everyone in this new world...[21]

Kalantari's concise mention of myriad transformations occurring between 1996 and 2016 in the documentary field in Iran does not explicitly acknowledge the emergence of women's voices and their increasing presence in the documentary medium as a major transformative factor in contemporary Iranian documentary. In Kalantari's account, this crucial aspect is folded back to a general demographic context and is considered a part of "the emergence of a new generation" of documentarians. Nonetheless, the considerable contributions of women documentarians to the *Film Monthly*'s special issue, who reflect on their activities and the state of contemporary Iranian documentary cinema, as well as various critical engagements with women's documentaries in the issue, attest to the indispensable role of Iranian women in Iranian documentary.

As feminist studies scholar Teresa de Lauretis eloquently puts it, "The historical fact of gender, the fact that it exists in social reality, that it has concrete existence in cultural forms and actual weight in social relations, makes gender a political issue that cannot be evaded or wished away, much as one would want to, be one male or female."[22] The direct connection between women's documentaries and "social reality," influenced by the lived experiences of Iranian women documentarians and their female subjects, therefore provides a crucial perspective on the particularities of Iranian women's lives in contemporary Iran, and allows the merging of theory and practice based on women's experiences. It is only through this merging that, according to feminist studies scholar Margaret A. McLaren, "feminist theory [can] effect social and political change; it must be relevant to the actual, concrete lives of real women. It should be able both to inform and reflect our experience."[23] It is also important to note that to talk about gender and gendered experiences does not mean to remain in the constraints of sexual difference, but to acknowledge that "[t]he sex-gender system ... is both a sociocultural construct and a semiotic apparatus, a system of representation which assigns meaning (identity, value, prestige, location in kinship, status in social hierarchy, etc.) to individuals within the society."[24]

Iranian women's documentary film practices also highlight issues of authorship through the ways in which they present female subjectivity in the fields of production, distribution, and exhibition. Film scholar Patricia White aptly asserts, "Authorship has been of critical importance to feminist film studies, in large part because women's access to the means of production has been historically restricted," and that negating women's exclusions by focusing on their perspectives is "an act of historical retrieval" and "a practical matter of equity."[25] Therefore, the lack of scholarly works on female authorship in documentary field brings a much-needed urgency to this context. In this regard, Boel Ulfsdotter and Anna Backman Rogers contend, "This issue was never addressed in the early days of documentary filmmaking, simply because the person behind the camera was excluded from delineating what a documentary image does beyond its function of documenting, and how it should function prescriptively (especially in relation to Direct Cinema)."[26] The assumption that recording and presenting reality are the foremost mission of the documentary medium, thus, has had a crucial repercussion for documentary authorship and particularly for women's documentary authorship.

In this study, the notion of authorship that I work with projects a form of collective authorship as well. That is, how considering the works and activities of Iranian women documentarians together can show us their collective and shared commitment to foregrounding women's voices and pushing for gender equality, albeit from diverse perspectives and through various documentary methods. This consideration also allows me to better delineate the complexity of various contexts within which these women work to make their documentaries. Patricia White aptly asserts that "no single woman filmmaker is characteristic of current film culture, and singularity should be displaced as a mainstay of authorial ideology."[27] As such, the chapters of this book are organized based on contextual and conceptual grounds rather than on individual women documentarians. In this way, the book is also an intervention in the *auteurist* approaches within the field of Iranian cinema studies, which are not only predominately male-oriented, but also fiction-film-oriented.[28]

The book consists of five chapters that follow the trajectory of Iranian women's documentary film practices from the early stages of financing and production to various forms of distribution and exhibition, and to what ultimately the viewers see as the contents of the films. Chapter 1, "Gendering the Documentary Film Industry in Iran: Sites of Production," provides a thorough discussion of production practices involved in women's documentaries from conceptualizing the projects and navigating funds to making the documentaries. Beginning with a brief history of women's documentary filmmaking in Iran, the chapter then offers a closer look at women's documentary production since the late 1990s, analyzing various governmental, non-governmental, and private institutions that women documentarians navigate to make their films. The goals of the chapter are to investigate possibilities and limitations as well as advantages and disadvantages involved in the matrix of independent documentary filmmaking, and to showcase various negotiations, adjustments, and/or solutions that Iranian women documentarians come up with to materialize their ideas and to produce their films.

Chapter 2, "Watching Iranian Women's Documentaries: Sites of Distribution and Exhibition," focuses on the ways in which the films of Iranian women documentarians are circulated and can be viewed and accessed through theatrical and non-theatrical and formal and informal settings. In this regard, the roles of various distribution and exhibition outlets, such as domestic and international film festivals, specialized and private screenings, television and digital platforms, as well as governmental and private distributors are studied. The chapter further points to the significance of access in shaping the popular engagement with Iranian women's documentaries both domestically and internationally, while also discussing the activities and perseverance of Iranian independent documentarians themselves, which have produced a diversity of modes of circulation and multiple power relations and negotiations in this regard.

Chapter 3, "Discovering the Self in Autobiographical Documentaries: Sites of Self-Reflection," and Chapter 4, "Narrating Women's Lives in Biographical Documentaries: Sites of Recognition," interrogate the "intricate links between the personal and political" as a central manifestation of feminist discourse, which as Kristin Lené Hole and Dijana Jelača discuss, delineate themselves in two ways: through "the insertion of the filmmakers' autobiographical stories in their documentary work," and through the projection of "the personal stories of others."[29] As such, Chapter 3 focuses on contemporary autobiographical documentaries made by Iranian women by first offering a brief historical overview of autobiographical practices by Iranian women, and then highlighting various transformations in Iranian society since the late 1990s that have contributed to the rise of women's autobiographical documentaries. The chapter then provides close readings of three autobiographical documentaries: Mina Keshavarz's *Unwelcome in Tehran* (*Nakhandeh dar Tehran*, 2011), Shirin Barghnavard's *21 Days and Me* (*Bist-o yek rooz va man*, 2011), and the collaborative, episodic documentary *Profession: Documentarist* (*Herfeh: Mostanadsaz*, 2014).

Chapter 4 extends Chapter 3's discussion by focusing on Iranian women's biographical documentaries on Iranian women's lives. The chapter first offers a brief historical overview of biographical films in Iranian cinema, with a particular focus on Iranian documentary, followed by a discussion on the impact of various sociocultural, gender, and political transformations in Iran since the late 1990s that have contributed to the formation of new biographical documentaries on and by women. The chapter concludes its argument by providing close studies of two biographical documentaries: Mahnaz Afzali's *Mother of the Earth* (*Madar-e zamin*, 2017) and Mina Keshavarz's *Braving the Waves* (*Dar miyan-e amvaj*, 2016).

Finally, Chapter 5, "Advocating for Iranian Women through Documentaries: Sites of Negotiation," focuses on social-issue, activist documentaries that strive to have a direct impact on community building, awareness raising, and social change. The chapter highlights diverse activist modes as well as a variety of aesthetic approaches that women's social-issue documentaries employ to shed light on women's rights and status in Iranian society and to motivate change. The chapter further provides close analyses of three case studies: Mahnaz Afzali's *The Ladies Room* (*Zananeh*, 2003), Rakhshan Banietemad's *We Are Half of Iran's Population* (*Ma nimi az jamiyat-e Iranim*, 2009), and Mina Keshavarz's *The Art of Living in Danger* (*Honar-e dar khatar zendegi kardan*, 2020). The chapter argues that these works foreground the voices of ordinary women and activists to present bottom-up resistances that crucially challenge patriarchal and authoritarian structures in Iran while serving as a ground for community building and activism.

Collectively, these chapters put forward a new discussion on Iranian women's filmic practices and activism that showcases their authorial agency and artistic vision through committed collaborations with each other and with the community. As Lindsey Moore puts it, "While it is problematic to generalize a 'native informant' position, Iranian women do engage dynamically with their complex environment and assert the need to localize the politics of feminism."[30] It is my hope, then, that by studying a dynamic and diverse women's documentary scene in contemporary Iran, we get a deeper understanding of women's activism through documentary in the country. The works these women documentarians produce are not only crucial for the current civil and political engagements in Iran and the diaspora, but they are also indispensable historical documents for future generations.

CHAPTER 1

Gendering the Documentary Film Industry in Iran: Sites of Production

A glance at the history of documentary production in Iran attests to the presence of Iranian women in this medium since the early 1960s. Yet as this chapter delineates, Iranian women's increasing involvement in the documentary field since the late 1990s is an unprecedented phenomenon that is the result of key political, social, economic, and technological transformations that have occurred in Iran in recent decades, giving rise to a burgeoning state of documentary filmmaking in the country, especially among women. In fact, the rise of women's involvement in the documentary field is part of a general revival in documentary filmmaking in Iran, which documentary historian and filmmaker Mohammad Tahaminejad calls "the third generation or wave" of Iranian documentary cinema reflecting "the vast presence of digital camera and the increase in tendencies regarding intimate documentary filmmaking by ordinary people across Iran."[1] However, in addition to the digital technologies, which have contributed to both the expansion of the documentary film production and the emergence of new documentary forms and themes, other major factors, including political, social, and economic changes, have helped bring about a documentary revival, at the center of which resides the active presence of Iranian women.

This chapter aims to study Iranian women documentarians' experiences in regard to the context of this new documentary era by focusing on two major goals: First, to offer a thorough discussion of production practices involved in women's independent documentary filmmaking—the organizations and individuals these women work with to support their projects' production; the ways through which they navigate and secure funding; and the delicate strategies they employ to maintain their independence in documentary film production—and second, to examine the shifting social and political dynamics in Iranian society and their effects on these practices. Film and media scholar Shweta Kishore writes that "unlike auteurist studies of individual authors, the study of practice draws attention to the relation between filmmakers as individual subjects but also as members of a collective public located at particular historical moments."[2] The resonances of "a collective public" in specific "historical moments" explicitly show themselves not only in the contents of Iranian women's documentaries, which will be discussed in later chapters, but also in the everyday practices and diverse approaches that these documentarians deploy to "bypass disciplinary and normative socio-economic rationalities."[3]

While independent documentary filmmaking has its own challenges for all Iranian documentarians regardless of their gender, there exist specific unequal practices and gendered biases that necessitate a closer examination of documentary industry based on Iranian women's experiences.[4] In an interview for this study, Mina Keshavarz, the director of such films as *Unwelcome in Tehran* (2011) and *Braving the Waves* (2016), eloquently explained how a documentarian's lived experiences may have an effect on the type of documentaries she creates: "I think the female gaze is dominant in my films not only because I choose topics that are more feminine, but also because I see the topics from a woman's perspective within a society that I grew up in. In fact, my main attraction to topics about discrimination and being a minority derives from the same feeling that I [have] experienced as a woman in Iranian society."[5] This sociocultural and gendered reflection is not separated from the apparatus of documentary production in Iran, as in one way or another, this apparatus is influenced by sociocultural and gender norms governing cultural and artistic production in the country. Keshavarz further asserted, "But what is important for me is the fact that we women can be our own voice through showcasing the world we live in, through expressing how we see life and society."[6] In this regard, this chapter highlights the agency of women documentarians and the multiplicity of their voices and experiences as they explore the matrix of independent documentary filmmaking foregrounding the negotiations, adjustments, and/or solutions that they come up with to materialize their ideas and to assert their artistic visions.

I contend that Iranian women documentarians employ various forms of negotiation, and what I call *adaptive strategies*, to perform and maintain their independence and agency. My term is inspired by Kishore's notion of "tactical practice," which she deploys in the context of Indian independent documentary filmmaking. Kishore defines the term as "a reflective, context-specific adaptation of both organisational and industry conventions, norms and regulations founded on decapitalisation and de-economisation, with the purpose of asserting the artist's self."[7] In this case, it is a strategy that is employed in regard to the use of private and non-governmental organization (NGO) funding by Indian independent documentarians. In the case of Iran, I am extending the documentarians' adaptation of institutional and industry norms to state-run organizations as well. By adaptive, of course, I do not imply a change in ideological and/or visionary stances of the documentarians. Rather, it is the ability to amend regulations when they think it is possible, in order to create productive sites for negotiation and materialization of their projects. Moreover, as I further discuss, women documentarians also use these adaptive strategies in their transnational filmic practices to assert their voice and artistic vision in cross-cultural encounters. As such, adaptive strategies reflect the agency and subjectivity of Iranian documentary filmmakers and producers, and similar to the tactical practice of Indian documentarians "[f]rom within regulated institutional environments," they aim at resisting "the subordination of documentary and, indeed, cultural production to a[n] ... institutionally defined episteme of communication."[8] Correspondingly, in reading the documentary practices of Iranian women, this study considers the concept of independence via a multiplicity of discourses. These are primarily ideological, economic, and thematic in nature, all of which affect the ways in which independent women's documentaries are produced and ultimately distributed, exhibited, and received.[9] To understand the diverse adaptive strategies that these women's documentarians employ in the process of their documentary production and funding, the chapter first offers a brief history of women's documentary filmmaking in Iran, then provides a closer look at women's documentary production since the late 1990s through specific case studies analyzing various governmental, non-governmental, and private organizations that women documentarians navigate to produce their films.

Women and Documentary Filmmaking in Iran: A Historical Overview

Prior to the 1979 Islamic Revolution, only one documentary was made by an Iranian woman: *The House Is Black* (*Khaneh siah ast*, 1962), directed by the famed poet Forugh Farrokhzad (1935–1967). Farrokhzad began her film career through a collaboration with prominent Iranian filmmaker Ebrahim Golestan in his newly-established, semi-independent Golestan Film Studio (established in 1957), which produced mostly documentary films. As film scholar Hamid Naficy points out, "Soon after joining the GFW [Golestan Film Workshop], she moved beyond secretarial duties (for which she had been hired) and into production, working both behind and before the cameras."[10] Farrokhzad edited the short documentary *A Fire* (*Yek atash*, 1961), directed by Ebrahim Golestan, and according to film scholar M. Ali Issari, "it was through her creative editing that a cinematically dull subject, an oil well burning, was turned into an artistic film that won two awards at the Venice Film Festival of 1961."[11] Farrokhzad collaborated with Golestan on several other projects and in 1962 received a commission from a non-governmental organization (NGO), *Anjoman-e komak beh jozamiyan* (The Society for Assistance to Lepers), to produce a documentary that would generate more public support for lepers in Iran.

With a small crew, Farrokhzad shot her black-and-white documentary "in twelve days" in Babadaghi leper colony near Tabriz, in the northwest of Iran.[12] The pioneering twenty-minute documentary used the style of "poetic realism" rather than the authoritative, educational Voice of God, incorporating powerful shots from the daily lives of the lepers, and shots accompanied by the poetic voiceover of Farrokhzad herself. Emphasizing the abundance of institutional sponsorship and their direct involvement in Iranian documentary in pre-revolutionary Iran, Naficy considers the emergence of poetic realism in the 1960s as "a style through which filmmakers subverted the official style of the documentary and its direct, propagandistic force by various lyrical and symbolic uses of indirection, by contrapuntal strategies of sound and image editing, and by poetic narration."[13] All of these stylistic features can be seen in *The House Is Black*. In fact, due to its specific style, the documentary allows for a nuanced and multi-layered critical reading of the state of Iranian society at the time through some of its most marginalized members. Iranian studies scholar Nasrin Rahimieh considers the images of the lepers in the film "the personification of the abject" in Iranian society.[14] Rahimieh thus argues that by showcasing the house of "the disenfranchised, deformed, and disabled," who have been neglected and refused by the Iranian society, Farrokhzad "questions the assumption that the nation's house is in order."[15]

While Farrokhzad's documentary remains the sole pre-revolution documentary made by a woman, two social documentaries on women's issues made by Kamran Shirdel in the 1960s also deserve mentioning. Sponsored by the Women's Organization of Iran (WOI), a non-profit organization whose president was Princess Ashraf Pahlavi—the Shah's sister—and made for the Ministry of Culture and Art (MCA), these documentaries, *Women's Prison* (*Nedamatgah*, 1965) and *Women's Quarter* (*Qaleh*, 1966)—also known as *Fortress: The Red Light District*—critiqued the conditions of imprisoned women and prostitutes in Tehran who, like the lepers in Farrokhzad's film, lived on the margins of Iranian society. Yet, media scholar Niki Akhavan explains that these two documentaries "went one step further in directly challenging the sponsoring organization. As a result, *Fortress* was banned during filming and the footage [was] confiscated."[16] The sociopolitical critique through documentary soon embodied itself in the surge of revolutionary protests on Iranian streets, at the forefront of which were Iranian women.

As Naficy explains, "Very few professional women are known to have filmed the revolution. One was Mehrnaz Saeed-Vafa, who ... had gone to the London Film School and become a film professor at NIRT's College of Cinema and Television. She took photographs and shot 8mm films of ..." the agitated sociopolitical scenes in various parts of Tehran.[17] At the same time, many amateurs used their photographic and Super 8 cameras to document the uprising, some of which can be found in family albums and recordings. After the 1979 Islamic Revolution and during the eight-year Iran-Iraq War (1980–88), a number of women filmmakers made social documentaries for the Voice and Vision of the Islamic Republic (VVIR)—later named Islamic Republic of Iran Broadcasting (IRIB). According to Tahaminejad, social documentaries made at this time can be divided into two main groups: First, "Children films and explanation of social behaviors via children," and second, "films on other everyday issues of the society."[18] In the former category, television series such as *Little Breadwinners* (*Nanavaran-e koochak*) depicted the hardships of working children and the role of child labor in familial and social economies. The Executive Producer of the series was a woman—Mitra Khamenei—and some episodes were directed by women directors working in television, including Farideh Shafai and Shahla E'tedali-Khou.[19] The thirty-two-minute documentary *Bread from Mud* (*Nani az gel*, 1981), made for the series by Farideh Shafai, portrayed "the work and life of a child in a brick-works, [and] won an award at the Oberhausen Film Festival."[20]

In the latter category, Rakhshan Banietemad was, and continues to be, a major documentarian. Banietemad got her start in filmmaking by first working in television during her academic study at the College of Dramatic Arts. Upon receiving her degree, she joined the group of television film directors and made several documentaries for Iranian television.[21] After making *Centralization* (*Tamarkoz*) in 1986, Banietemad left television, but continued her social documentary filmmaking and received commissions from governmental organizations to produce works on social issues. Naficy mentions that in 1992 "Banietemad was hired by the Tehran municipality, and eventually was aided by the Farabi Cinema Foundation, to document an urban renewal project in Fatemiyeh, an area that housed about 450,000 residents living in terrible conditions."[22] The result was a documentary trilogy on housing problems, which included *The '92 Report* (*Gozaresh-e '71*, 1992), *Spring to Spring* (*Bahar ta bahar*, 1993), and *To Whom Do You Show These Films?* (*In film-ha ra beh ki neshun midin?* 1993).

After the war, Iran entered a period of economic and industrial reconstruction. Government policies encouraged the expansion of privatization, and correspondingly, many private film companies sprang up, mostly in the capital Tehran, and got engaged in documentary production via commissions. Documentary producer Saeed Rashtian observes, "There was a tendency among many economic and industrial managers at the time to ask for collaborations from documentarians and television programmers to both document and introduce their activities."[23] Furthermore, in addition to in-house documentary production, Iranian television at this time began commissioning programs and documentaries to private film production companies. The major production of this post-war era was the documentary series *The Children of the Land of Iran* (*Koodakan-e sarzamin-e Iran*, 1995–97) which was produced by a newly-established, private company named Dega Films. Dega Films was owned by the Razagh-Karimi brothers, and made the series for television's Channel 2, with Mohammadreza Sarhangi as the series' producer. The series is considered as a rare, successful collaboration between a state-run organization and a private film company bringing together various generations of documentarians for a fifty-two-episode series. Two of these episodes were directed by women: *The Little Hands of Robabeh* (*Dast-haye koochak-e Robabeh*, 1995), directed by Nahid Rezaei, and *White-Clothes Wearers* (*Sepid-jamegan*, 1996), directed by Mahvash Sheikholeslami.

As the conditions were beginning to provide a solid base for the creation of a private documentary production during the post-war construction era, "the IRIB curbed back its outside commissioning and the [production] market that seemed fluid and available at this time ... became much more closed and exclusive."[24] Given the heavy involvement of the government in the process of privatization, a true independence for private film production companies did not materialize. Documentary scholar and filmmaker Persheng Sadegh-Vaziri considers the rhetoric of privatization in Iran at this time to be "a mix of economic liberalism and centralized government control and funding" that persistently kept the private media companies "economically dependent on the state."[25] Therefore, as soon as technological advances allowed the possibility of a more independent and personal documentary production, many Iranian documentarians began producing cheaper films with a much smaller, even one-person, crew. Technological developments and their popularity—first video then digital technologies—coincided with the opening of sociocultural and political spaces during Mohammad Khatami's two-term presidency (1997–2005). Film scholar Blake Atwood explains that the Ministry of Culture and

Islamic Guidance (MCIG) "lift[ed] the ban on video technology" in 1993, but "it was not until Khatami's presidency that video achieved widespread popularity and became associated with the ideals of democratization that marked the use of video around the world."[26]

Documentary production in Iran has also experienced steady growth since the late 1990s/early 2000s. Saeed Rashtian points to the technological development in filmmaking equipment to consider "the unprecedented prevalence and sociality of documentary film production" as "the most significant event since the early 2000s."[27] Rashtian further explains that "the first sign of this welcoming matter showed itself in the number of films submitted to domestic documentary festivals. From about 100 films that were usually submitted to the festivals prior to 1996, the number gradually reached to about 1000 films in the late 1990s ([and] to the present)."[28] A considerable number of these documentaries have been made by Iranian women. A report by the public relations section of the Cinema Vérité: Iran International Documentary Film Festival on the average number of films submitted by women to this festival in recent years reveals that women's participation has equated to about 10 per cent each year.[29] This estimate is of course limited to one festival and cannot account for all the documentaries made by women, many of which are not even entered into domestic and international film festivals. This makes an exact calculation of women's documentary films even more difficult. Furthermore, while statistics attest to a growing documentary production in Iran, there remain considerable challenges, especially in the process of documentary production and funding.

In terms of production, for instance, the issue of production and exhibition permits is a significant matter in Iranian documentary. The Ministry of Culture and Islamic Guidance (MCIG) is one of the main governmental organizations authorized to issue these permits. Documentary filmmaker Mahvash Sheikholeslami, in an interview for this study, stated, "The documentarians who are members of the House of Cinema (its documentary filmmakers' guild) can get their [production] permit via them … or a film might be made without any permit, which in that case it will have difficulty getting distributed in the country or [screened] at the domestic film festivals."[30] Persheng Sadegh-Vaziri also notes:

> Besides MCIG many institutions are able to issue production permits, including IRIB and Hawzeh Honari that act independently of the Ministry of Culture. … Exhibition permits are issued only by the Ministry of Culture, which covers most official screening spaces and film theatres. However, a number of spaces, such as the screening room of the House of Cinema and galleries show films without screening permits.[31]

Considering that such permits put documentaries under the state's scrutiny and possible censorship, some filmmakers might altogether ignore them using affordable audio-visual technologies to produce their own films and then distributing them via social media or online streaming platforms, or exhibiting them via private screenings.

What exacerbates this issue of permits is the fact that there are no clear censorship policies. Some red lines are familiar to filmmakers, such as the veiling of women in all external and internal scenes and the observation of (Islamic) female-male relationships on-screen.[32] But as Rakhshan Banietemad observed in my interview, others "vary in different periods and are mostly based on the taste and the political perspective of the supervising committees in each period."[33] Emphasizing that red lines are much stricter and less-known when it comes to social cinema—both documentary and fiction—Banietemad further mentioned:

> Stamina and patience have been my solutions to bypass arbitrary red lines, and I have been able to pass my films through inspection without any cuts and with long and rational discussions and reasoning … In some cases, such as [the documentary] *Touran Khanom*, we were forced to cover women's hair in some familial scenes [via special effects], which naturally, as they were shot inside the home [women] did not have the common hijab.[34]

Given that *Touran Khanom* (2018) was produced by private producers, Banietemad's account reflects the fact that the state's control casts its shadow widely on Iranian documentaries attesting to a complex entanglement between Iranian independent filmmaking and the Iranian state and their relational power dynamics. Moreover, as documentarian Nahid Rezaei pointed out in my interview, "We should also not forget that to some extent these red lines have [influenced] the mentality … of documentarians [themselves], and at the beginning of each project, expressing some issues unconsciously recedes from the mind."[35] Considering that documentary is an indispensable medium for recording, preserving, and impacting historical moments and social issues, censorship and red lines can negatively impact such significant functions. That is why independent documentarians work hard and take considerable risks to stay true to their perspectives, their subject matter, and their profession. In doing so, they use various adaptive strategies to preserve their social commitment and artistic and ideological independence while navigating funding opportunities and production processes to make their documentaries. The following section examines some of the practices and experiences of women documentarians in navigating the relevant governmental and private resources in order to fund and produce their films.

Governmental Organizations

Since the 1979 Islamic Revolution, the state has dominated documentary film production with various state-affiliated institutions involved in this field. Chief among them are: the Ministry of Culture and Islamic Guidance (MCIG) and its subsidiaries—*Markaz gostaresh-e sinema-ye mostanad va tajrobi* (Documentary and Experimental Film Center (DEFC), established in 1984), and *Anjoman sinema-ye javanan-e Iran* (Iranian Youth Cinema Society (IYCS), established in 1976); Center for Intellectual Development of Children and Young Adults (CIDCYA)—also known as *Kanoon*—established in 1965, and after the Revolution, supervised by the Ministry of Education and Training; *Moavenat-e sinema-iye hozeh honari* (Cinematic Management of Hozeh Honari, officially established in 2000);[36] and the television (IRIB).

Iranian television has heavily invested in documentary production and even established a Documentary Channel. But due to its strict state-control models and conservative ideological approaches, it has alienated independent documentarians. Although the need for programming might allow some—especially younger documentarians—to get involved in documentary production for the television, as documentary filmmaker and producer Orod Atarpour puts it, the "concern is filling the airtime and not the quality of the airtime. In this situation, documentary production is turned into a matter of quantity and statistics; the cheaper and the more, the better. The television's current [and] main problem is that it has become empty of experienced individuals,"[37] who prefer to work outside of it. And as long as the television's censorship is strong and its political and ideological perspectives are unilateral and exclusive, it seems very unlikely that independent documentarians would be attracted to it.

Among governmental organizations, the Documentary and Experimental Film Center (DEFC) has played a distinctive role in supporting Iranian documentary. Established in 1984, *Markaz sinema-ye tajrobi and nimeh-herfei* (Center for Experimental and Semi-Professional Cinema) had the initial goal of supporting 16mm film production. As its former director Mohammadmahdi Tabatabaeinejad puts it, "to act as a step between amateur and professional cinemas, where filmmakers after preliminary training in the Iranian Youth Cinema Society [with 8mm films] …" received semi-professional training at the Center with 16mm films. Both stages were meant to prepare the filmmakers for entering the professional filmmaking stage with 35mm films, supervised by *Bonyad sinema-iye Farabi* (Farabi Cinema Foundation). In the 1990s the center became the Documentary and Experimental Film Center, thus putting documentary cinema at the core of its activities.[38] Today, the center is one of the foremost governmental institutions producing, distributing, and promoting documentary, animation, and experimental films. The center also organizes the Cinema Vérité: Iran International Documentary Film Festival, a major documentary event both nationally and internationally.

Although the DEFC has played a major role in the production and support of documentary film culture in recent decades, the accounts of women documentarians demonstrate that the center also needs to implement major structural and visionary changes to accommodate a more inclusive climate in its working relationship with the independent documentarians. Emphasizing the selective approaches of the center and the difficulty of providing the required budget for an independent documentary production, documentarian Nahid Rezaei said:

> I gave the proposal of the film that I finished shooting recently to the DEFC some years ago. ... It is interesting that while the film's topic does not have a specific political or social critique, and it's about the independent activities of a man in a Chabahar village, [who is] active in children's book reading, the DEFC did not respond [to the project] because I have always been critical of their policies and approaches ... As such, it took me a while to find the budget for this film through my own efforts, and in this way, the working process for those of us who are not dependent on television or governmental organizations gets slower and longer.[39]

Discussing her experiences of working with the DEFC in the production of *The Scent of Lemon at Dawn* (*Sepideh-dami ke boo-ye limoo midad*, 2014) and *Hidden Half of the Moon* (*Nime-ye penhan-e mah*, 2017), Azadeh Bizargiti also lamented the lack of production budget provided by the center. She mentioned:

> With my own budget, I started doing the research on the documentary *The Scent* ..., which was about the lives of chemically injured women 25 years after the chemical bombardment of [Iranian city] Sardasht [by Iraq]. But ultimately, I was not able to find anyone who would support [the project]. And thus, when the DEFC agreed [to support it], I began working with them with a very limited budget that was not enough to cover all of the film's expenses. In the end, the film became so influential that everyone praised it, but given its low budget [and given] we had to do all of the work [ourselves], I ran out of energy after finishing the film.[40]

The involvement of the center in the project, despite its low budget allocation, seems considerable given that the topic of the film was war-related, which might have won its attention a little easier. But this is also a documentary that focuses on the less-discussed women's experiences of the war, especially in regard to the gendering of discussions on chemical warfare and its consequences, from an independent woman documentarian's perspective. As such, a paradoxical supportive mechanism was used on the part of the center to assist the production of this documentary.

In regard to the production of *Hidden Half of the Moon*, Bizargiti pointed to the same monetary constraints along with a more difficult approval process: "The re-reading of women's participation in the Iranian Constitutional Movement [1905–1911] was not a topic that interests the DEFC … but again I did not have any budget and with the friendship and support of some of our friends, the project, after lots of back and forth (it took 8 years), was finally approved."[41] Bizargiti links the nature of the difficulties she endured during the long production process of *Hidden Half of the Moon*, spanning three different managements at the DEFC, to the topic of her documentary depicting Iranian women's Constitutional struggles for a more inclusive and progressive society. She astutely calls her endeavors and perseverance in the making of the documentary her "post-Constitutional struggles."[42] In my interview, Bizargiti foregrounded her sociocultural concerns and the commitments and responsibilities they entail, along with the lack of financial resources, as major reasons to work with a governmental organization such as the DEFC.[43] Yet in doing so, she gives priority to asserting her independent ideology and artistic vision in the process of documentary production. As Bizargiti mentioned, an independent documentarian "is a committed documentarian, who … regardless of all imposed ideologies, attempts to tell us the truth so that s/he can facilitate social reform and changes."[44]

Noticeably, when the DEFC gets involved in a project, they consider the film a DEFC product, and in addition to the documentarian, assert control over it. However, such a level of involvement, usually "from inception to distribution stages," may create an imbalance of power dynamics over the project and therefore hinder the possibility of a "true collaboration."[45] Pointing to the fact that the majority of the DEFC production projects are through 100 per cent financial sponsorship, Mohammadmahdi Tabatabaeinejad speculates, "We have done all we could to change our position from a producer to a supporter, but there is a reality that in documentary cinema there are not enough financiers … We do hope to reach a point that we do 20 per cent of the financing."[46] The successful implementation of this plan may establish a climate that encourages independent financing and production, as well as independent circulation of the finalized films, thus breaking away from a governmentally dominated production management model. In other words, the ideal position of the DEFC seems to occur in strengthening the private sector's funding opportunities in documentary cinema and promoting the infrastructure of private, independent production outside of, but in relation to, the current governmental structures.

During the directorship of Mohammad Afarideh at the organization, some efforts were made to boost the (co-)production of documentary in Iran, particularly through the Cinema Vérité: Iran International Documentary Film Festival, the first edition of which was organized by the DEFC in 2007. Two initiatives during the festival's early years of operation included for the first time a "documentary support box" with a national focus on funding and production, and a "support box for the international section" centering on global documentary co-production.[47] These supportive boxes, along with the festival's documentary market, aimed to complement "the cycle of documentary cinema" from its pre-production stage to distribution and sale "in the festival [circuit] itself."[48] Also, in order to promote the role of professional documentary producer, the national box required that "the documentarian should not be the producer herself/himself, rather s/he needs to find a producer" whether from a private sector or (semi)governmental organizations.[49] These two supportive initiatives then evolved into a Pitching Panel in 2018, held at the twelfth Cinema Vérité festival after holding three international workshops on pitching and fundraising at the festival in previous years. In its initial year, this initiative consisted of national and international financiers, and received 100 proposals from Iranian applicants, of which eighteen were entered into the Pitching Panel's initial round and ultimately seven projects were accepted for the final stage.[50]

However, regarding the support of independent documentary cinema, especially women's documentaries, these efforts need to be also accompanied by a more inclusive and open perspective in the managing structure of the DEFC and other governmental organizations involved in documentary production. In this regard Azadeh Bizargiti shared the following perspective:

> The fact is that women are less present in managerial and decision-making [roles]. Usually, except in some specific cases, they are allocated less budget. And the fact is that cinema industry in the world is still to some extent considered a masculine industry, and women's situation would improve when in managing, approving of projects, dividing the budget, and in decision-making those managers are selected who are informed and egalitarian, and consider prioritizing one sex over the other to be a wrong stance; only the presence of this kind of individuals can make the situation better for women.[51]

Emphasizing that uneven and selective approaches in documentary management system can be damaging to independent documentary practices, regardless of the documentarians' gender, Nahid Rezaei in my interview asserted:

> Yet, the [organizational] climate in cinema and other places is so masculine that forming a comfortable and friendly relationship becomes much easier for men than women … There might be many men in decision-making positions who, like many women, disagree with forced state-sanctioned definitions, but you cannot distinguish them via their hijab, clothes, or make-up. But even a simple photo of a woman can also portray her way of thinking.[52]

Two significant points arise from Rezaei's comments. First, an unequal, gendered management affects the working efficiency of women documentarians within governmental spaces. Since the 1979 Islamic Revolution, Iranian women have made groundbreaking advancements in various contexts such as the arts, education, and sports, just to name a few. This is a phenomenon which I have called elsewhere the rise of an indigenous "gender consciousness" in contemporary Iran "that stems from an essential need of Iranian youth, especially women, in regard to defining themselves in the society and practicing their freedom."[53] Nevertheless, the majority of top executive and management positions are still overwhelmingly occupied by men, which can correspondingly impact how women documentarians come to experience the governmental institutions and networks.

Second, Rezaei's reflection foregrounds the effects of a woman's appearance on the ways in which she might be received by government personnel, a pattern of recognition which is also very clear to the women themselves. Women's studies scholar Norma Claire Moruzzi argues that "the modern question, the modern argument, is not over women's public participation…," but rather "over women's public (self-)representation: the manner of their presence, the limits to their actions, and the autonomy of their role."[54] Providing a detailed and nuanced analysis of the "language of *hijab*" in contemporary Iran, where women's dress is regulated and legislated, Moruzzi writes that in this context "the codes of self-representation are both publicly explicit and keenly personal. Within set limits, I define myself, and I am defined, by my adaptation to the representational code."[55] As such, the way a woman documentarian's dress and appearance might signal her liberal and progressive social ideas, as defined by government personnel, can consequently affect her working relationship with those individuals in the governmental agencies.

In the same vein Mina Keshavarz observed, "The mere fact that I, as a woman, appear in official spaces with a covering that I like, makes my opportunities for participating in every [official] space less and less. Unfortunately, what is important in the official space of Iran's documentary cinema is not specifically film, but the interactions that filmmakers form with the officials."[56] Women documentarians' dress and appearance thus become a tool for defining their ideological tendencies and their independence affecting how they might be received in their navigation of governmental documentary spaces. In this way, the documentarians are literally and practically divided into insiders (*khodi-ha*—those close to the ideologies of the state and supportive of its policies), and outsiders (*gheir-e khodi-ha*—the independent ones). This in turn determines the budget, facilities, and support they can receive to make their documentaries. Nevertheless, as Sadegh-Vaziri writes, the "filmmakers use inconsistencies in the regulations and their relationships with state executives to push the boundaries of what is allowed and accepted in the dominant discourse."[57] In doing so, they employ various adaptive strategies, such as using changes and fissures in the management, intermediaries, added personal funds, and persistent negotiations to produce their films.

Non-Governmental and Private Organizations

Despite the election of the reformist president Mohammad Khatami in 1997, few substantial legal and structural reforms actually materialized—mostly due to the obstructions from the conservative faction of the state, such as the Guardian Council, Expediency Council, and the Judiciary. However, the new atmosphere, fueled with democratic ideals, did result in "a freer public sphere, the formation of various civil society organisations (including women's) and NGOs, and an easing of some restrictions (for example, on women's dress code)."[58] Since then, these civil organizations and NGOs have been an integral part of Iranian society, and although many of their activities were curtailed under the conservative government of Mahmoud Ahmadinejad (2005–2013), along with the "imprisonment of secular activists, closure of women's NGOs and of hundreds of print media outlets," these restrictive measures did not stop the women's "movement, which developed a new strategy"—that is, the use of social media and online activism for political and civic engagements.[59]

Within the field of documentary, one of the most successful collaborations between independent documentarians and a non-governmental organization can be found in the Karestan documentary film series (initiated in 2015), showcasing less publicly known, yet eminent, Iranian entrepreneurs. This series was formed as a collaboration between the Kara Film Studio—an independent documentary collective consisting of a group of documentarians involved in production and distribution of documentary films—and *Bonyad-e tosea'-ye kar-afarini-e zanan va javanan* (Entrepreneurship Development Foundation for Women and Youth), an NGO "whose primary goal is the promotion and development of the culture of creativity, innovation and entrepreneurship at national level."[60] Established in 2013, the Kara Film Studio is a groundbreaking and pioneering form of collectivity in the history of Iranian documentary production and is co-founded by two independent veteran documentarians, Rakhshan Banietemad and Mojtaba Mirtahmasb. Along with Banietemad, Shirin Barghnavard and Mahnaz Afzali are the two other female members of the Kara team. As Banietemad explained:

> The Kara Film Studio provides an opportunity for the gathering of our group, which has common concerns and the common perspectives regarding documentary filmmaking, and comes together to make a [documentary] project. We don't have a financial capacity and we don't have a forced intention of mass production. For any work whose production we consider necessary, through hardship and finding new ways, we try to make the film's production possible.[61]

In fact, the collaborative model employed at the Kara Film Studio is driven by the needs of a project, and as such, individuals collaborating on a project might not be involved with another project of the Studio.[62] The Karestan film series comes at a critical moment when Iran struggles under American economic sanctions and a domestic economy suffering from rampant inflation and severe mismanagement, all of which have made the daily lives of millions of Iranians difficult. The series aims to introduce young Iranians to the "role-models … who, without relying on any special opportunity or privilege, played a significant role in promoting personal and social lives as well as in the country's development."[63] Given that the majority of commissions in Iranian documentary cinema are associated with state-affiliated organizations or industries, documentarian Shirin Barghnavard pointed to a more nuanced definition of commission and its various aspects. Discussing her involvement in the Karestan film series, Barghnavard said, "Sometimes a film series is defined in a framework and then some filmmakers are invited to that specific project for production and collaboration. Out of seven documentaries that I have made, five films, including *21 Days and Me* (2011) and *Poets of Life* (*Shaeran-e zendegi*, 2017) [which is part of the Karestan film series], are made in this way."[64] These kinds of projects, in addition to having the support of an independent, non-governmental organization for their production, which is itself a major incentive for the involvement of independent documentarians, are also based on deep professional connections, friendship, and trust among documentarians and producers. Mahnaz Afzali, who has made *Mother of the Earth* (2017) for the Karestan film series, disclosed that after being invited by Mirtahmasb and Banietemad to join their project, she accepted because of "the interest she had in Mrs. Banietemad's works and the assurance she had of Mirtahmasb's performance as a documentarian."[65] In the same vein, Barghnavard considered her participation in the project and her collaboration with Banietemad and Mirtahmasb "a professionally beneficial event" for herself.[66] The cross-generational and professional mentorship is thus embedded in the functioning of the Kara Film Studio and its projects.

Moreover, the Karestan film series' impact is multi-faceted and goes beyond documentary film productions. As Banietemad revealed in the interview:

> The publication of a collection of photos of the characters and their lives and works, the publication of a collection of children's books on the concepts of the series with a simple language, and the writing of some fiction scripts inspired by the lives of entrepreneurs, are among our working agenda. At the moment, five fiction scripts are being written by professional screenwriters.[67]

The multiple ways of recording and documenting the entrepreneurs' lives, their contributions, and their sociocultural and professional impacts offer invaluable resources to enlighten Iranian audiences, especially the youth, for generations to come. At the same time, they preserve the pioneering works of these individuals as an important part of Iranian history.

In another example, Katayoon Shahabi, a pioneering producer and distributor of Iranian independent films, worked for two governmental cinematic organizations for nearly fifteen years before launching her own private company, Sheherazad Media International (SMI) in 2001, one of the most important Iranian film companies involved in film festivals, co-productions, and international distribution of Iranian fiction, documentary, and short films. In her work with the Farabi Cinema Foundation and the Cima Media International (CMI), "a semi-private company that produced and marketed Iranian films and Television productions,"[68] Shahabi played a pivotal role in establishing Iranian cinema and its filmmakers on a global film stage.

During the conservative presidency of Ahmadinejad, private and non-governmental organizations, as well as the House of Cinema, came under heavy scrutiny by the Iranian state. In particular, after the fraught presidential election in 2009, which led to massive protests known as the Green Movement, a crackdown on activists, journalists, and artists, including independent documentary filmmakers and producers, intensified. At the same time, the attention given by Western media to Iran and the coverage of national events, especially by outlets such as the BBC Persian and the VOA Persian, further increased. This eventually led to a conspiracy theory put forward by the Iranian state that connected Iranian protesters and their sympathizers to the Western media and forces seeking to challenge the sovereignty and legitimacy of the Iranian state. As Naficy writes, Katayoon Shahabi, "[i]n September 2011... became embroiled in the soft power public diplomacy struggles between Iran and Britain, as she along with five independent filmmakers were arrested."[69] Shahabi was ultimately released "two months later,"[70] but the incident prompted her to internationally expand her private film company. In the interview for this study Shahabi explained:

> The establishment of the France-based Noori Pictures was the result of the problems created for me and the Sheherazad Media International during Mr. Ahmadinejad's government. Under those circumstances, I realized that for continuing [my] activity and maintaining [my] professional independence, it is not enough for me to have a company in Iran; and it was time to further expand my professional experience by establishing a company outside of Iran, so that I can work the way I want to.[71]

Both the SMI and Noori Pictures have been instrumental in boosting independent Iranian documentary and fiction filmmaking within a transnational context. In their support of documentary film production, they have helped establish the professional careers of such women documentarians as Mina Keshavarz and Shirin Barghnavard, and provided opportunities for transnational documentary co-productions. In regard to the former, the SMI commissioned and produced Barghnavard's *21 Days and Me* (2011) and Keshavarz's *Unwelcome in Tehran* (2011). Shahabi explained:

> We initiated a project about [Iranian] youth's personal experience[s] and [lives], and with the help of a colleague, a reputable Iranian TV producer, we contacted young filmmakers to provide us with a topic regarding their daily life so we could select four projects among them. Shirin Barghnavard's and Mina Keshavarz's projects were chosen because the subject[s] of their films examined the concerns of young women in contemporary Iran, which until that time were not discussed.[72]

Shahabi is among a small number of Iranian independent producers with an expansive knowledge of transnational co-production. Reflecting on her experiences, Shahabi cited three major outcomes of co-production projects between Iran and other countries, the sum of which is: providing professional experience for Iranian crew, generating currency and income for Iran (a country that has a very low production cost in comparison with other nations), and enhancing Iranian filmmaking culture via the acquisition of common international regulations and production systems.[73] At the same time, Shahabi considered the difficulty of an effective, cross-cultural communication, especially between Iranian producers and foreign directors working on films with an Iran-specific subject. Shahabi elaborated on this challenge inherent to transnational co-productions:

> For instance, in producing the documentary feature *Sepideh* [in Iran], whose director was Danish and the rest of the crew and me (the producer) were Iranian, [we] not only had to solve the production difficulties, but [we] also constantly held meetings with the Danish director and producers regarding [the film's] shooting schedule to [make sure] that the film's scenes would not diverge from the reality. The divergence from reality means the touristic look of the foreign crew on the social issues of the host country.[74]

This awareness of the possibility of a "touristic look" at Iranian society in the context of a transnational documentary co-production allows Shahabi to successfully supervise internationally co-produced documentary films like *Sepideh: Reaching for the Stars* (2013), directed by Berit Madsen—which depicts the aspirations of a strong-willed young Iranian woman to become an astronaut, while dealing with various familial and sociocultural obstructions to this—without falling into clichéd representations of Muslim women's "victimhood."

In another example, unilateral governmental organizations' contracts and their subsequent control of the means of documentary production and distribution, along with a lack of funding for documentary production, prompted Mina Keshavarz to become a professional documentary producer in addition to being already a successful documentary director.[75] For her feature documentary, *Braving the Waves* (2016),[76] Keshavarz served as the director and (co-)producer, employing a multiplicity of ways to co-produce her documentary. She began with personal funds while simultaneously exploring new funding methods such as crowdfunding, one of the first such cases in Iranian documentary production. Keshavarz used the Iranian crowdfunding platform Hamijoo (literally "looking for supporters") to partially fund *Braving the Waves*, whose initial title was *Will She Win the War?* (*Aya ou dar in mobarezeh pirooz mishavad?*). The Hamijoo website indicates that the project attracted sixty-six supporters and gathered 90,850,000 Iranian rial (approximately $2620),[77] well beyond the target of 90,000,000 rial.[78] Discussing the use of online financing and its relation to community building, Inge Ejbye Sørensen contends, "Supporters are not only financially supporting a film, but also its cause. Thus, crowdfunding and crowd investment schemes usually attract campaigning and issue-led films."[79] Considering the subject of Keshavarz's film, I argue that the successful financial support of the documentary via crowdfunding derives from both the subject matter—the struggles of an Iranian woman trying to help other women in her community to maintain their economic independence—and its cause of women's empowerment within a broader economic and social context. Another significant factor is Keshavarz's reputation as an independent, committed, and successful documentarian whose documentaries often deal with nuances of gender issues and female subjectivity in Iranian society.

Keshavarz further explained the context within which she co-produced *Braving the Waves* with a producer from Norway. She said:

> The Norwegian producer entered the project when the shooting was almost over, and I had pitched the film in various forums. Besides the personal fund, which covered my wages and the equipment used in four years to produce the film, I was able to get funds from the IDFA and the Screen Institute Beirut ... The Norwegian producer succeeded in acquiring three funds for the project one of which required us to do the sound mixing and [color grading] there ... The Beirut fund, as part of its regulations required us to name [Lebanon] as one of the producing countries in all the catalogues, therefore the film, as I was its main producer, ultimately became an Iran, Norway, and Lebanon co-production.[80]

Braving the Waves took five years to complete and a part of the film's post-production—its editing—was completed in France because Keshavarz wanted to work with an editor in that country.[81] In 2013, Keshavarz also established her own private production company, Mindoc Film Production, with *Braving the Waves* becoming the company's first documentary project. The experiences gained from *Braving the Waves*' transnational co-production enabled Keshavarz to get involved as a producer in other filmmakers' projects. At the time of interview, Keshavarz indicated that she was involved in some interactive documentary projects with Dutch companies, was working on two of her own co-production projects, was producing a documentary for an Iranian documentarian, and yet another for a Bangladeshi documentarian.[82] Keshavarz has thus turned limitations and obstacles into creative and groundbreaking opportunities within a professional and transnational context. In doing so, she has acquired valuable experiences in documentary production that contribute to the expansion of methods and approaches in Iranian independent documentary.

Nevertheless, not all independent documentarians in Iran view transnational co-productions as the best practice. Emphasizing the significance of familiarity with professional documentary production in other countries, such as "the style of budget planning and the exact scheduling," as well as the possibilities of a stronger support especially in terms of distribution, sale, and exhibition, Mahvash Sheikholeslami maintained, "because my works are personally very intuitive and I cannot, unfortunately or fortunately, bring everything on the paper, these kinds of projects are considered disadvantages for me … I made a film for France's Arte channel for which I was not under pressure this much, but due to the film's limited [running] time requirement, I was not able to be very successful."[83] The tight production schedule that some co-production projects entail, especially those made for television, can be constraining for some documentarians accustomed to an artisanal mode of filmmaking. In another example, Nahid Rezaei explained that, for better or worse, she has not yet had a co-production experience, but thinks that "while these projects can give independence to a documentarian, in their implicit forms, they lean towards satisfying the foreign audience, [which can] ultimately harm our independent cinema perspective-wise."[84] Rezaei points to the vexing conditions that Iranian independent documentarians might run into in regard to transnational co-productions in which Iran and Iran-related topics are reduced to clichéd and fetishized representations, thus taking away the nuances and complexities of the country and its culture—a concern which was similarly raised by Katayoon Shahabi as an Iranian producer working with foreign documentarians making films on Iran.

Yet, I argue that as is the case when working with governmental organizations in the country, Iranian independent documentary filmmakers and producers similarly employ adaptive strategies in their professional relationships with international institutions and individuals. Discussing two primary modes of support mobilized in the production process of Indian independent documentary films—"NGO-sponsored and self-funded filmmaking"[85]—Shweta Kishore points to the "paradoxical, patronage-based financing [that] evidently complicates the claims of 'independence' attached to a practice that strives to preserve artistic and political autonomy from regulations, norms and external obligations."[86] However, as Kishore asserts, Indian documentarians use various "procedures of negotiation and adaptation or 'tactical practice' [to] transform institutional relationships into production opportunities."[87] A similar argument can be made in regard to the various and multi-faceted adaptive strategies used by Iranian independent documentarians in their professional relationships with international institutions. For instance, in making *Braving the Waves*, Mina Keshavarz had to meet the requirements of her financial sponsors in Lebanon and Norway, and while she did not have a French producer, due to artistic priorities and the fact that she wanted to work with a particular editor in France, she used some of her own wages received for the project to finance a part of the film's post-production in France.[88] In another example, Shirin Barghnavard considered her three-month participation in the Harun Farocki Residency in Berlin in 2017 "very useful and valuable" as it offered her the possibility to solely focus on the research and script writing of her upcoming documentary short film without being concerned about financial issues regarding the project.[89] According to Barghnavard, such programs can be crucial for supporting Iranian women documentarians and their projects "as they allow them to expand their network of relationships and access better and more professional facilities to concentrate and work on their projects. In other words, such kinds of support allow them to be more independent and work with more ease of mind within a more professional space."[90] Barghnavard's reflection on her residency thus points to what Kishore calls the transformation of the "institutional relationships into production opportunities,"[91] while maintaining the independence of artistic vision and practice.

Additionally, given that the navigation of transnational organizations requires time and that the funding received for a production might not cover all the expenses and needs of the project, personal funding usually plays a less explicit but significant, and at times inevitable, part in the process of independent documentary production. And of course, there are many independent documentaries made in Iran that solely rely on personal funds, such as *Profession: Documentarist* (2014), a collaborative and self-reflexive documentary consisting of seven episodes. Each episode is made by an Iranian woman documentarian who reflects on the profession of documentary filmmaking in Iran from a personal perspective. The filmmakers of the project include Shirin Barghnavard, Firouzeh Khosrovani, Farahnaz Sharifi, Mina Keshavarz, Sepideh Abtahi, Sahar Salahshoor, and Nahid Rezaei. Another example is *Scenes from a Divorce* (*Sahne-haei az yek talagh*, 2015), directed by Shirin Barghnavard and Mohammad Reza Jahanpanah. Discussing the challenges of independent documentary filmmaking, Barghnavard pointed to the highly competitive processes of applying for transnational grants, which might prompt filmmakers to use personal funds to produce their films. Barghnavard said:

> For instance, *Scenes from a Divorce*, which was a joint production between me and my spouse, did not receive any funding from anywhere, which caused the production process to take three years to complete. Or *Profession: Documentarist*, which was produced by each filmmaker's personal fund, faced serious financial challenges in shooting, editing, and even screening stages. Such challenges and limitations take away the ambitious possibilities from the filmmaker, convincing her to make her film in a smaller scale.[92]

In another example, Mahnaz Afzali pointed to the lack of financial resources and support for independent documentary cinema that prevented many of her filmic ideas from materializing. Afzali noted, "Ultimately with limited familial budget and resources, I have used whatever I've had in my power to make my films. Currently, I have three works in the editing stage (which I am working on) that for years, and due to the existing circumstances, I had not been able to edit."[93]

As all the above examples of non-governmental and private documentary productions indicate, the independent women documentary filmmakers and producers in Iran have used a range of adaptive strategies to materialize their artistic visions and to produce their projects. They have used personal funds, crowdfunding, and non-governmental and transnational support, have established their own production companies and film studios, and have collaborated with other documentary practitioners within a national or transnational setting; all "with the purpose of asserting the artist's self," to borrow Kishore's words,[94] and maintaining the independence of artistic vision and commitment.

Film studies scholar Chris Berry writes regarding independent Chinese documentarians: "The more active they become and the more opportunities they explore, the more complex are the negotiations and relationships they have to develop with others in the matrix of power in order to remain independently Chinese."[95] Such is the case for Iranian independent documentarians, whose "matrix of power" has become even more complex in recent years due to various economic conditions, such as American sanctions and domestic economic mismanagement and corruption. Inflation is drastically shrinking the already inadequate funding resources across both governmental and private sectors as the Iranian rial has decreased in value. And as these conditions gain momentum, much more attention and support from a wide range of domestic and international entities and players are still in demand. Yet, regardless of all the limitations, the documentarians remain independently Iranian, offering the world some of the most significant and fascinating observations and reflections on Iranian society, culture, and history.

CHAPTER 2

Watching Iranian Women's Documentaries: Sites of Distribution and Exhibition

The circulation of Iranian independent documentary films in terms of distribution and exhibition lags behind their production as "they do not all receive screening permits or broadcast opportunities" in Iran, a condition that according to documentary filmmaker and scholar Persheng Sadegh-Vaziri, "the filmmakers have termed *moshkel-e khorooji* [the problem of output]."[1] Considering the significance of such circulation for both the documentarians and (national and global) audiences, this chapter discusses some of the existent channels for distribution and exhibition of Iranian independent documentaries, especially those made by women, foregrounding the diversity of such channels—formal and informal—and the dynamics of power relations and negotiations embedded in them. Acknowledging that distribution "determines what films we see, and when and how we see them,"[2] media scholar Ramon Lobato posits, "If we understand politics as a struggle for power and resources, then distribution is politics at its purest."[3] Before offering a deeper look at the politics of distribution and exhibition in regard to Iranian women's documentaries, however, it is necessary to highlight two important points in this regard.

First, in its conventional notion, "film distribution might be understood as the space between production and exhibition where negotiations are made to secure the release of films in cinemas and/or organise the production of a physical consumer copy of the film on DVD, or more latterly, Blu-ray."[4] However, as media scholar Virginia Crisp argues, "such a straightforward definition only gives part of the story,"[5] overlooking overlaps and interconnectedness of these film stages from production to distribution, exhibition, and consumption. Therefore, I refrain from drawing clear-cut boundaries between distribution and exhibition in my discussion while acknowledging their particularities of modes of operation. This is mainly because various platforms such as film festivals and online sites have increasingly played active roles in both distribution and exhibition of documentaries, not to mention their production. Attesting to such overlapping practices, Lobato defines "film distribution as the movement of media through time and space (a definition which at times necessarily encompasses film exhibition)."[6] Inspired by this notion of temporal and spatial media movement, I employ the term *fragmented modes of circulation* to refer to a state of distribution and exhibition in Iranian independent documentary, wherein instead of rigidly systematic and linear media movements through distribution and exhibition outlets, there exist various fragmented, and at times simultaneous, modes of documentary circulation.

The unprecedented rise in independent documentary production in Iran since the late 1990s has not benefited from the distribution and exhibition infrastructures in a country that is mostly dedicated to fiction cinema. In fact, Iranian fiction cinema is at times referred to as *sinema-ye ekran* (screening cinema), due to its heavy reliance on theatrical screenings and ticket sales. Under such circumstances, Iranian independent documentary has had to develop its own modes of circulation adopting diverse platforms that are varied in their outreach and complex in their operations, especially in relation to the state's control and censorship. Drawing from the analytical lens proposed by Lobato, I discuss these fragmented modes of circulation as "formal and informal" modes. As Lobato explains, "Formality refers to the degree to which industries are regulated, measured, and governed by state and corporate institutions. Informal distributors are those which operate outside this sphere, or in partial articulation with it."[7] Within this context, I consider the Iranian television, the Documentary and Experimental Film Center (DEFC) and its Cinema Vérité film festival, and the theatrical screenings of the Art and Experience Cinema (*Gorooh-e Sinemaei-ye Honar va Tajrobeh*) as primary formal sites of Iranian documentary circulation that are in one way or another "usually subject to higher levels of regulation and consolidation" by the Iranian state.[8]

Yet, considering the social, political, and economic complexities of Iran in terms of both the state's involvement in these filmic spaces and the global interest in them, my understanding of what constitutes such formal domestic outlets becomes more nuanced when considering the function of international sites of formal circulation such as international film festivals and foreign television channels, with their own specific practices of formality. For instance, an independent documentary film might not get screening permission for domestic film festivals, theatrical venues, and/or television, but it might get exhibited at international film festivals, cinema theaters, and/or television channels outside of Iran. Or an independent Iranian distribution company might work with international film festivals and television channels instead of such state-run entities in the country to distribute and exhibit the films. In these instances, there are delicate nuances and degrees of (in)formality, the contexts they are derived from, and the negotiations they necessitate in order to maintain the independence of the documentarian and the distributor. In other words, if Iranian independent documentaries do not go through the formal channels of distribution and exhibition in the country, this does not mean that the alternative modes of circulation available to them are necessarily informal. Rather, these alternative ways might as well perform their own degrees of formality over media circulation. Therefore, by applying a formal-informal analytical lens, I maintain the gray areas between these two notions to reveal the complexity of circulation practices at work. This is also the case for informal distribution and exhibition platforms that range from various non-theatrical screenings (at universities, cultural and art centers, public libraries, and personal home gatherings), to private media companies' practices, DVD distributions, online platforms, and documentarians and individuals sharing films with their acquaintances and friends. All these formal and informal modes of documentary circulation mentioned here point to the diversity of the platforms and the degrees of (in)formality within them, both of which I will examine in this chapter.

Second, while these modes of circulation are conditions of an infrastructure faced by all Iranian independent documentarians regardless of their gender, the focus of this chapter is on the experiences of Iranian women documentarians and the politics of gender that affect how these women navigate these conditions. In an interview for this study, documentarian Mahnaz Afzali explained, "Perhaps because I work independently, the main challenge [comes] at the time of film [distribution] and exhibition. I think as women filmmakers, we have to decrease the degree of error so that the [existent] limited resources are not taken away from us. Whereas there is a [possibility] of trial and error for men, [this possibility] is lesser for women."[9] This reflection emphasizes that few opportunities are available to independent women documentarians, especially in regard to distribution and exhibition of their films, which might prompt them to be less ambitious or experimental in their filmmaking approaches. In terms of distribution and exhibition, even though women documentarians have deployed creative and informal strategies to make the most out of the fewest possibilities and to engage with audiences, such gendered pressures and gatekeeping can directly influence the public reach of women's documentaries as well as their sociocultural and political impact. As Lobato contends, "Distributors, formal and informal, determine which films win and lose in this game of cultural consumption. In the process, they shape public culture by circulating or withholding texts which have the potential to become part of shared imaginaries, discourses and dreams."[10]

Pointing to the sociopolitical and cultural significance of documentary films, Rakhshan Banietemad in a 2018 interview mentioned, "Documentary cinema is a mirror of reality that in encountering with the society's various issues has the power of representation, critique, and documentation. Perhaps this is the reason that it is always watchfully dealt with by the state and politicians."[11] And as I indicate in this chapter, whenever the social representation, documentation, and critique come from an independent woman documentarian's perspective, the state becomes more watchful, which in turn, affects the distribution and exhibition of her films. Moreover, the documentary's impact should be considered based on a mutual interaction between a documentarian and her audiences through which not only can the film and the perspective it offers have the potential to bring about progressive changes in the society, but the audience can also reflect on the work and impact the documentarian's perspective and future approaches. As Iranian documentary producer Morteza Razagh-Karimi argues:

> The increasing number of documentary films produced in the country delineates that the production in the documentary cinema is active, but a production without distribution and exhibition does not allow the economic cycle to get completed and the connection with the audience to get formed. A documentarian can have the audience's feedback [on a film] only when this film gets [distributed and exhibited].[12]

By examining various modes of documentary circulation in the following sections, I foreground the shifting ideologies and practices of state-run media organizations in regard to independent documentaries' distribution and exhibition, and to some extent, international media responses to them; the scattered, yet crucial, functions of informal practices of documentary circulation; and the activities and perseverance of Iranian independent documentarians themselves, which have produced a diversity of modes of circulation and multiple power relations and negotiations. The result of these factors is ultimately the creation of a dynamic, if fragmented, public and artistic documentary culture and discourse.

Television(s)

In the interviews that I conducted with Iranian independent women documentarians for this study, many lamented that Iranian television has failed to effectively exhibit Iranian independent documentary films.

Even Mohammad Afarideh, a former DEFC director, complains that the perspectives of state-run media organizations are not aligned with each other, resulting in television essentially ignoring documentary cinema, especially those films produced outside of its organization.[13] In the same vein, Banietemad mentioned:

> While fortunately in recent years with the help of digital revolution watching many of these [documentary] works has become possible, the foremost place of this cinema everywhere in the world is television. In Iran, because of the impossibility of the broadcast of most of these works in the national [television], the Iranian audience [cannot see them]; Iranian documentary cinema is deprived of its most important platform.[14]

Iranian television makes and/or commissions its own documentary films and rarely purchases externally produced independent documentaries. This is in fact a common practice in global television industries. Film distributor Mohammad Attebai noted a similar phenomenon in a 2006 survey he conducted of 110 television channels in thirty-one European countries. According to Attebai, "Germany's ZDF channel usually provides its documentary programs through production methods and 'acquisition' is the least way of supplying programs for this channel. Greece's ERT channel usually provides its needed programs via 'commissions' to Greek production groups, and England's BBC channel usually uses 'in-house production' to supply its programs."[15] While purchasing of documentary films may not be a common practice for many global television industries, what is considerable in the Iranian case is the state's financial and ideological monopoly over this medium. The television falls under the direct supervision of Iran's Supreme Leader and is mostly used, according to media and communication scholar Gholam Khiabany, for "the 'propagation' and defence of the values and ideals of not only Islam in general, but a strand which is considered pure and revolutionary as defined by the ruling clergy."[16] As such, although the IRIB has been expanding its national and international channels and using up-to-date and modern media technologies, its production and exhibition policies have firmly remained within an ideologically and politically charged context.

In particular, the IRIB has operated the Documentary Channel (*Shabakeh Mostanad*), which "broadcast its pilot programs in 2009, and was [officially] established in 2011."[17] It is a "24-hour digital channel with the goal of production and exhibition of documentary films."[18] According to the channel's website, in addition to providing a professional base for documentaries and documentarians to boost documentary filmmaking culture, it is also "seeking to promote religious insight, ... Iranian-Islamic identity, and a real image of the society, with the goal of correcting and presenting the historical, cultural, ethnic, and religious" aspects of the country.[19] Ironically however, as documentary filmmaker and producer Shahram Derakhshan explains, it seems one of the early objectives of establishing and operating this channel was "the [television] organization's self-sufficiency from independent documentaries or those produced in other filmmaking sectors."[20] Considering the television's strict red lines and extensive censorship, it seems the channel finds it both ideologically and economically "safer" to produce and broadcast its own documentaries.

During Mohammadmahdi Tabatabaeinejad's directorship at the Documentary and Experimental Film Center, the DEFC slightly diversified the exhibition outlet of the Documentary Channel through showcasing some documentaries presented at the Cinema Vérité film festival on this platform. In a 2016 interview, Tabatabaeinejad stated that the center has worked with the television and it "has a box [slot] named Cinema Vérité in the Documentary Channel ... We have tried to continue this despite financial constraints because a cost had been spent for making a documentary and there is this expectation that the television pays the broadcast fee."[21] Elsewhere, Tabatabaeinejad said that the DEFC expected the television to pay at least "one third of [a documentary's] production budget," a condition that Iranian television rejected as it prefers to only pay a relatively low "copyright fee" for the documentary films. A copyright fee is a one-time payment making the purchase available to the entire television industry, thus allowing it to be exhibited by multiple IRIB television channels in multiple instances.[22] Despite these very unbalanced terms, it was the prospect of increasing the public reach of the documentaries that persuaded the DEFC to maintain its relationship with Iranian television. Yet, given the considerable number of documentaries produced by the DEFC itself,[23] and many more made independently outside of it, such a push for the television exhibition could hardly be expected to change the hegemonic and closed structure of this organization's documentary exhibition practices. As Mina Keshavarz pointed out in my interview:

> Unfortunately, the exhibition space for documentary film in Iran is very limited, [and] this limited space is often allocated to those films that are made with the support of the television and governmental organizations. ... Independent documentaries practically do not have a place in the television and are often deprived of the festival spaces due to censorship or other issues. As such, the audience's access to independent documentary cinema is very limited and the assessment of these films' impact on the society is not an easy task.[24]

Given the IRIB's ideological and propagandistic approaches to documentary, Sadegh-Vaziri notes that the IRIB "broadcasts critical documentaries by well-known American and European filmmakers, if they fit the leadership's anti-American rhetoric. Films like Michael Moore's *Roger and Me* (1997) and *Sicko* (2007), Alex Gibney's *Taxi to the Dark Side* (2008) …, and … *Citizen Four* (2014) by Laura Poitras have all been shown on IRIB channels."[25] Interestingly, this political and ideological struggle within a global context has not been one-sided. Media scholar Niki Akhavan writes:

> A spike in foreign funding for "democracy promotion" available from sources in the United States, the United Kingdom, the Netherlands, and other European countries expanded media projects and platforms that embraced stories about oppressive aspects of Iranian society. Launched in 2009, the Persian BBC Television Channel (funded by Britain's Foreign and Commonwealth Office), for example, has been an outlet for the dissemination of both short- and long-form documentaries …[26]

Another example is the US-government-funded Voice of America (VOA Persian/VOA 365), which also exhibits short and feature-length Iranian documentaries. Akhavan further argues that with these new outlets, "a new generation of women filmmakers [have] also found an audience for their work."[27] These new exhibition platforms for documentary films outside of Iran have in fact provided a way around restrictive policies of Iranian television to reach a wider Iranian audience domestically and in the diaspora. And of course, not all the foreign channels necessarily screen documentaries that showcase the "oppressive aspects of Iranian society;" even the BBC Persian has broadcast many nuanced documentaries made by Iranian documentarians such as Rakhshan Banietemad's *All My Trees* (*Hame-ye derakhtan-e man*, 2015), Mohammad Shirvani's *Iranian Cookbook* (*Dastoor-e ashpazi*, 2010), and Mojtaba Mirtahmasb's *Six Centuries, Six Years* (*Shesh gharn, shesh sal*, 2014).

In another instance, the American satellite television network Link TV presented a series entitled *Bridge to Iran*—"a co-production of CEM Productions and KCETLink"[28]—exhibiting documentaries on Iran and Iran-related issues produced by documentarians living in Iran or the diaspora. According to *Bridge to Iran*'s official website, the series was "a direct response to the cultural misunderstandings and political tensions that have developed between Iran and the U.S. since the Iranian revolution."[29] The series' third season primarily focused "on Iranian Women and the Circle of Life. Over six evenings of one-hour programs, broadcast nationally on KCET-LinkTV and select PBS stations …"[30] Works by Iranian independent women documentarians such as Rakhshan Banietemad's

We Are Half of Iran's Population (2009), Mahvash Sheikholeslami's *Where Do I Belong?* (*Be koja ta'alogh daram?* 2007), and Nahid Rezaei's *Dream of Silk* (*Khab-e abrisham*, 2003) were among the documentaries showcased by the series.

However, due to the anti-Western rhetoric of the Islamic Republic, the Iranian state is suspicious of these foreign channels and usually considers them weapons of Western soft power. As a result, the documentary exhibition in these international outlets has come at a price for some Iranian independent documentarians whose films were broadcast by them. As discussed in Chapter 1, in 2011 independent producer and distributor Katayoon Shahabi and five other documentarians—Mojtaba Mirtahmasb, Hadi Afarideh, Naser Saffarian, Mohsen Shahnazdar, and Mehran Zinatbakhsh—were detained and charged with "collaborating with the BBC Television."[31] They were ultimately released but the incident once again highlighted the sensitivity of the Iranian state toward documentary practices, especially within a transnational context. Moreover, based on his 2006 survey of European channels, Attebai suggests:

> [T]he documentary films with the running time of 50 to 59 minutes have the highest possibility of sale to and exhibition on European channels, and the documentary films below 30 minutes have the least possibility of broadcast. It is important to note that the majority of Iranian cinema's documentary productions are below 30 minutes and this issue itself decreases the chance of these films' sale [to Europe].[32]

This issue thus further adds to a politically and ideologically charged television environment within a transnational context, restricting the possibilities of exhibition for Iranian independent documentaries. Nevertheless, Iranian television itself must play a main role in supporting and promoting Iranian documentaries. And unless the structures and ideologies of this organization fundamentally change, any substantial opportunity to screen and promote Iranian independent documentaries, especially those made by women, seems unattainable. The major governmental organization overseeing the production, distribution, and exhibition of documentary films remains the DEFC, which in recent years has increased its efforts in regard to the distribution and exhibition of Iranian documentaries.

Documentary and Experimental Film Center (DEFC) and the Cinema Vérité Film Festival

The Documentary and Experimental Film Center (DEFC) has incorporated different modes of documentary circulation that include occasional film screenings with discussions at the center, DVD sales via the center's library as well as a "video library" allowing "documentarians, researchers, and critics" to access and watch "over 1000 documentary, animation, and fiction films produced by the center in different periods."[33] However, not all the documentaries produced by the center are available on DVD or get a wide distribution. For instance, one might purchase from the library the DVD of Azadeh Bizargiti's documentary, *The Scent of Lemon at Dawn* (2014), which was officially distributed by the center. However, Bizargiti's *Hidden Half of the Moon* (2017) was not available, despite having screened in various venues. To watch the film for this study required having to contact the DEFC and request permission to access the documentary in the form of a DVD for the research. In addition to broadcasting some documentaries on Iranian television, the DEFC promotes its documentaries "by producing film catalogues in Persian and English and presenting the films in international festivals."[34] Yet, as mentioned above, the distribution, exhibition, and promotional efforts of the center do not cover all the documentary films produced by this organization. Commenting on the center's policies, Mina Keshavarz said:

> The center considers itself the financial and even intellectual (*ma'navi*) owner of a film, and ultimately the majority of the films produced by the DEFC do not enter any distribution circuit because the center [as a governmental organization whose budget comes from the Ministry of Culture and Islamic Guidance (MCIG)] does not need a return on investment. And these films are usually screened at the Cinema Vérité festival which again its trustee is the center, and if [the films] get very lucky or the filmmaker follows up the process himself/herself, they might also get screened in some international festivals and that's all.[35]

This illuminating observation reveals that for most Iranian independent documentaries, even those produced or co-produced by the DEFC, festival screening remains the dominant if not the sole way of reaching audiences and critics. This explains why so few of these films find other means of circulation such as non-theatrical screenings, home video, and/or online exhibitions. In fact, the circulation of many Iranian documentary films begins and ends within the festival circuit. In this context, a key outlet for exhibiting and marketing documentary films organized by the DEFC is the Cinema Vérité: Iran International Documentary Film Festival.

Many film festivals in Iran showcase documentary films, including the Roshd International Film Festival and the Tehran International Short Film Festival. There have also been some festivals that focus exclusively on documentary films, some of which are now defunct, such as the Kish International Documentary Film Festival (1999–2005) and the Yadegar

Documentary Film Festival (2002–2005). According to documentary historian and filmmaker Mohammad Tahaminejad, "In the 1990s, about twenty-two Iranian documentary film festivals on average introduced more than a thousand documentary films most of which were produced by the government as their financier."[36] Yet, the possibility of a specialized *and* continuous international documentary film festival in Iran had to wait until the mid-2000s.

In 2007, the DEFC organized the first Cinema Vérité film festival, which quickly became a major player in the documentary scene both domestically and internationally. As festival programmer and journalist Pamela Cohn reflects on the event, "The festival and market's organizers have tasked themselves with two main responsibilities: the introduction and showcasing of Iranian documentaries to the world, and the introduction of international fare to the local population of moviegoers, specifically to its younger generations."[37] The Cinema Vérité festival, therefore, positions itself at a cultural and artistic crossroads in order to enhance transnational documentary exchanges between Iran and the international community. In doing so, the festival paid "tributes to filmmakers Richard Leacock, Peter Wintonick and Jørgen Leth" among others.[38] In addition to showcasing works from the capital Tehran, other documentary films and documentarians from Iranian provinces have also been highlighted, including those from "East Azarbaijan, Isfahan, Kerman, and the southern regions."[39] Iranian women documentarians have also been some of the main participants in the festival, despite their lack of presence on the festival's selection committees and among the jury and programming committee members. According to a report on the eleventh festival held in 2017, "86 women filmmakers with their latest documentary works were applicants for participating in the festival," which depicts "a participation of 10.05 per cent for women documentarians."[40] This percentage still has much room to improve and the inclusion of more female documentary experts in the festival's decision-making roles and committees can be a potential contributing factor regarding this goal.

The film screenings, Q&A sessions with the documentarians, workshops and documentary industry meetings with international distributors, festival programmers, and filmmakers, alongside the presence of documentary enthusiasts, all create a dynamic documentary atmosphere and exchange. These few festival days, while temporally short, create longer critical and discursive effects manifesting themselves in the forms of journal reviews and magazine articles, television and media coverage, and post-festival screenings and discussions. Persheng Vaziri cites the festival's free admission as one of the main reasons behind the "high attendance." She writes:

> Over the years, filmmakers have objected to the free admission structure as being counterproductive to the documentary field. They want audiences to value documentaries, and believe that charging an admission fee would not impact the popularity of the event. The festival can afford to be so generous because the sponsor, Documentary and Experimental Film Center (DEFC), is government-supported, as are most of Iran's cultural institutions.[41]

Such embedded governmental support regarding the Cinema Vérité film festival, however, has at times directly affected its domestic and international reception. For instance, after the contested 2009 re-election of Mahmoud Ahmadinejad as the country's president, which led to massive protests known as the Green Movement, many Iranian documentarians boycotted the festival and did not submit their documentaries for the third festival. As film scholar Hamid Naficy writes:

> In a letter, initially signed by 136 people, ... veteran and young documentarists declared ... that they were boycotting [the festival]. This was not because they disagreed with the festival or with its hardworking director, Mohammad Afarideh, ... rather, it was because they objected to the government's impediments to filming the Green Movement's protests, which would make this festival, whose mission was to reflect and document Iranian realities, look like all other years, as though nothing unusual—no protest—had taken place in Iran that year.[42]

For many documentarians the boycott of the festival, as well as the reluctance in collaboration with the DEFC, continued until the end of Ahmadinejad's second presidential term in 2013, when the "moderate" government of Hasan Rouhani (2013–2021) installed new leaders in the MCIG and its Cinematic Organization. In 2022, during the presidency of conservative Ebrahim Raisi (2021–2024) and concomitant with the massive Woman, Life, Freedom protests—which were a response to the arrest, beating, and subsequent death of a twenty-two-year-old Iranian Kurdish woman, Mahsa (Zhina) Amini, at the hands of Iran's notorious morality police[43]—a group of documentarians "in a statement signed by over 150 documentary filmmakers and cultural figures" boycotted the sixteenth Cinema Vérité film festival. In their statement, these documentarians expressed "their solidarity with the honorable and bereaved people of Iran" and asserted that they "boycott the participation in this edition of the festival in any form, in-person and online."[44] Meanwhile, escalating economic crises in Iran, in part as a result of US sanctions against Iran, have severely affected the Cinema Vérité film festival. As Vaziri explains in her essay on the twelfth festival held in 2018, "You could see the effects of the sanctions on prices, which had tripled for many items or had at least doubled for food and necessities over the past year. In response to price hikes, the festival had cut back on expenses, such as offering air travel for their international guests. But they did provide for hotel accommodations, daily meals and organized outings."[45] These moments in Iranian documentary's history—the boycotts of the festival and the festival's planned austerity—reflect the interwoven nature of sociopolitical, cultural, and economic settings with the artistic facets of the festival, rendering such events as sites of (geo)political tensions and negotiations.

Such a context also affects the ways in which Iranian documentaries are programmed and received at the international film festivals. In light of the Woman, Life, Freedom movement in Iran, for its thirtieth edition in 2023, the Sheffield International Documentary Festival dedicated a retrospective to the documentaries of Rakhshan Banietemad, who was the festival's "Guest of Honour." The festival showcased six of Banietemad's works including *Our Times* (*Ruzegar-e ma*, 2002), *We Are Half of Iran's Population* (2009), and *Hey, Humans* (*Ay adam-ha*, 2016).[46] Additionally, the festival curated "Perspectives on Iran," "a selection of new and vital documentaries showing different perspectives on Iran. Ranging from female filmmakers surveying the limitations placed on their lives and work, a reassessment of the male gaze in cinema and an account of the insidiousness of censorship to a dark portrait of political interrogation and a celebration of friendship across two continents."[47] The recognition of Iranian women's documentaries at major international film festivals is a welcoming effort. Nevertheless, the politics of this recognition at specific historical times needs to be recognized as well.

Breaking away from the idea that international Western film festival programming works according to "objectively positioned merits" or art-for-art's sake tendencies, documentary programmer Svetla Turnin asserts, "The recognition that programming is no longer simply an innocuous curatorial process but instead a political practice affected by the commercialization of the documentary festivals, which suffer from financial and populist pressures, is the first step to strategizing how to develop more equitable programming practices, including around gender."[48] Therefore, a deep and *sustained* commitment to engage with and showcase Iranian women's independent documentary films could facilitate a better understanding of the complexities of Iranian women's lives and the documentary practices associated with them. Turnin for instance suggests, "build[ing] support networks and create[ing] mentorships by and for women filmmakers" and balancing festivals' competition programs as possible ways to bring about diversity and gender equity in the documentary field. As she writes, "if women's history is a counter-history, and documentary is historically situated to engage with it, then what we need is counter-programming, and more of it!"[49] At the same time, international film festivals' recognitions, while bringing much-needed distribution and exhibition opportunities for Iranian documentary films, may also unintentionally put their makers under the surveillance of the Iranian state. The state often regards such Western praises as a result of the films' portrayals of the "dark aspects" of Iranian society (*Siahnamaei*), thus considering them as a catering tool to Western perceptions of Iran. This dual complexity—the workings of both Iranian and international film festivals and their different approaches to Iranian documentaries in the festival circuit—demonstrates that "film and film festivals not only reflect (or fall victim to) political developments, but also instigate and shape them."[50]

Theatrical Screening: Art and Experience Cinema

Unlike fiction cinema in Iran, which remains the mainstay of theatrical exhibition and commercial revenue, Iranian documentary has not benefited from similar public exposure or economic possibility. Writing on the history of commercial screenings of Iranian documentary films after the 1979 Islamic Revolution, documentary critic Amirhosein Sanaei claims, "The documentary *Our Times* (Rakhshan Banietemad [2002]) got public screening in January 2003 in a few theaters for a short time. Seven years later in the spring of 2009, *Tehran Has No More Pomegranates* (*Tehran anar nadarad*, Massoud Bakhshi [2006]) was screened in three theaters, Azadi, Osveh, and Sepideh, and was one of the very few Iranian documentaries in the 2000s to get a theatrical, public screening."[51] In fact, these few instances of theatrical exhibition during this period were concomitant with a surge in documentary production in Iran, as pointed out in Chapter 1. But many of these documentaries remained unseen by most audiences. The increasing number of documentary films, along with the limited theatrical screening possibilities, which could hardly cover all the approved fiction films for such a form of exhibition, prompted the government to address the theatrical exhibition issue.

In 2014 and during Hasan Rouhani's first-term presidency, the Cinematic Organization of the MCIG formed the "Art and Experience" cinematic workgroup, whose members were appointed by the head of the Cinematic Organization. They were tasked to select and officially screen art and experimental films[52]—fiction, documentary, animation, and short films—that have a lesser chance of commercial and theatrical exhibition "in order to diversify screening box and simultaneously pay attention to general and specialized cinematic audiences … and enhance audiences' [filmic] taste ."[53] The initiative officially began its programs "on October 5, 2014 with the collaboration of four movie theaters in Tehran and one in Mashhad."[54] At the time of writing, "the Documentary and Experimental Film Center (DEFC) holds the responsibility of management, coordination, and supervision regarding the initiative's activities."[55] At a glance, such a project may appear unprecedented in the history of Iranian cinema by seemingly creating a platform for many art films, including documentaries, which are often overshadowed by the fiction cinema, to reach a wider audience. Yet here again documentary films are shoehorned with other cinematic forms, all of which are considered by the Cinematic Organization as "specialized-audience films" (*film-haye mokhatab-e khas*), which "unlike commercial films, cannot attract a large audience in … movie theaters in the short term, but may accumulate audiences over time with alternative screenings."[56] In their assessment of Art and Experience Cinema in 2021, Payam Ghanipour and Sayyed Ali Rohani write, "It seems the majority of Art and Experience Cinema's audiences are young and university individuals, cinema personalities, and in specific cases families."[57] But they do not offer further details on which filmic category often attracts these groups of audiences to this initiative. In 2016, Mohammadmahdi Tabatabaeinejad, the then DEFC director, pointed out, "Based on [Art and Experience] group's statistics, about 25 per cent of Art and Experience space is allocated to documentary films and the center has screened more than 10 of its documentaries in this program."[58] However, two major issues loom over this cinematic initiative, namely the requirement for permits—only films that hold both production permit and exhibition permit from the MCIG can be considered for screening in the Art and Experience Cinema[59]—and audience attraction, both of which need to be addressed in a much more open and active manner for the Art and Experience Cinema to perform more inclusively.

All films, whether fiction or documentary, must obtain exhibition permits from the MCIG for official, theatrical screenings. Therefore, many filmmakers might to some extent self-censor their works to get screening approval. Nahid Rezaei, along with six other documentarians, produced the groundbreaking collaborative documentary *Profession: Documentarist* (2014), which offers personal reflections on sociopolitical and artistic aspects of contemporary Iranian society in seven episodes, each of which is made by one of the filmmakers. Recalling the production of this documentary and its relation to the exhibition stage, Rezaei explained:

> In *Profession: Documentarist*, even though we did not want to comply with the existing red lines at the time to, for instance, discuss the events of 2009 or the [1979] revolution from our own perspectives, we were still hopeful to have our film screened in a better circumstance inside the country, and therefore, we observed some issues such as wearing the hijab. We discussed the ban on women's singing but did not enter many [other] realms. I, for example, could not depict an intimate space of a party with friends in my own house, which was in my initial plot …[60]

Profession: Documentarist did not obtain an official exhibition permit but was screened at the House of Cinema's celebration ceremony and other informal venues in Iran. Further, it was exhibited at various international film festivals such as Sheffield International Documentary Festival, Jihlava International Documentary Film Festival, and Zurich Film Festival.

Discussing official permits in documentary production and exhibition, documentarian Mahvash Sheikholeslami explained:

> Basically, I [have] not worked without permits and my films have always followed the legal processes. That's why I have been able to survive and work in this profession for forty years. But, for example, *Article 61* (*Madeh 61*, 2005) could not get an exhibition permit and still is not granted such a permission, yet this film, after many years, has been exhibited in many festivals and once or twice in Iran.[61]

The negotiations between what to say and not to say, what to depict and not to depict, while also preserving the complex and nuanced reality of life in Iran, indeed constitute a very difficult task that Iranian independent documentarians have to meticulously and creatively work on. Film producer and distributor Katayoon Shahabi, regarding the complexity of approval permits, said, "In some cases, especially regarding documentary films, there is less restriction for the permit, and because their screening is limited to inside the country, the permits are given on a case-by-case base and sometimes the exhibited version inside Iran differs from its international version."[62] This observation sheds light on another aspect of exhibition, that some restricted or banned documentaries do not get screened in Iran but manage to secure exhibition outside of the country, predominantly at international film festivals.

This level of gatekeeping is based on very vague and mutable red lines, preventing some independent documentaries and other filmic works to get any exhibition permits before even they can be considered for the placement on the Art and Experience theatrical screening program. One such example is Azadeh Bizargiti's documentary, *The Scent of Lemon at Dawn* (2014), which was produced by the DEFC and was screened in many international film festivals, receiving multiple awards. In addition to positive reviews, the film represented Iran at the Cannes film market.

Yet, it was denied a screening permit for the Art and Experience exhibition.[63] Bizargiti mentioned that she even received an invitation from the United Nations-The Hague as a peace ambassador in the section on the prohibition of chemical weapons. "But unfortunately," as she recounted:

> here in Iran, I was asked to shorten the film. In other words, to censor it and [then] send it [to the UN for screening]. And I did not do it, and my film sadly did not get exhibited exactly where it should; a place where I thought I could be influential and bring the world's politicians' attention to the topic of war and its consequences so that perhaps they refrain from their militaristic policies; or at least withdraw from using chemical weapons ...[64]

Bizargiti's documentary highlights the brutalities of the Iraqi invasion during the Iran-Iraq War, and in particular narrates the lives of some women affected by Iraq's chemical attack on the Iranian city Sardasht. Yet, the fact that her film, which was produced with the support of the DEFC, could not obtain exhibition permit for the theatrical screening in Iran, speaks volumes about the monopoly of the state, over not only the narratives of the Iran-Iraq War and the ways in which they are mediated and controlled, but also the politics of granting exhibition permits to independent documentaries.

While from the start one of the main objectives of the Art and Experience Cinema has been to target mostly specialized audiences, the initiative also hoped to cultivate a general appreciation of and engagement with Iranian art and experimental films through "the enhancement of audiences' cinematic knowledge and the improvement of the artistic quality of Iranian cinema."[65] However, emphasizing the lack of public advertisement for the documentaries screened in the Art and Experience Cinema, the documentarian Naser Saffarian in an interview with the *Mehr News Agency* asked, "Now that the documentary is on the screen, do people go to the theater to watch it?" To which he negatively responded, continuing, "There are two groups of audiences for a documentary film: one is the people involved in documentary cinema themselves and/or documentary enthusiasts, and the other is the ordinary audience that can be attracted. The former does not need much advertising as they follow up themselves, but to inform the latter you need to have more appropriate advertisements."[66] These observations illustrate that the Art and Experience Cinema has not succeeded in broadening its reach into the society and attracting a more general audience. At the same time, maintaining the sustained attention of documentary cinephiles also requires appropriate outreach strategies and constant monitoring of their effectiveness. In this regard, I argue that not granting exhibition permits to some documentaries and restricting promotional approaches regarding some films screened in the program have directly impacted the audience's attendance.[67] This is mainly because these actions send a signal of exclusivity and official control over this exhibition platform. These restrictions also paradoxically work against one of the objectives of the Art and Experience Cinema itself; that is to be a platform for the exhibition of high quality, non-commercial films that have a lesser chance of theatrical and public screening.

Non-Theatrical Screenings

Documentaries that do not get official exhibition permit for theatrical screening might get semi-formal and/or informal screenings at universities, cultural and art centers, libraries, and home gatherings. In this regard, Mina Keshavarz, in her interview for this study, explained that her documentary "*Unwelcome in Tehran* (2011) was banned by the MCIG and not granted an exhibition permit inside Iran, yet the documentary was screened in smaller venues domestically, and ... after eight years since the film was made, [the documentary is] being used for teaching at the College of Social Sciences for Urban Sociology major."[68] As Keshavarz put it, "this film, regardless of all the limitations, has found its way and is having an impact, but this process is moving very slowly."[69] In the same vein, Mahnaz Afzali had only one of her documentaries, *Mother of the Earth* (2017), exhibited theatrically as part of the Karestan Film Series. Her other films have been exhibited on a case-by-case basis at venues such as universities, research centers, and/or film festivals.[70] Afzali, like Keshavarz, asserted, "What is clear is that when a film has something to say, [it] finds its way" to reach the audience and have an impact.[71] Indeed, the fact that these semi-formal and informal screenings have materialized foregrounds the audience's desire to access and watch these independent documentaries through the formation of alternative exhibition spaces.

A few years after its establishment in 1999 as a documentary guild in the House of Cinema, the Association of Iranian Documentary Producers (AIDP)—*Anjoman-e tahiyeh-konandegan-e mostanad-e Iran*[72]—formed an Exhibition workgroup that began a regular documentary screening in the House of Artists "with its first documentary screening in the fall of 2001."[73] This initiative strongly continues today, attracting "an average of a hundred individuals per screening."[74] The House of Cinema has been another alternative space for documentary screenings. The documentaries are exhibited in this place as part of the Iranian Documentary Filmmakers Association's (IRDFA) screenings and the House of Cinema's annual celebration. Mina Keshavarz named some of the main cultural spaces that screen independent documentary films, "such as Rokhdad-e Tazeh-ye Mostanad, Khanesh Institute, and UpArtMaan [Cultural Center]."[75] Rokhdad-e Tazeh-ye Mostanad is a pioneering workgroup that focuses on "sociological documentary films"—documentaries that use critical sociology as a method "to expand and transfer such point of view to the field of criticism and theory, so that documentary cinema's critics and cinephiles, in their interpretation of reality and representation of issues, can encounter liberating features substituting passiveness with intervention and activeness."[76] As such, the documentaries screened and discussed by this workgroup are deeply interwoven with different aspects of Iranian society dissecting its challenges and power dynamics that inevitably, yet differently, affect each documentary and its documentarian's practice. The group was formed in the summer of 2015 and even though the Rokhdad-e Tazeh Institute got closed in winter 2016, the documentary workgroup has been "determined to continue its previous activities with the same persistence."[77] Shirin Barghnavard and Zeinab Tabrizi are two women documentarians of this workgroup.[78]

Other cultural centers, such as Arasbaran and Golestan, have also occasionally hosted documentary screenings. According to Amirhosein Sanaei, "Since the beginning of 2016, the Hoseinieh Ershad's library has been also a regular place for documentary exhibition."[79] Nahid Rezaei is the documentarian involved in this library's monthly documentary screenings.[80] Among home screenings, Haleh Bastani, the wife of documentary producer Saeed Rashtian, has provided a space for intimate documentary gatherings, especially for female audiences. In a published interview she recalled:

> The collective started in 2009. In our office ... many films were being made. As such, I watched many films and told myself, it's unfortunate that fewer people can see these [works]. Documentary cinema does not have a wide screening and the television does not care much about it. We began with two or three people ... When I started [the gathering], I said to myself, if we get short on films, we will review them again. But we are now behind, as so many good films are being made.[81]

This private bi-weekly meeting has continued over the years and the documentarians are often in attendance at the screenings followed by Q&As and relevant discussions.[82] Many other sporadic events in small venues showcase documentary films, some weekly, some monthly, yet others on a case-by-case basis. All these exhibition practices together form parts of the fragmented modes of circulation in Iranian documentary, and in these instances, they create a fragmented, yet much-needed, documentary exhibition structure. It is also important to note the active involvement of women and women documentarians in these exhibition efforts in order to create a deeper exchange between the documentary medium and the Iranian society. In this regard, Nahid Rezaei mentioned, "Interestingly, the experience of exhibiting documentary films in various art places, which has become very common these days, shows that the majority of these screenings' audiences are also women."[83] The fragmented modes of documentary exhibition make it difficult, if not impossible, to statistically track the number and gender of audiences attending these diverse non-theatrical screenings. Nevertheless, Rezaei's perspective as a documentarian involved in such exhibition practices underscores Iranian women's high degree of interest in documentary films and their engagement with a wide range of sociocultural issues through these films.

In relation to these alternative, non-theatrical screenings, a pressing issue has been the payment of exhibition fees to the documentarians so that they can have a small, yet reliable, revenue to continue making their documentary films. In fact, the majority of these non-theatrical screenings occur in the name of "cultural works" and without any exhibition fees. Considering the few official exhibition venues for independent documentaries, many documentarians go along with free-of-charge non-theatrical screenings in order to offer audiences greater access to their films. In 2016, four documentarians—Pezhman Mazaheripour, Mehdi Bagheri, Mona Zahed, and Behrooz Malboosbaf—created a campaign via social media titled, "Exhibiting Documentary Film Is Not Free," which attracted "more than 600 signatories" many of whom were/are involved in the Iranian documentary field.[84] According to the *Mehr News Agency*, part of the campaign's statement reads:

> In broadcast, rerun, and use of [documentary] films in media and academic and educational centers, there are no exhibition rights. Documentary festivals, in order to attract audiences, do not sell tickets and inevitably hold the documentary screenings free of charge. Unfortunately, in this circumstance, the favorite works are also presented to the audience through official screenings with a free tag. There is no basis for calculating the appropriate exhibition rights based on the type of screening and the type of a film's use. The existing methods would negatively affect the production, the quality of works, and the audiences' taste in the long run.[85]

The campaign, therefore, asked for more transparent plans for documentary circulation within various formal and informal settings, with a particular focus on supporting the documentarians' financial rights in regard to the exhibition and distribution of their works. Considering many scattered non-theatrical spaces, a reasonably-priced exhibition fee might indeed make a significant difference and provide a crucial incentive for independent documentarians facing financial uncertainties.

Private and Digital Modes of Circulation

Domestic and international distribution of documentaries requires skilled and professional independent distributors, yet there are precious few in Iranian documentary. It is often very difficult for busy documentarians to work on exhibition and distribution processes efficiently and actively, in addition to being already involved in various stages of production. In this regard, Azadeh Bizargiti lamented:

> Although my films have been screened in some accredited international festivals and have also received some awards, I mostly consider all of this as fate and chance. I usually work hard for years and then my film collects dust in the closet, because I personally think the process of a proper distribution is an important process and a job, which unfortunately in Iran we documentarians seem to have to do ourselves, and of course, the person whose professional job is filmmaking does not have enough time for distributing his/her film as s/he immediately starts the next film.[86]

Katayoon Shahabi is one of Iranian documentary's most influential, independent distributors/producers. Her dedication and efforts have helped broaden the circulation of Iranian independent fiction, documentary, and short films globally. Shahabi was "the first person in Iran who organized for CMI [Cima Media International, a semi-private company] an International Market for Iranian films and television programs, TIM (Tehran International Market) in 1995."[87] She then launched her own private distribution and production companies—Tehran-based Sheherazad Media International (SMI) and Paris-based Noori Pictures in 2001 and 2012 respectively—that have been active within an international context. In an interview for this study, Shahabi explained the motivations for setting up her own private companies: "First, I wanted to share ... the cinema that I liked with others. Then, to give an opportunity to the youth so that they can present their first and second films within an international space and enhance their own and their country's cinema."[88] Specifically, Shahabi believes film distribution is a task independent from any governmental politics, and as such, it is not compatible with a government job. She said, "The speed and correct decision-making that are foundational elements for this job are not compatible with the management of governmental sectors that goes through substantial changes every few years. On the other hand, my personality was not the one that could follow wrong decisions and obey without questioning. As such, establishing my own company seemed inevitable."[89]

Shahabi's companies are involved in three main activities: festival, international distribution, and co-production. She sees the first two as the ways through which Iranian independent films, including documentaries, may gain wider exposure to global audiences. In the festival section, based on the quality of films, her companies submit the films to the top international film festivals and then to other lower-ranked festivals as appropriate. Shahabi maintained, "The festival is a good launch pad for Iranian films, but unfortunately without a film's presence at the top or 'A' festivals, its sale is not easy."[90] While in recent decades the number of international film festivals has dramatically increased and the notion of an A-category festival has been contested,[91] the so-called "A" festivals still assert their dominance.[92] This dominance occurs not only in terms of their competitive "premier hierarchies,"[93] but also in regard to the prestige and symbolic capital that these festivals can bestow upon the films they exhibit. Moreover, film scholar Dina Iordanova highlights the fact that usually "[e]ntering a film at a festival is seen as a way of opening doors to what lies beyond, … to proper distribution via theatrical and DVD deals for a wide range of territories," and thus argues for the consideration of festivals as primarily exhibition sites rather than distribution ones.[94] Iordanova further observes, "Most of the films made in independent contexts, however, depend on festival participation, as it secures circulation beyond their original environment."[95] That is why for an international distributor such as Shahabi, festivals are *one* way of distributing Iranian independent films (in addition to exhibiting them).

Shahabi's companies use other means of international circulation such as "exhibiting films in [foreign] cinemas, television channels, [and] cultural centers, and [distributing films via] the Internet, VOD [platforms], and other formats."[96] Shahabi further explained, "We usually try to give a film's rights to a domestic distributor in each country for a time period that is agreed between the two sides so that the film can benefit from all aspects of exhibition and distribution."[97] Their global reach to audiences around the world is what makes the work of private companies, such as Shahabi's, significant, yet this same factor also makes them more vulnerable to the international geo-politics. For example, Shahabi discussed the following negative consequences of the US sanctions on the Iranian film industry to *Variety*: "The economic situation is a disaster for [Iranian] independent cinema … it's basically impossible to sell [films] to any country, not just to the U.S.," because for Iran-based companies "you can't receive any money."[98] Shahabi's Paris-based company may, in this situation, provide an easier way out of the sanctions' stalemate by working with international companies and film industries. But as Shahabi pointed out, US distribution "companies that work with Iranians are penalized, so they don't want to take any risks."[99] Considering the prevailing political and economic constraints on Iranian film distribution, international film festivals' exhibitions can provide alternative and essential venues for independent Iranian films; albeit Iranian filmmakers themselves might face travel restrictions that prevent them from attending such events.

In another example, the Kara Film Studio, a private documentary studio co-founded by two veteran documentarians, Rakhshan Banietemad and Mojtaba Mirtahmasb, "endeavor[s] to provide improved and increased means of screening films inside and outside Iran," in addition to its production activities.[100] In this regard, the Kara Film Studio presents its produced films at various domestic and international film festivals, and according to its website at the time of writing, its films have attended "117 festivals" receiving "22 awards."[101] The Kara Film Studio's screenings also include exhibition at universities both inside and outside of Iran. The documentary *Touran Khanom* (2018), for instance, was screened at the thirty-first International Film Festival for Children and Youth in Isfahan, the forty-eighth Roshd International Film Festival in Tehran, Boston University's College of Art and Sciences in the US, and University of Ottawa in Canada, among others.[102] In 2017, "Maryam Bagheri, the distribution and international manager of Kara Film Studio attended the IDFA to represent the two selected documentaries of *Mother of the Earth* by Mahnaz Afzali and *Poets of Life* directed by Shirin Barghnavard" at the IDFA's Docs for Sales market, a venue for the introduction of the works to interested documentary distributors.[103]

In the Iranian domestic market, some independent documentary films can be accessed on legally-produced DVDs, but there remains a parallel black market of bootleg DVDs including documentaries. Regarding the legal video market, Amirhosein Sanaei writes, "After the ban on video was removed in 1993, Moaseseh-ye Resaneh-haye Tasviri [Visual Media Institute] was established to organize legal activities in the country's video network. This Institute, which until 2000 was the sole licensed center active in this field, had a limited activity in regard to documentary film distribution."[104] Sanaei, therefore, names Houshang Golmakani's documentary, *Stardust-Stricken* (*Gong-e khabdideh*), which was produced in 1993 and distributed in 1996, as "one of the earliest [Iranian] documentary films that was released on a VHS tape."[105] Since the 1990s, however, other governmental institutions—including the Documentary and Experimental Film Center and the Iranian television—and private organizations have become active in the home video market. As I mentioned earlier, the DEFC distributes some of its documentaries on DVD. Azadeh Bizargiti's *The Scent of Lemon at Dawn* is one example.

In the private sector, the documentarian Naser Saffarian received "the first video permit issued to an individual person in 2002 by the Cinematic Organization's Department of Supervision and Evaluation …, and *The Green Cold* (*Sard-e Sabz* [2002]) came to the market outside of the current [governmental] institutions' system."[106] Saffarian reflects on this experience himself, stating that "the executive part of the [distribution] was given to a professional music distributor through [selling the documentary] at the bookstores."[107] Considering the independent nature of this type of distribution by a documentarian, as well as the lack of proper distribution infrastructures and professional distributors, the inter-media collaboration and networking with the music sector and bookstores seem inevitable. Saffarian was thus able to independently distribute other documentaries made by himself and his colleagues using the same method. Reflecting on the economic viability of such distribution practices, Saffarian postulates, "While in comparison with book circulation and the book market, the sale of 1300–2000 films over a three-year period did not seem bad, it could not be considered an economic activity so that we could continue the work based on its profit."[108] Yet, given the limited options available for this kind of private and independent distribution model in Iran, some music stores, bookstores, and publishing houses have also become involved in documentary distribution selling DVDs of these films in their shops. Shah-re Ketab (The City of Book) in Tehran, for instance, sells the DVDs of the Karestan Film Series, which can also be purchased online via the bookstore's website.[109]

Digital forms of exhibition and distribution have brought about unprecedented possibilities for accessing Iranian documentary films outside of metropolitan areas and have enabled documentarians to engage with a wide range of audiences in a global context. Such novel digital configurations have also considerably challenged the hierarchies of power in regard to the documentary medium both domestically and internationally. Discussing the idea that Western documentary in its traditional essence has been backed by three pillars of "scientism, eurocentrism, [and] patriarchy,"[110] documentary scholars Brian Winston, Gail Vanstone, and Wang Chi argue that these three aspects have been "*potentially* deeply undercut by the digital."[111] As such, performances and discourses of subjectivity and identity politics have become central in documentary practices granting a space to documentarians from the Global South as well as the minority filmmakers in the Global North to present their voices.

In Iran, "commercial imperatives and motives, as well as the desire for effective control of the Internet," have prompted the Iranian state to take "the leading role in providing internet access and services."[112] In its 2023 report, Comparitech placed Iran and three other countries (Myanmar, Turkmenistan, and UAE) in the second place—after North Korea and China, which ranked first—as the worst countries for Internet censorship.[113] Nevertheless, young and technologically-savvy Iranians have managed to find ways to stay online and connected to the rest of the world.[114] In fact, the Internet has turned into an influential platform for communication and filmmaking in the country. The "Iranian sites and blogs have become new sources of information on various aspects of public life in the country,"[115] while they have also brought about new modes of documentary circulation. Hamid Naficy writes, "The emergence of the Internet, with its vast resources of information and connectivity as well as its gargantuan capacity for the posting, linking, exhibiting, distributing, archiving, marketing, blogging, uploading, downloading, and streaming of audiovisual materials ... [has] expand[ed] documentarists' horizons far beyond domestic and niche markets."[116] In regard to online distribution and exhibition of Iranian films, the number of SVOD services offering access to viewing outlets for these films is on the rise.[117] In terms of contents, these platforms are required to obtain licenses and legal permits from the Ministry of Culture and Islamic Guidance (MCIG) and IRIB-affiliated SATRA (the Iranian Audio-Visual Media Regulatory Authority).[118]

Established in 2018, Hashure is a SVOD platform primarily focused on Iranian documentary films in order to enhance their circulation. In addition to VOD streaming with subscription, the platform provides Internet screenings with online ticket sales occurring simultaneously in Iran and the rest of the world. The screening section has also dedicated segments to documentaries from the Art and Experience Cinema and the Cinema Vérité film festival.[119] In her interview for this study, Mina Keshavarz spoke positively of Hashure as "a new space that has facilitated the possibility of access to the films for audiences and to the audience for filmmakers."[120] But she further emphasized that, "The site also needs wide advertisements" so that it can broaden its reach more efficiently.[121] The Internet screening of *Touran Khanom* (2018), directed by Rakhshan Banietemad and Mojtaba Mirtahmasb, through Hashure's website, was the first of such experience for the Karestan Film Series, and brought about a significant amount of advertising in Iran and the diaspora for both the film and the platform partly due to the film's well-known documentarians and the novel method of its exhibition. The event also highlighted Hashure's role as a crucial online documentary platform. Mirtahmasb, in an interview with the *Iran Newspaper*, reflected on this experience, stating that "... [the Karestan] group's concern is film distribution; meaning the concern over [having an] audience and expanding [the reach] of the topics that we make film[s] about."[122] Highlighting the fact that the Art and Experience Cinema has not been successful "in attracting new audiences and even in maintaining its own potential audiences" and that the television "has not also been a reliable option," Mirthamasb argued that "our solution for attracting a wider audience was direct communication with them via the Internet."[123] The excitement over such documentary experience was immense on social media platforms, especially among Iranians in the diaspora who felt connected to this documentary event initiated from Iran, and shared the link of the online screening with others on their social media pages. Banietemad in her interview for this study mentioned that in terms of the audience for this screening, compared with previous Karestan film screenings, the result was multiplied.[124] This experience, therefore, shows that the VOD platforms have the potential to consolidate their role as a viable option for documentary circulation.

Outside of Iran, IMVBox offers legal VOD streaming of a wide range of Iranian films—fiction, documentary, and short, as well as television series—to global audiences (currently, the platform is not available in Iran). Established in 2013 in West London (UK), IMVBox operates similar to Western SVOD services such as Hulu and Netflix, yet it is a platform dedicated to Iranian cinema.[125] Upon setting up an IMVBox account, users can stream some of the media contents for free, while accessing other films, including some of the documentaries, requires users to subscribe to the platform by choosing one of the payment packages offered. The copyright protected contents of the IMVBox, a majority of which "with subtitles in more than twenty different languages,"[126] can broaden the reach of Iranian films, especially documentaries, within a global context while protecting the creative and financial rights of Iranian filmmakers. In another example, Docunight, a diasporic documentary "initiative under the Kiarostami Foundation" and based in the United States, initially "began its programming [in 2014] with monthly screenings in San Francisco and by 2020, it expanded to 25 cities in North America. Most of these screenings were held at universities in the US and Canada."[127] Due to the Covid-19 pandemic in 2020, the initiative moved its documentary screenings online by establishing the SVOD platform Docunight, that features documentaries with English subtitles, thus making "Iranian documentaries available to a broader international audience."[128]

Other online platforms such as YouTube and Vimeo also host many documentary films uploaded by individual documentarians. It was through Vimeo that some Iranian women documentarians featured in this study were able to grant me access to their documentaries. Platforms such as Vimeo and YouTube further provide the viewers with the possibility of interacting with the documentaries and the filmmakers through "like" and "comment" features, thus offering a more active communication method and feedback exchange between the viewers and the documentarians. Moreover, these sites allow documentarians to upload their works and share them with desired audiences for which, unlike online public screenings of documentaries via Iranian SVOD platforms, they do not have to obtain screening permits from the MCIG.

Online distribution and exhibition outlets and various VOD services have dramatically expanded the opportunities to access and view Iranian documentaries, especially those made by independent women documentarians. Yet, as Mina Keshavarz reminded us, these platforms need to have proper advertisements and outreach to attract potential viewers. There is also the issue of class privilege regarding these digital technologies, which raises the question of who can afford the means of such kind of access. As Ramon Lobato contends, "[D]istribution circulates cultural capital unevenly. It has the power to fragment audiences along age, class, gender, and ethnic lines, reinforcing certain differentials of power and creating new ones along the way."[129] Considering cinema's "production of difference at the point of distribution,"[130] and in regard to Iranian documentary films' circulation, the majority of Iran's Internet and new media users, who also engage with the country's documentary scene, belong to the younger generations, many of whom are technologically savvy and from middle and upper classes.[131]

Reflecting on the documentary film festivals' audiences in Iran, for example, Mina Keshavarz estimated that "the majority of these festivals' audiences are the documentarians themselves and perhaps 10 per cent is the audience that is not documentarian but belongs to the elite class of the society."[132] Indeed, this significant observation on the type of documentary festivals' audiences is also emblematic of online documentary audiences. Yet, when it comes to the online sites and social media platforms, the reach of the films, news, and media exchanges can potentially break the barriers of age and class, among others. Discussing the paradoxical context of the Internet in China, as a venue that to some extent has facilitated the circulation of independent documentaries while also being subjected to Chinese authorities' control and surveillance, film scholar Dan Edwards observes that "the Internet has provided an important additional discursive space for cinephiles, filmmakers and screening clubs to constitute an active public around independent documentaries."[133] Such discursive and active online spaces can also be found in the independent documentary scene in Iran. However, the availability of online documentary-related content does not on its own guarantee the engagement of the audience with Iranian documentaries, especially those made by women. It is rather the political, social, gender, and artistic commitments combined with the potential of the medium of documentary for progressive social change that have led some audiences to find and engage with such documentary resources. Persheng Sadegh-Vaziri, in this regard, explains:

> Social media sites such as Facebook and YouTube are officially banned but are widely used by the younger generations to communicate, help disseminate information, and organize. For example, Facebook pages are created that provide information about films and filmmakers or call for support for journalists and documentary filmmakers if they are sanctioned by the state. On-line petitions are circulated to support different causes. If a filmmaker or journalist is arrested, they provide information and support. Furthermore, filmmakers use online video platforms to present their films to a global audience.[134]

This mediated, online environment is thus an interplay between various relations and power dynamics. The Iranian state, Iranian documentarians, Iranian and global audiences and critics all form and affect, albeit differently, axes of power in documentary circulation, and as such, they can transform, with varying degrees, the experiences of a documentary encounter.

In regard to the relation between distribution and the audience in a media market, Lobato argues, "In contrast to the neoclassical economic model of perfectly competitive equilibrium, in which production responds directly to demand by satisfying the needs and wants of a particular market, analysis of distribution circuits often reveals that demand can be an *effect* of distribution. In other words, distributors shape public taste as well as reflect it, creating a feedback loop between distribution and demand."[135] This "feedback loop" has not yet been efficiently formed in the Iranian documentary field and its market, mainly because of the incongruous states of production and distribution in relation to each other; that is, the increasing number of documentary films produced yearly in Iran does not match the limited and fragmented distribution and exhibition modes. Therefore, while the process of attracting *and* maintaining an audience for documentaries in Iran is gradually happening, it is still far short of its potential.

The debates, reports, and analyses of Iranian documentary films on various publishing platforms, particularly film magazines and websites, can be *one* way to entice the audience's interest in the documentary medium in general and Iranian documentary films in particular. However, such a task itself depends on critics, journalists, and readers having access to documentary films. Mina Keshavarz, one of the creators and an administrator of the documentary website *Vamostanad*, recounted: "In 2009, the social and political circumstance was disappointing, and as documentarians, we felt we do not have any platforms and cannot even make films. One day the documentarian Reza Bahraminejad contacted me and said that our group has gathered to [initiate the website]; are you in? ... I strongly welcomed that."[136] The initial group consisted of Pirooz Kalantari, Reza Bahraminejad, Elham Hoseinzadeh, Rokhsareh Ghaemmaghami, Mehdi Ganji, Makan Mehrpooya, and Mina Keshavarz. According to Keshavarz, the group "wanted *Vamostanad* to not only focus on documentary cinema, but on any documentary visual space, and each of us, based on our own interest and approaches, published a dossier. We knew that the site is not supposed to be for news, and the production of content is towards introducing new [aspects] of documentary cinema."[137] In addition to technical issues, the group got smaller along the way, and ultimately Keshavarz and Kalantari continued the website until 2012. Other websites such as *Peik-e Mostanad* and *Rybon Mostanad*, which are no longer active, also tried to provide a space for documentary discussion and review. Yet, for the most part, the people involved in these types of websites and activities have been documentarians themselves, and while these online reflections on documentary visual culture might encourage documentary cinephiles to seek out the works discussed, the (im)possibility of accessing these films can enhance or hamper such engagements. As Nasim Najafi writes:

> The creation of a persistent audience [and] an analytical space, and the prevalence of documentary cinema's analytical theories depend on exhibition and viewing of documentary films. When a reader cannot access the documentary films anywhere, the contents that are sometimes written on a documentary do not have any functionality for him/her and so s/he often ignores them. A few readers might pay attention, who are often documentarians themselves.[138]

Therefore, in order to create a much more efficient "feedback loop"—to create audiences' demands and to inform documentarians of such demands—there needs to be a much better targeted and cohesive circulation of documentary films so that the documentaries produced can reach their intended audience. By this, I am not implying a linear and regulated form of documentary circulation from production to distribution, exhibition, and reception. Rather, by efficiently harnessing the possibilities of the diverse circulation modes currently available in Iran, or what Shweta

Kishore in the case of Indian independent documentary calls "tactical circulation"—"a subversion of the regulatory logic of gatekeeping that draws ordinary people into significant relationships with documentary film and wider documentary cultures through adaptive usage of available resources and technology"[139]—Iranian documentarians and individuals involved in independent documentary can foster and maintain spaces of deeper engagement with the public.

Diverse in their outlets and fragmented and dispersed across spatial and temporal sites, the Iranian documentary modes of circulation operate unevenly. Yet despite all the domestic and international limitations that loom over distribution and exhibition of Iranian independent documentaries, these works have managed to gradually attract diverse groups of audiences across the world. As the queues for the Cinema Vérité film festival (and other international documentary festivals) get longer, the seats for universities' and cultural centers' screenings get fuller, the number of attendees at private, home screenings gets bigger, and the number of online subscriptions for documentary streaming platforms gets higher, we need to witness a transformative documentary state that generates a more participatory and dialogic communication between Iranian independent documentarians and their audiences, thus turning the circulation itself into "a site of meaningful cognitive exchange and dialogue that leads to an embodied publics."[140] It is in this way that the visionary works of Iranian independent documentarians, and particularly those made by women, which I will analyze in greater depth in the following chapters, can expand deeper into the fabric of society and transform audiences into active players and/or allies in regard to the realities presented and discussed in these works.

CHAPTER 3

Discovering the Self in Autobiographical Documentaries: Sites of Self-Reflection

Writing in 1992 with a focus on Persian literature, Persian studies scholar Farzaneh Milani argues, "Erased from the public scene and privatized, the Iranian woman has for long been without autobiographical possibilities. Textual self-representation of individuals is not divorced from their cultural representation; and in a culture that idealizes feminine silence and restraint, not many women can or will opt for breaking the silence."[1] Yet as this chapter delineates, since the late 1990s, autobiographical approach has become a major trend in Iranian documentary; one that has been particularly embraced by women documentarians. This unprecedented rise in Iranian women's autobiographical documentaries in contemporary Iran substantially points to both the centralization of female agency and subjectivity behind and in front of the documentary camera and the broader social, cultural, political, and technological transformations in the country that have made the emergence of this crucial documentary approach possible.

Pointing to the intersection of personal and political with autobiographical in women's documentaries, film scholars Kristin Lené Hole and Dijana Jelača assert that "nowhere is the focus on the feminine and feminist more pronounced than in autobiographical works in which female documentarians mine deeply personal and often painful stories about their own lives and intimate family histories."[2] Following these observations, in this chapter, I examine the politics and aesthetics of Iranian women's autobiographical documentaries in regard to familial, social, cultural, and political sites, where female voice and body have been reclaimed through self-reflexive practices further discussing the ways in which women's autobiographical documentaries have creatively undermined the gender hierarchies of power and the historical erasure of women and their voices in Iranian society. What forms of gender representation and discourse arise when the filmmaker's subjective point of view (the "eye" of the camera) mingles with the filmmaker's embodiment (the "I" of the filmmaker)? Through close examination of three case studies—Mina Keshavarz's *Unwelcome in Tehran* (2011), Shirin Barghnavard's *21 Days and Me* (2011), and Shirin Barghnavard, Firouzeh Khosrovani, Farahnaz Sharifi, Mina Keshavarz, Sepideh Abtahi, Sahar Salahshoor, and Nahid Rezaei's *Profession: Documentarist* (2014)—I contend that in these autobiographical examples, the documentarians present a politics of the self that is always active and responsive to a larger societal setting. In these works, the strong articulation of a personal perspective and the performative embodiment of a personal self as a response to social, cultural, and political issues are facilitated by the documentary medium asserting a female voice and body whose subjectivity questions the patriarchal authority at the same time that it offers productive moments of self-discovery and self-recognition.

In my interviews, Mina Keshavarz and Shirin Barghnavard pointed to the significance of personal discovery via the documentary medium. Keshavarz mentioned, "For me, documentary filmmaking is the arena of discovery and quest. From the initiation of an idea until the end of [making] the film, and even years after that, with every screening of the film, something happens inside me as a documentarian that is truly delightful; a sort of constant learning."[3] Therefore for Keshavarz, the possibilities offered by the documentary in terms of personal "discovery and quest" were among the reasons she was drawn to this medium.[4] In the same vein, Barghnavard in regard to selecting her films' topics said, "The type of strong relationship that I am supposed to form with my film's main character and her environment is important to me. It is very important to me that in the process of making my film, I myself discover and learn."[5] In the autobiographical documentaries *Unwelcome in Tehran* (2011) and *21 Days and Me* (2011), made by Keshavarz and Barghnavard respectively, we can indeed see not only an attempt at self-discovery but also a self-explorer trying to understand and navigate her relationships, her environment, and her society.

Such lucid representations and analyses of the self have become possible in part due to the investigative and reflective potentialities of the documentary medium and its contested, yet powerful, connection to the profilmic reality. Film scholar Bill Nichols writes that in documentaries speaking in the first-person mode, "The emphasis may shift from convincing the audience of a particular point of view or approach to a problem to the representation of a personal, clearly subjective view of things. From persuasion the emphasis shifts to expression."[6] Moreover, film scholar Alisa Lebow argues, "First person films can be poetic, political, prophetic or absurd. They can be autobiographical in full, or only implicitly and in part."[7] However, what significantly stands out in these films according to Lebow is their particular "mode of address: these films 'speak' from the articulated point of view of the filmmaker who readily acknowledges her subjective position."[8] This form of personal expression thus constitutes an imperative aspect of first-person documentaries. As documentaries such as *Profession: Documentarist* (2014) and Jafar Panahi's *This Is Not a Film* (*In yek film nist*, 2011) show, the climate of heightened repression and censorship cannot necessarily hinder bold self-expressions; it might rather paradoxically prompt a defiant aesthetics of the self that directly challenges the repressive and authoritarian structures. Both documentaries were made in the politically and aesthetically restrictive and tension-ridden environment that ensued after the 2009 contested presidential election in Iran, which resulted in massive protests known as the Green Movement. As such, both works are in part self-mediations and self-reflections on this context and the ways in which it relates to the practice of filmmaking by their filmmakers.

Because it has not been a common practice to create an assertive and explicit "I" in Iranian literature and cinema, the first-person documentaries ideologically destabilize the dominant hegemony by challenging authoritative and patriarchal norms in Iranian society through presenting an embodied subjectivity. This issue distinguishes these works from the majority of their Western counterparts. As Lebow aptly asserts:

> [T]he vast majority of first person films pouring out of especially anglophone western countries only serve to reaffirm hegemonic values by positing a liberal humanist subject who can afford to assume a commonality with his (and it is usually a he) audience based on notions of individual liberties and rights assumed to be shared by all, wilfully ignoring systemic inequities and their own implicit parochial and exclusionary positionalities.[9]

In Iranian autobiographical documentaries, the discourses of subjectivity and individuality are never taken for granted. In fact, as I argue, in many Iranian women's autobiographical documentaries, the acknowledging of the self and the body directly arises out of familial, social, cultural, and political issues and constraints, and is an attempt at finding the filmmaker's voice and agency in regard to these contexts. This is a process that has been crucially facilitated by the possibilities offered by the documentary medium.

Although censorship remains a constant, yet highly unpredictable, phenomenon in Iranian cinema, as I discussed in previous chapters, the documentarians have learned to creatively navigate, negotiate, and resist it via various strategies. In autobiographical documentaries, for instance, women filmmakers (and other female subjects) might wear the veil in private spaces, but that does not mean that they also cover their true self and true feelings. Rather, they overtly assert their individuality, their subjectivity, and their voices, thus presenting various forms of self-revelation and self-presentation unprecedented in Iranian cinema. If Iranian fiction filmmakers have creatively invented and developed "the sophisticated practices of allegorical encoding … over more than three decades of censorship and political scrutiny,"[10] then autobiographical documentarians have creatively developed direct forms of address and expression that not only challenge the external censorship, but also the internal one that has evolved in relation to the outside restrictions imposed on individuals and their personal opinions and creative practices.

Such crucial documentary sites of authorial reckoning and personal expression, however, have not come about easily and demanded major changes in both Iranian society and Iranian cinema. Film scholar Hamid Naficy recognizes a shift in women's presence and representations in post-revolutionary Iranian cinema from their "structured absence" in the early 1980s to their "background presence" in the mid-1980s, their "foreground presence since the late 1980s," and further their practices of "veiling and modesty as political criticism since the mid-1990s."[11] Along with Iranian women's unprecedented presence in the documentary medium since the late 1990s, which I discussed in previous chapters, Iranian society, as I argue in this chapter, has gone under substantial social, cultural, political, and technological transformations that have opened up new venues for various forms of self-expression; among these is the documentary medium. Autobiographical documentary has in fact become one of the most salient ways through which Iranian filmmakers in the country express their individuality and subjectivity. Iranian women's autobiographical documentaries offer unique perspectives and mediations on female individuality and subjectivity, proving that Iranian women are no longer "[e]rased from the public scene and privatized."[12] Rather, by connecting private and public spaces and by making personal political, they have created some of the most influential and powerful female voices and representations in contemporary Iran.

In order to explain what contexts have made such groundbreaking forms of visual and discursive expression by Iranian women documentarians possible, I first provide a brief historical overview of autobiographical practices by Iranian women and subsequently highlight various transformations in Iranian society since the late 1990s that have contributed to the rise of women's autobiographical documentaries. Finally, I analyze the aesthetics and politics of women's autobiographical documentaries by providing close readings of three case studies: *Unwelcome in Tehran* (2011), *21 Days and Me* (2011) and *Profession: Documentarist* (2014).

Women and Autobiography in Iran: A Brief History

Discussing the scarcity of autobiographical works in Persian literature, especially among women writers, Farzaneh Milani argues that various sociocultural issues have contributed to the dearth of this genre. As Milani postulates, the absence of autobiography "is perhaps the logical extension of a culture that creates, expects, and even values a sharply defined separation between the inner and the outer, the private and the public. Perhaps it bespeaks a mode of being and behavior that is shaped, or misshaped, by varying degrees and types of censorship, both external and internal."[13] In the same vein, Iranian studies scholar Hamid Dabashi, in regard to Iranian cinema, writes, "In a culture in which even painting and still photography were forbidden, the translucent representation of reality was dangerously sacrilegious. This anxiety made the nascent formation of individual subjectivity in modernity even more precarious."[14] I agree with these scholars that literature and cinema in Iran have long been deeply influenced by Iranian society, whose gender segregation and religious discourses have not only reinforced the dualities of public/private, inner/outer, and self/other, but also made the textual and visual representations of individual subjectivity in these media highly contested. That is why until recently, the autobiographical genre had not turned into viable and common literary and cinematic practices in Iranian literature and cinema. Indeed, gender hierarchies of Iranian society and culture have had a major impact on the lack of autobiographical practices in these media, and while we can refer to the practices of veiling and privacy as "a relative constant of Persian experience,"[15] we need to be specially attuned to the gender specificities of self-expression in Iranian culture and in regard to Iranian women. Milani aptly observes that "women who have been deliberately, if not obsessively, kept away from the arena of public life and discourse have a still more restrained relation to public self-representation."[16]

While within an Iranian patriarchal setting, pudency (*hojb*) and poise (*vaghar*) serve as desired characteristics of both men and women, a particular form of chastity and virtue is expected from women that has no other equivalent to that of men's desired features. In this regard Milani maintains, "In a sexually segregated society where access to a woman's world and words is limited, and the concept of honor is built around woman's virginity (proof of her inaccessibility) women's autobiographies, with their assertive self-attention and self-display cannot easily flourish, and they have not."[17] Within this context, the women's veiling turns into a symbol of ideal femininity. The veil is supposed to protect women's bodies and their modesty by obstructing the male gaze in public spaces, which are relatively open to male mobility, and as such, are considered male spaces. It is also in this context, I contend, that the politics of imposed veiling for women operates in post-revolutionary Iranian cinema: to protect women's bodies and preserve women's modesty and chastity by making them inaccessible to (male) audiences' gaze.[18] The perception of an ideal woman is also a silent and restrained one extending the cultural expectations of physical inaccessibility and visual invisibility of a woman to her muted voice. Yet regardless of these cultural contexts, throughout history, Iranian women have creatively and persistently challenged and subverted various forms of sociocultural marginalization in order to express their personal voices and selves.

Historian Karl J. Weintraub considers "*experienced* reality" as the quintessential aspect of autobiographical practices,[19] which is necessarily reflected upon from a self-conscious perspective. This interconnectedness of "self-consciousness" and "interrelated experience" further shows itself in various forms such as "self-explication, self-discovery, self-clarification, self-formation, self-presentation, self-justification."[20] As Weintraub explains, "All these functions … are centered upon an aware self aware of its relation to its experiences."[21] Weintraub's significant argument on the essential interplaying aspects of autobiography allows me to consider, like Farzaneh Milani and Hamid Dabashi, the influential poet and religious preacher, Fatemeh Baraghani, known as Tahereh Qorrat al-Ayn (1816–1852), as an early example of a female autobiographer in Iran, regardless of the fact that she did not write an autobiography. Dabashi writes, "The masculine nature of the Iranian encounter with modernity is impossible to disregard. But to the rule of that masculinity there are crucial feminine exceptions, which ought to be taken equally seriously."[22] In the mid-nineteenth century, Qorrat al-Ayn thus shines a feminine voice on this encounter challenging its masculine hegemony. As Milani observes, "Through her unveiling and her public preaching, she exposed her body and her voice and committed the first public autobiographical act on record in contemporary Iran."[23] Qorrat al-Ayn self-consciously and publicly asserted her individuality and her vision, thus breaking the traditional notions of domesticity and silence as ideal features of Iranian women. Trying to subjectively express her own "experienced reality" rather than passively accept what was restrictively offered, Qorrat al-Ayn paved the way for the first expressions and performances of women's subjectivity to come to the fore in Iranian society. Nevertheless, such an unprecedented and brave assertion of selfhood tragically prompted Qorrat al-Ayn's death. "She was strangled to death at the age of thirty-six for her open advocacy of a new religious faith, Babism."[24] The efforts to silence female voices, both literally and metaphorically in the case of Qorrat al-Ayn, however, did not last long as women, from various backgrounds and social classes, began to publicly express their voices and advocate for women's rights. Their efforts crucially culminated in the large participation of women in and their advocacy for Iran's Constitutional Revolution (1905–1911).

Among these figures were Bibi Khanum Astarabadi, the wife of "Musa Khan Mir Panj, [who] was a *ghulam* (mounted messenger) at the British embassy in Tehran,"[25] and Princess Taj al-Saltaneh, the daughter of Naser al-Din Shah Qajar. Written in 1895 by Bibi Khanum Astarabadi, *Ma'ayeb al-Rejal* (*Vices of Men*) is perhaps better considered as "the first major 'protest' essay written by a woman,"[26] Yet, in the chapters of the manuscript, Astarabadi shares some aspects of her personal life and further expresses her subjective opinion against patriarchal notions in Iranian family and society.[27] Her manuscript is a protest and response to "an essay written around 1891 by an anonymous male author, titled *Ta'dib-e zanan* or *Ta'dib on-nesvan* (How to Chastise Women),"[28] in which the author expresses some discriminatory opinions about Iranian women that are accompanied by selective demands as a way to discipline them. Astarabadi's *Vices of Men* therefore serves as a powerful answer to this male author. In doing so, it not only brings some insights into the lives of Qajar women and men and the gender dynamics of Iranian society at that time, but also becomes an important venue for the expression of female voice and subjectivity.

Princess Taj al-Saltaneh wrote *The Memoirs of Taj al-Saltaneh* (*Khaterat-e Taj al-Saltaneh*) in 1914. The work presents a significant autobiographical practice that is explicitly self-referential and self-consciously reflexive. As historian Afsaneh Najmabadi contends, "This autobiography is rare within its type because it projects itself and its worth as autobiography, not as social history or social commentary. In other words, it is one of the few writings in Persian in which the author, male or female, attributes a value to the discussion of her own life as such."[29] As the daughter of a Qajar king, Taj al-Saltaneh was a highly educated woman. While it can be argued that the upper-class status of Taj al-Saltaneh was instrumental in her upward educational mobility and intellectual growth providing the ground for her self-expression, her status also paradoxically worked to control her social life and subjectivity. Breaking the confines of the *andarun* (interior space), she socially mingled with "young male admirers and perhaps lovers, [for which] she became an outcast."[30] As such, according to Najmabadi, Taj al-Saltaneh "was one of the first Iranian women in the modern period to experience the tremendous social and psychological pressures of crossing over the boundaries of social morality."[31] And of course, Taj al-Saltaneh's boundary crossings further showed themselves in breaking the boundaries of private and public, interior and exterior, and self and other. It was through these acts of transgression, of breaking limitations imposed upon a female self, that Taj al-Saltaneh struggled to find her individuality. These women pioneers of autobiographical practice had to pay immense psychological and emotional costs such that breaking down the boundaries of segregated spaces at times resulted in these women's own nervous breakdown.[32] Nevertheless, they persisted and their efforts set the ground for other autobiographical works to appear in the following years.

In mid-twentieth-century Iran, as Milani points out, "Banu Mahvash, a singer-dancer, and Malekeh E'tezadi, a political activist, published their highly unconventional life stories."[33] But perhaps the most important autobiographical expression at this time belongs to that of poet and filmmaker Forugh Farrokhzad, who channeled her "experienced reality" and personal feelings in her poetry. In terms of openness and poetic self-revelation, Farrokhzad's poetry is a pioneering act of female emotional unmasking. The female body, sexuality, and voice take center stage in Farrokhzad's works, turning the author, in the words of Dabashi, into "the iconic representation of the suffocated sensibilities of a feminine presence in the Iranian poetic imagination."[34] In fact, Farrokhzad's poetry was inspired by her own subjectivity and individuality as a woman. As Milani puts it, she "systematically integrated a female self—her own—in her five collections of poetry, otherwise avoided talking about her personal life."[35] In feminist studies, autobiography is considered a significant practice as it provides women with a venue to speak for themselves and to draw from their own lived reality. Scholar Margaret McLaren observes, "Women's autobiography can be viewed as a feminist technology of the self because the subject plays an active role in her own self-constitution."[36] I thus argue that Farrokhzad in both her poetry and her social practices employed a form of "feminist technology of the self" through which she actively masked and unmasked different aspects of her personal life. Such a conscious way of "self-constitution" thus bestows an autobiographical mode to her work and an autobiographical act to her life. Farrokhzad's life was tragically and unexpectedly cut short in 1967 by a car accident, but her legacy has powerfully continued to influence many Iranian women, including women documentarians.[37]

By the early 1990s, Iranian women's autobiographies in their written form still constituted a very limited number. While memoirs on the Iran-Iraq War (1980–88) began to appear shortly after the outbreak of the war, as Azra Ghandeharion and Maryam Sadat Mousavi Tekiyeh write, it is only recently that "a significant increase in production and proliferation of texts on the Iran-Iraq War written or narrated by Iranian women, or about Iranian women, in the form of biography, autobiography, memoir, or fiction," has appeared.[38] Among the well-known memoirs are *Da: Memoirs of Sayyideh Zahra Husseini, as Recorded by A'zam Husseini* (*Da: Khaterat-e Sayyideh Zahra Husseini, be Ehtemam-e A'zam Husseini*, 2008) by A'zam Husseini, and *I'm Alive* (*Man zendeam*, 2013) by Ma'sumah Abad. In a 2013 article, titled "Iranian Women's Life Narratives," Milani acknowledges a recent rise in Iranian women's autobiographical and first-person practices within a literary context. She writes, "There is now an unprecedented explosion and diversity of autobiographies and memoirs by Iranian women inside and outside the country. ... They refuse silence and exclusion by exploring new territories, re-scripting the plots of their lives, recreating their own language, and reconstructing their style with little help from tradition."[39] Yet, the majority of current studies, including Ghandeharion and Mousavi Tekiyeh's and Milani's, solely focus on a literary context and do not discuss the recent rise in women's autobiographical documentaries in Iran. This is a gap that this chapter aims to fill out.

An Overview of Iranian Society's Transformations Since the Late 1990s

Since the late 1990s, major demographic, psychological, sociocultural, and gender transformations have brought about new practices of subjectivity and individuality, especially among women, in Iran. In this regard, sociologist Asef Bayat notes the emergence of "nonmovements" as "the collective actions of noncollective actors; they embody shared practices of large numbers of ordinary people whose fragmented but similar activities trigger much social change ..."[40] According to Bayat, in authoritarian and patriarchal settings, where works of women's rights and political activists are often met with heavy and brutal crackdown, "women have tended to pursue a different strategy, one that involves intimately the mundane practices of everyday life, such as pursuing education, sports, arts, music, or working outside the home."[41]

During the presidency of Mohammad Khatami (1997–2005), many non-governmental organizations (NGOs) and civil society initiatives emerged, some of which centered on women's issues and significantly contributed to the efforts and discourses on women's rights and gender equality. But in addition, there have been the powerful day-to-day negotiations and activities of millions of ordinary women, who consciously or unconsciously challenge patriarchal norms and assert their subjectivity. As Bayat aptly argues, "Every claim [women] made became a stepping-stone for a further claim, generating a cycle of opportunities for demands to enhance gender rights. Thus, women's quest for literacy and a college education enabled them to live alone, away from the control of their guardians, or led to a career that might demand traveling alone, supervising men, or defying male dominance."[42] Therefore, Iranian women have broken the confines of gender segregation and domesticity and have become an active force in the society whose voice and subjectivity cannot be ignored any longer.

Concomitant with the rise of this gender transformation in the late 1990s, there also emerged a demographic change. Bayat observes that "by 1996 Iran had experienced a dramatic rise in its number of young people, with two-thirds under the age of thirty."[43] With this young population has come about a form of youth culture aspiring for more individual, intellectual, and sexual freedom. Predominantly university students and well educated, the majority of these young people "lived in cities, exposed to diverse lifestyles with spaces for relative autonomy, extrakinship identities, and social interactions on a broad scale."[44] With increasing mobility of these individuals for education and work, and with the expansion of media technologies, the urban-influenced aspirations of young people extended to the youth in the rural areas and smaller towns in other provinces, where many young individuals, especially women, have increasingly begun attending universities in other provinces or taking leisurely arts or music classes in the nearby metropolises, which in part has been facilitated by their work or educational mobility.

Facing various demands generated and pushed by the young generation across the country, the Islamic Republic of Iran, according to sociologist Kevan Harris, initiated its "developmentalist efforts" in part as a way "to appease, channel, and utilize the social aspirations of the postwar generation."[45] In this regard Harris further observes, "The expansion of the welfare system during the 1990s and 2000s attempted to meet the rising demand for health care, education, and social insurance among the population. It also helped to defer entry of some of Iran's 1980s baby-boom generation into the labor force while many pursued professional or technical credentials."[46] Such developments have therefore led to a growing middle-class population whose growing material and intellectual power resonates itself in progressive daily activities, or nonmovements. With these gender, demographic, economic, and cultural changes, a form of "urban individuality" has appeared,[47] at the center of which reside the public visibility and mobility of Iranian women and youth. However, such visibility and mobility have at times, if not often, run counter to the state's ideology, regardless of its efforts to adapt newer forms of propagation to convey its revolutionary and anti-Western ideologies to the younger generation.

Within this multi-faceted context of social change and power dynamics, a psychological shift has also occurred in the ways in which individuals discuss themselves and their inner thoughts and feelings. In this regard, medical anthropologist Orkideh Behrouzan recognizes a major shift among Iranians in regard to practices of the self in recent decades. She writes, "In 1990s Iran, a cultural shift took place in public articulations of psychological well-being, manifest in the evolution of a psychiatric discourse in the media and a rise in psychiatric talk among people."[48] Significantly, such an increase in psychiatric discourses has been spearheaded by the younger generation, the majority of whom were born after the 1979 Islamic Revolution and during the Iran-Iraq War in the 1980s. Although this population did not experience the revolution or participate in it and were too young during the Iran-Iraq War to fully grasp the immediate trauma and tensions of the war, they have witnessed a form of lingering anxiety and post-traumatic effects that largely loom over their lived experiences. Therefore, as Behrouzan eloquently explains, "Today, the constant circulation of compelling accounts of the nostalgias as well as anomies of the past and the present is creating a new mode of self-recognition, a new sense of voice, and a new identity politics for young Iranians."[49] Not surprisingly, this new form of self-articulation has also found its way in autobiographical documentaries. A relevant example is Farahnaz Sharifi's *My Sad Face* (*Chehreh-ye ghamgin-e man*, 2008), which directly deals with the issue of depression in the filmmaker's life and the Iranian society, and is inspired by German author Heinrich Theodor Böll's short story of the same name about "a regime which dictates the expressions on one's countenance."[50] Sharifi's autobiographical documentary weaves together the account of her personal depression as a newly-wed before and after the marriage with medical, psychological, and sociological information and underpinnings, thus situating her personal state within a larger social context to self-reflexively probe a society in which depression among its people is rife.

Developments of media technologies have also contributed to new forms of self-presentation and introspection in Iranian society and cinema. Discussing the "proliferation of digital video technology" in the 1990s in Iran, media scholar Blake Atwood emphasizes the democratizing force of such technologies in regard to filmmaking "by providing affordable access to cameras and editing software," thus contributing to "a system of production, distribution, and aesthetics that operated outside of the bounds of state control."[51] Moreover, Atwood underlines that "these democratizing technologies reshaped culture in Iran at the same [time] that Khatami identified democracy as an important part of his political agenda."[52] As this study has also argued, the emergence of digital video technology coincided with the opening up of political discourses on civil society and individual rights during the presidency of Mohammad Khatami, both of which facilitated individual self-expression and subjective approaches in Iranian society and Iranian documentary.

Digital technologies also brought about new practices of blogging, further contributing to the emergence of unprecedented forms of self-expression, especially among Iranian women. Given the possibility of anonymity, the blogsphere allowed women freer opportunities for exposing their voices and experiences, although some of these women explicitly revealed their gender and identity. Urban sociologist Masserat Amir-Ebrahimi writes, "Through bold narration in their blogs, they unveiled the hidden woman, suppressed by the traditions of Iranian society, and revealed first-hand information about themselves which had never before been told publicly."[53] Similarly, I contend that these first-hand accounts in the virtual world, drawn from Iranian women's lived experiences, directly connect the virtual transgressions of women to their public and private transgressions blurring the boundaries of virtual/actual and private/public. Also, such forms of self-narration within online platforms and blogs emphasize individuality, yet further connect it to a broader group of individuals who read, react to, and comment on each other's experiences and thoughts. This form of interaction turns Iranian blogs into "*affective* spaces: emotive, interpretive, and performative sites for ongoing examinations of lived experience ..."[54] Here the "I" of the blogger is in constant dialogue with the "we" of the society creating significant, if ephemeral, forms of affinity that take as their grounds personal, yet socially connected, experiences. In recent years, many Iranian women have also used social media platforms "to speak about the sexual assault and harassment they experienced;" activist efforts that have been dubbed as "an Iranian #MeToo movement."[55] These first-person accounts have not only situated Iranian women's voices alongside and in conversation with other similar outcries in a global context, but have also crucially subverted the longstanding gender hierarchies and patriarchal structures in Iranian society.

According to film scholar Michelle Langford, "Compared with the widespread uptake of text-based social media in Iran—blogging, tweeting, social networking—video-based Internet activity has been hindered by the Iranian government's strict filtering and speed limiting of the Internet."[56] Nevertheless, Iranian professional and amateur filmmakers have used such text-based social media platforms to bring more visibility and publicity as well as much-needed advocacy to their works. For instance, as discussed in previous chapters, they have deployed such online platforms as Hamijoo for crowdfunding and Vimeo for private sharing and exhibition of their films. The possibilities offered by the digital technologies have also contributed to new forms of personal, non-fiction practices, in addition to first-person documentaries. In this regard, Naficy points to the emergence of "noncommercial, semi-amateur, and artisanal forms of nonfiction cinema," including wedding documentaries and home videos, that "circulate within informal, private, and noncommercial sectors, as well as on the Internet."[57]

Along with these transformative aspects that Iranian society has gone through, a new notion of selfhood has appeared in the autobiographical and first-person documentaries that bears little resemblance "to the moral, self-sacrificing films that promote Islamic idealism and are brimming with moral certitude,"[58] or suppress individual subjectivity to predominantly highlight grand narratives of a social collectivity.[59] Instead, as documentary filmmaker and scholar Persheng Sadegh-Vaziri writes, "In the personal or essay films, the self is usually a fragmented, post-modern self that is central yet elusive. This 'self' poses questions which have no clear answers."[60] In these documentaries, this fragmented personhood is affected by and constantly morphs in relation to various sociocultural and political contexts, and as such, it eludes a coherent and fixed notion of the self. These works in fact offer nuanced mediations not only on the self, but also on the individual's environment within which the self is situated and through which the self re-articulates herself.

Analyzing the crucial evolution that occurred in Iranian documentaries in the late 1990s and early 2000s, documentary filmmaker and critic Omid Balaghati recognizes two major shifts: "First, the hegemonic, omnipresent narrator has been replaced by first-person narratives or humbler and less pretentious narrators, and second, the experimental cinema of the 1960s and 1970s and the village and suburban settings have been substituted with a different narrative of the city, the urban individual, and of course a different perspective on the village."[61] Documentarian Mehdi Bagheri considers Mona Zahedi's *Pain* (*Dard*, 1999) and Bahman Kiarostami's *Leech* (*Zaloo*, 2003) among early examples of first-person documentary in Iran, followed by Farahnaz Sharifi's *My Sad Face* (2008).[62] Since then, the trend of autobiographical and first-person documentaries has continued showing itself in works such as Mehdi Bagheri's *Old Boy* (*Pir pesar*, 2011), Mina Keshavarz's *Unwelcome in Tehran* (2011), Shirin Barghnavard's *21 Days and Me* (2011), and Shirin Barghnavard, Firouzeh Khosrovani, Farahnaz Sharifi, Mina Keshavarz, Sepideh Abtahi, Sahar Salahshoor, and Nahid Rezaei's *Profession: Documentarist* (2014). The latter three will be more closely discussed in the following section.

Unwelcome in Tehran (2011) by Mina Keshavarz

Mina Keshavarz's *Unwelcome in Tehran* centers on the issue of women living independently and by themselves in Iran's capital, Tehran. As we learn early in the film, Keshavarz herself is married and has never had a chance to experience what an independent living looks like as a lifestyle for a woman. Keshavarz then embarks on a journey to search for her many questions in this regard by interviewing different women who live by themselves in the metropolis as well as some women living with their families in smaller, more conservative towns. *Unwelcome in Tehran* foregrounds female subjectivity not only through its autobiographical mode, but also through its subject matter. It investigates how young women in Iranian society perform their agency through breaking familial and sociocultural boundaries and expectations to gain and maintain their independent lifestyle. The film in fact channels a personal question and quest to broader perspectives and experiences of Iranian women making the style of the film "first person plural."[63] According to Lebow such a designation "means the 'I' is always social, always already in relation, and when it speaks, as these filmmakers do, in the first person, it may appear to be in the first person singular 'I' but ontologically speaking, it is always in effect, the first person plural 'we'."[64]

The relational thread in the documentary's structure in part derives from Keshavarz's relationship with her husband—a person who is directly and inevitably drawn to her situation and is expected to acknowledge and respond to Keshavarz's questions and dilemmas—but it is more significantly connected to other young women and their experiences of living by themselves in Tehran. This relational perspective of the film differs from women's autobiographies in Persian literature that, according to Milani, always situate the female self in relation to a male other. Milani writes,

"If in the first-person narratives related by male authors, women are at best marginalized, in female-centered discourses, the self is represented in its relations with men. The unfolding of the narrator's consciousness usually takes place through relationships with a chosen masculine other."[65] Iranian women's autobiographical documentaries, however, go beyond such a one-dimensional, relational mode of discourse. In the case of *Unwelcome in Tehran*, Keshavarz opens the film by explaining her concerns within the context of her married life and in relation to her husband, yet she immediately expands her point of view by finding and interviewing other women.

The documentary begins by inserting a very powerful and assertive personal perspective on the part of the filmmaker. Keshavarz, while holding a camera, depicts different sections of the house in which she and her husband live. The camera enters the bedroom showing Keshavarz's husband sleeping on the bed, then we see other parts of the house and a big wedding photo of Keshavarz and her husband that is hung up on the wall. Keshavarz's voiceover accompanies these images saying, "Five years have passed since I married Mehdi. I love every corner of our house, but I know that I just got married to get away from my parents and migrate to Tehran. Now when I see my friends and girls of my age who are single, I wonder why I married so young. Why didn't I experience a life as a single girl like them?" Thus, within the first few minutes of the film, we see the filmmaker and her husband and learn about her major dilemma that frames the rest of the film. Immediately after this opening scene, Keshavarz

Figure 3.1 Keshavarz holds the camera in a self-reflexive moment. *Unwelcome in Tehran* (2011), directed by Mina Keshavarz. Courtesy of Mina Keshavarz.

Figure 3.2 Keshavarz interviews other women who live by themselves in Tehran. *Unwelcome in Tehran* (2011), directed by Mina Keshavarz. Courtesy of Mina Keshavarz.

Figure 3.3 Keshavarz interviews other women who live by themselves in Tehran. *Unwelcome in Tehran* (2011), directed by Mina Keshavarz. Courtesy of Mina Keshavarz.

tries to find some interview subjects and then we witness the accounts of various women, many of whom have come to Tehran from other provinces and are living independently by themselves in this city. They point to the economic and sociocultural hardships that have come with such an independence, but still, they prefer to live on their own. These women have used their education and jobs as a safe and convincing way to leave behind their families and to come to Iran's capital.

One interviewee mentions, "Well, my living condition is very difficult. If I had my family's support, things would have been different. Nevertheless, I am very happy because it is the life that I have chosen; no one else is involved." This personal statement highlights the multifaceted formation of an independent female self and subjectivity—economic-wise and family-wise—further highlighting the significance of becoming the governor of one's own life. Another female interviewee assertively says, "My name is Maryam, my last name is Sheikh. I have worked hard to become Maryam Sheikh, and I am not going to give it up at any cost." The assertion of a female identity, individuality, and voice that have been achieved through the hard work attests to a transformation of female subjectivity in Iran that is no longer passive, no longer silent, and no longer in the background. Such mediations and overt assertions of the female subjectivity in the film through diverse female voices and in relation to multiple sociocultural, familial, and gender contexts, strongly position *Unwelcome in Tehran* in the category of an "autoethnographic" documentary. Inspired by the use of the term by comparative literature scholar Mary Louise Pratt, film scholar Catherine Russell writes, "Autobiography becomes ethnographic at the point where the film- or videomaker understands his or her personal history to be implicated in larger social formations and historical processes."[66] As such, the film at its core challenges the restrictive sociocultural and historical norms imposed on Iranian women to define their lives through domesticity and dependency as well as through various forms of governmentality, performed in particular by parents, siblings, relatives, neighbors, and even unfamiliar individuals in the society.

Among her interviewees, Keshavarz gravitates towards Azar, a single young woman from the small town of Sabzevar, who left her home due to the pressures from her mother and brother, who overwhelmingly controlled her life. Keshavarz, in a considerable portion of the film, follows and observes Azar, converses with her, and tries to understand Azar's desire for and perspective on female independence. In a scene in which Azar goes to a real-estate store to inquire about the possibility of renting a place for herself, the real-estate male agent asks Azar if she has a father or a mother (a guardian in general) to sign the rental agreement for her, to which Azar responds that she needs the home for herself and not for her family. In another scene depicting an intimate gathering of Keshavarz's friends in her home, Keshavarz brings up the issue of female independence, thus prompting some male guests to share their points of view. While one of them is resistant to the idea of Keshavarz experiencing a single, independent lifestyle, especially now that she is married, another openly sympathizes with Keshavarz's curiosity about and desire for this form of living, highlighting the gender disparities in Iranian society in this regard. He recalls, "Ten years ago when I used to come home at 2am in the morning, once my sister said to me: 'It's cool that you can stay out until 2am.' Well, I couldn't tell my sister what we did when we were out, we walked, went to the cinema. I couldn't tell her as she thought going out was a big deal. Well, what I could do was to put myself in her shoes; I would have had to be home by 8pm!"

Such kinds of social interactions, presented in these scenes, extend the challenge of female independence and agency beyond the confines of the filmmaker's home and family to the fabric of the social structure that is defined through the patriarchal notions regarding female individuality and mobility. That is why in addition to various accounts and observations on female independence and female freedom and social mobility, the film portrays women's actual movements across various locations and cities. Keshavarz travels with Azar on a train to visit a small town, which seems

Figure 3.4 Keshavarz and Azar travel on a train. *Unwelcome in Tehran* (2011), directed by Mina Keshavarz. Courtesy of Mina Keshavarz.

to be Azar's hometown. Azar chats with some of the young women there regarding their lifestyle and their plans for the future.

Keshavarz also travels alone on a bus to visit her family in her hometown of Shiraz, and to discuss with them her regret of getting married at the expense of compromising her independence. Such forms of spatial mobility therefore expand the film's focus on female independence beyond Tehran to the locations from which some of these young women come, and for various reasons have left behind. In her reflection on the documentary, film scholar Gönül Dönmez-Colin contends that "the right to mobility, which is often denied to women under various pretexts in most Islamicate cultures, is at the center of the film, which as a form of defiance places the key events on the trains, on the long-distance buses and at bus terminals."[67] Regarding the process that prompted her to make *Unwelcome in Tehran*, Keshavarz in her interview for this study explained:

> It was a thought that had occupied my mind and I had been waiting for an opportunity to express it. When the opportunity came and I was invited to present a proposal for a mid-length documentary production in a group, the first idea that came to my mind was *Unwelcome in Tehran*. Perhaps many in that group were wondering why I was going to make a film about myself, but I was excited and thought this film can be my tool to say what had been inside me for years and I had not had any opportunity to express.[68]

Therefore, like the women in her film, Keshavarz expresses her voice and navigates her individuality, and while she poses more questions than she finds definitive answers, the process of expressing her opinion and professing her subjectivity allows her to find possibilities for her independence. As Russell mentions, "Autoethnography is a vehicle and a strategy for challenging imposed forms of identity and exploring the discursive possibilities of inauthentic subjectivities."[69] Therefore, the interviews with other young women and the closer connection and friendship with Azar allow Keshavarz to get a better grasp of the issues she has not been able to experience herself. In a conversation with Azar while traveling on a train, Keshavarz confesses, "Your character is very interesting to me … because you put your foot down and said that you wanted to do this; that they said what they wanted, but you objected. But I didn't tell my family what I wanted to do, what I wished to think, how I wanted to live my life …" To get out of her confinement, Keshavarz chose to marry Mehdi, but as she discloses to Azar (and the viewers), "Six months after my marriage, I was suffering from severe depression. I felt that I had become dependent … It was as if I couldn't go anywhere without Mehdi …" Breaking out of the familial dependency, Keshavarz yet aging finds herself in another dependent status, this time within a marital setting. Such confessional and self-reflexive moments in the film allow Keshavarz to gain a better understanding of her positionality within various familial, marital, and sociocultural structures and provide a substantial ground for the formation of her subjective voice. Moreover, such moments of self-revelation and self-analysis become possible for Keshavarz through situating her personal condition in relation to other women's experiences and within a female social collectivity. It is in this vein that Keshavarz finds the process of making the film "therapeutic." In this regard she said:

> Despite going through a difficult process, from the initiation of writing the idea to the production and then to the film's editing—anyway, I was going through one of the biggest crises of my life at the age of twenty-six and [this] was not at all easy—when the film was done, I felt as though I became light, as though the feeling that had [bothered me] for years had vanished. I felt empowered and thought I am at a point where I can make the correct decision. After that experience, which was like a therapy for me, this style of filmmaking became more significant to me.[70]

This powerful and intimate reflection emphasizes the potentiality of the documentary medium as a vehicle for self-discovery that facilitates journeys of the self. By turning the lens towards the self, autobiographical documentary becomes a tool that intervenes in both the presumed objective reality of the profilmic world by foregrounding the filmmaker's subjectivity, and in the rigid patriarchal structure by foregrounding the female self-recognition and point of view. In other words, as the film indicates, "by using one's body as a tool for autobiography, including a relationship to the camera as an extension of physicality and performance in front of the lens, women can reconstruct themselves by deconstructing the patriarchal language ..."[71] And this is an approach that Keshavarz masterfully employs in her autobiographical documentary not only to find and assert her own voice and subjectivity, but to also present other women's subjectivities and perspectives.

21 Days and Me (2011) by Shirin Barghnavard

Shirin Barghnavard's *21 Days and Me* chronicles twenty-one days of Barghnavard's life as she contemplates the issue of motherhood and whether to have children or not. Barghnavard's husband does not want to have any children, but she is fearful that he might one day decide otherwise, and that time might be too late for Barghnavard as a woman to bear a child. Emphasizing the sexual potency of men even at an old age in an intimate gathering of friends, Barghnavard points to the specificities of a female body and biological issues limiting the desired time for female fertility. Within this context, the filmmaker raises female-specific questions and concerns thus foregrounding, throughout the documentary, female perspectives and experiences in regard to these matters. Barghnavard's dilemma of motherhood becomes further convoluted when she learns of a fibroid in her uterus that needs to be surgically removed. The doctor informs Barghnavard and her husband that she has two options regarding this matter: to remove either the fibroid alone or the whole uterus itself. Therefore, this condition further complicates the prospect of fertility and motherhood for the filmmaker and highlights another specific female-related issue. In the final scenes of the film, we see Barghnavard preparing for her surgery and ultimately learn that the surgery for removing the fibroid has been successful and that the uterus has remained intact. But except for this clear conclusion, most of the questions raised throughout the film remain without definitive answers. Whether Barghnavard and her husband finally make up their minds to have children or not, and how they manage to convince their family if they decide to not have children are, for instance, among issues that remain open to the audience's speculation.

Barghnavard's documentary underlines a female authorial point of view derived from the specificities of female lived experiences. Nevertheless, Barghnavard connects these female-specific conditions to broader socio-cultural discourses on family and motherhood, and similar to Keshavarz, offers a mode of "first person plural" in the film.[72] Barghnavard not only interviews various women about their decisions to have or not have children, but also presents such questions to male friends and her husband. What then shapes the nucleus of the documentary's argument is the changing perspectives of the young, middle-class generation in Iran on the notions of family and parenthood. Discussing the self-reflexivity presented in this film as well as in her episode in *Profession: Documentarist* in my interview, Barghnavard attested to a "we" as the subject of these works beyond the explicit "I" of the filmmaker. She said:

> It is true that both films have a self-reflexive style, but this self-reflexivity is done in such a way to have a more general aspect. In other words, to reflect a part of the society, so that the audience can also engage with it. In these films, the filmmaker has seen herself not as a director, but as a member of the society, just instead of turning the camera towards the society, she has turned it towards herself.[73]

It is indeed through such a "first person plural" approach that the significance of *21 Days and Me*'s interviews and discussions can be understood. In these filmic moments we learn about the views of young, middle-class Iranians that for various reasons—political and economic uncertainties, unpleasant childhood experiences, inherent emptiness of life, and resistance to families' expectations—prefer to not have any children.

The social and familial expectations regarding parenthood might be to some extent less strict for men than women, as these entities overwhelmingly define female subjectivity and identity through the role of motherhood. Reflecting on her complicated situation and dilemmas in a scene, Barghnavard tells her husband, "It is an exhausting process that you have to explain to people why you do not want to have any children, and nobody asks you this question. They only ask me!" Moreover, Barghnavard's parents are in Australia and their absence becomes difficult to endure for the filmmaker, especially when her husband is away for work. As Barghnavard confesses to the camera (and the viewers), it is especially in these moments of loneliness that she thinks about having a child. Connecting such pressures that she feels personally to a larger societal context, Barghnavard meets with a friend who will be forty-one years old soon and has managed to defer social and familial expectations by living an independent lifestyle. The woman says, "I've lived freely but I've been skinned. We pay for things that we want, for things that we want to achieve and decide freely." Like Keshavarz, Barghnavard, searches for her questions and dilemmas by situating them in relation to others' points of view and experiences, and like Keshavarz, she never offers any final answers. Dönmez-Colin, regarding this documentary, observes "The camera of Barghnavard registers with precision the ambivalence in these women caught between the liberation of personal choices and the comforting aspect of confirming [sic] to the expectations of parents and society."[74]

Keshavarz employs her first-person voiceover at the beginning of *Unwelcome in Tehran* to assert her personal authorial vision in the film, yet Barghnavard uses direct addresses to the camera as a way to assert her personal perspective. Both styles are significant in terms of subverting the supposed objective and omnipresent documentary style by entrusting us, the viewers, with personal and intimate information on the filmmakers' lives. In Barghnavard's film, the direct camera addresses and their confessional nature affectively mobilize the audience through the embodied enunciation of the filmmaker and engage them more radically with the discussions and personal reflections presented in the film. In her discussion on embodied spectatorship, film scholar Laura Rascaroli points to the implication of a "you" that is usually generated by first person and essay films' mode of address through their self-reflexive authorial style. This is an embodied form of spectatorship in which "the (real) spectators of these films are called upon in an unremitting effect of interpellation. … In the case of essayistic forms such as diaries, notebooks and self-portraits, they are invited to engage with the truth that the author is telling about himself [/herself] and his [/her] experiences."[75] Therefore Rascaroli posits that "spectators of first-person films may feel closer to the text and to its author—and may themselves have a more personal, subjective spectatorial experience than with other types of cinema."[76] In *21 Days and Me*, Barghnavard's invocation of the "you" of the audience arises through its merging with a first-person and subjective rhetoric and style, through an embodied communication, one side on which resides the personal *and* embodied authorial discourse of the filmmaker and the other side which is occupied by an implied, embodied group of spectators who are directly addressed by the filmmaker. Direct addresses to the camera also emphasize the idea that personal confessions and deliberate self-revelations within a filmic setting, which is considered a public setting, are no longer a stigma within an Iranian context. As such, through a multi-layered, personal, and self-reflexive approach, Barghnavard offers a fresh glimpse of a changing society not only in regard to the issues of motherhood and female identity within the family and society, but also in regard to the female body and voice in Iranian cinema and culture.

Profession: Documentarist (2014) by Shirin Barghnavard, Firouzeh Khosrovani, Farahnaz Sharifi, Mina Keshavarz, Sepideh Abtahi, Sahar Salahshoor, and Nahid Rezaei

Profession: Documentarist is a groundbreaking collaborative documentary between seven Iranian women documentarians, who each contributed to the project by making one of its seven episodes. Each episode uses self-reflexive and autobiographical mode to present a first-person account of some aspects of each filmmaker's life as well as the filmmaker's reflection on documentary filmmaking in Iran as a profession. The episodes therefore not only interweave personal and professional perspectives within a documentary context, but they also connect these reflections to a larger social and political setting in Iran. The episodes particularly highlight the post-2009 repressive sociopolitical atmosphere that ensued after the 2009 contested presidential election resulting in the victory of the conservative Mahmoud Ahmadinejad, thus reflecting on the specific time within and in reaction to which the film itself was made. At the same time, the episodes collectively cover a broader historical era, such as the pre-revolution time, the 1979 Islamic Revolution, the Iran-Iraq War, the 2009 presidential election and the protests that occurred in its aftermath, and the 2013 presidential election. Reflecting on the context within which this documentary was made, Shirin Barghnavard in the interview for this study mentioned:

> The idea of the film grew out of the feeling of despair and frustration [that was felt] by documentarians in general, and some women documentarians working together in a film office in particular, after the 2009 election's events. At that time, the circumstances for documentary making had become more difficult and a good outlook for cultural and artistic activities in the society seemed non-existent. To liberate ourselves from the impasse that we were stuck in, we decided to get together to make a collective feature-length film.[77]

The "first person plural" mode of the film thus resonates not only through its individual filmmakers' personal narrative presented in each episode in relation to Iran's sociopolitical context, but also through its collective mode of production. In fact, *Profession: Documentarist*, in its collaborative and independent process of making, as well as in its subject matter, is an unprecedented example in Iranian documentary cinema. In my interview, Barghnavard acknowledged previous collective films made in Iran such as episodic films about the Kish Island and Persian carpet, and the documentary *Kahrizak, Four Views* (*Kahrizak, chahar negah*, 2012), made by Mohsen Amiryoussefi, Rakhshan Banietemad, Pirooz Kalantari, and Bahman Kiarostami. But she asserted:

> These films had a specific commissioner, investor, and producer, and another thing is that each episode was made separately by a professional director with different [filmmaking] groups, and then was put together [with other episodes] during the editing process. But *Profession: Documentarist* was not made this way. All different processes of making this film, from the first steps of proposing the idea to its inaugural screening, which took almost two and a half years, were done collectively with the presence of all the makers of the film.[78]

Such a close and intimate collaboration, regardless of its possible challenges, serves as a crucial form of solidarity and alliance, through which these women documentarians were able to embark on a process to reflect on their profession, personal lives, and their society. It is a process that derives from both individual and collective underpinnings and their respective interactions. In doing so, the episodes use archival footage, family albums and photos, home videos, and the day-to-day lives of the filmmakers to reflect upon various issues including the practice of the documentary filmmaking itself. Some of the topics presented in these episodes include the 1979 Islamic Revolution, war, censorship, banning of female solo singing in public after the revolution, nostalgia, US sanctions against Iran, immigration, political repression, and resilience and hope amid disappointing conditions.

In the documentary's episodes, the voices of the filmmakers narrate their stories and thus explicitly point to a "you," an embodied audience, that is rhetorically addressed sometimes even with questions the filmmakers ask. These questions of course arise from the filmmakers' own musings on the topics that they discuss, yet they inevitably invoke audiences to actively engage with the filmmakers and the issues they underline. What in fact makes each episode and the whole film unique is the deep entanglement of the personal memory, history, and experience with a collective memory, history and experience. Barghnavard, for instance, in her episode reflects on the possibility of the United States' war with Iran by depicting a video game in which American soldiers have occupied Tehran and are approaching the Gisha bridge. The episode further connects the discussion of an impending US-Iran war to the trauma that is left behind from the Iran-Iraq War (1980–88), which still affects Iranian lives. In doing so, the episode uses archival footage of the Iran-Iraq War as well as family albums and childhood photos to highlight an unending state of geopolitical anxiety that has loomed over Iranians' daily lives. Moreover, Barghnavard depicts her immigration to Australia to study filmmaking, her close bond there with some Iraqi friends, the protests of the people in Australia against the US war with Iraq, and the protests of Iranians in regard to the 2009 presidential election in Iran, thus prompting a form of national and global connectivity within a political context at the same time that she points to the specificities of these matters. Barghnavard ultimately wraps up her episode with the images of herself and her husband, Australia, close-ups of various Iranian individuals, and the city of Tehran while asking, "Nowadays, although the city is calm, I think if there will be another war, would I stay to document it? Or perhaps, I wouldn't even let my husband, a cameraman, film anything? … Would I leave? What about the others? …"

It is indeed through this deeply personal and female perspective on the war and other political events that Barghnavard and other filmmakers of the documentary subvert official and hegemonic accounts to re-write history from below. The recollections and memories presented in the film are ostensibly fragmented, therefore blurring the boundaries between truth and fiction, authenticity and construction, and objectivity and subjectivity. For instance, in the episode made by Sepideh Abtahi, the filmmaker strives to recall the events of the 1979 Islamic Revolution during which she was only three years and eight months old. She tries to remember her aunt, Maryam, who was a revolutionary activist and died on the exact day of the revolution due to cancer. Throughout the episode, Abtahi highlights the difficulty of seeing through the thickness of the past by questioning her memory, which visually shows itself through superimposition of multiple images or fragmentation of images via split screens. At a point during the episode Abtahi uses both of these visual techniques accompanied by her voiceover saying, "I am trying to recall. It's impossible to recall anything. If I were able to tell all these by words, I wouldn't have to carry all these cameras." Here, the cameras are put into the task of recording what memory might fail to remember; to document the history and the past. Yet at another point in her episode, Abtahi also questions the role of the cameras by asking, "Are these cameras telling the truth?" Therefore, she negates the idea of a single Truth and objectivity as recorded through documentary images by presenting instead a multiplicity of truths and meanings. Russell discusses the workings of autoethnographic films as "an archival practice," writing, "The filmed memory situates the filmmaker-subject within a culture of mediation in which the past is endemically fictional. To recall that past by way of memory traces is to render it 'another culture' in an ever receding palimpsest of overlapping cultures, of which past, present, and future are merely points of perspective."[79] Interestingly, Abtahi herself alerts us at the beginning of her episode to an "endemically fictional" reflection on her childhood, the revolution, and her aunt. As Abtahi says, "I'm telling the history as I'd like. My surrealistic history." Such form of personal and contested mediations on a major national and historical event such as the Islamic Revolution therefore challenges the official grand narrative discourses on the event as the Truth, rendering them uncertain. It also points to the construction of a selfhood that is fragmented, incomplete, and doubtful, and actively, if irresolutely, in negotiation with her own and her country's pasts.

Through their narratives, the episodes also connect private and public spaces and personal and professional activities, blurring their boundaries. For example, in the episode made by Farahnaz Sharifi, home videos, family photos, and archival footage are used to showcase a family's passion for various Iranian female singers, and music in general. The episode highlights the post-revolutionary ban on female solo singing in public, and further navigates the implications of such restriction for ordinary Iranians, whose love of music and dance was relegated to the confines of a private sphere. Moreover, Sharifi connects this restriction to the censorship in filmmaking in regard to depicting female solo singing by recalling her own first documentary film, which was about Qamar ol-Moluk Vaziri, the first Iranian woman to sing in public. As Sharifi says in the film, "The censorship office told me that I should remove her voice to show my film in Iran." In these reflections, the personal and familial become public, professional, and political, creating a multi-layered, gendered account of individual and cultural histories. Dönmez-Colin regarding the film argues, "Women and film-maker are two identities that suggest daily struggles in Iran, but together they provoke issues that are usually overlooked."[80] That is why each episode of this documentary finds a unique significance in bringing about personal accounts of women documentarians as they intimately open up about various sociocultural and political issues, as well as about the practice of documentary filmmaking itself in contemporary Iran.

In the episode made by Mina Keshavarz, we learn she got a divorce from her husband and is thinking of leaving the country due to the repressive environment that emerged after the 2009 election. But at the same time, Keshavarz does not want to sacrifice her documentary filmmaking career, which is grounded in Iran. Her immigration plan gets further complicated by American economic sanctions imposed on Iran, making such geographical movements and border-crossings economically challenging. Here, similar to *Unwelcome in Tehran*, Keshavarz utilizes the potentialities of documentary as a "therapeutic" and investigative medium to navigate her hesitations and dilemmas in regard to leaving the country. As Keshavarz in her interview mentioned, "The making of that episode and its long process of production … helped me decide to stay [in Iran]."[81] Here the entanglement of the documentary filmmaking with the personal life works in such a way that prompts crucial life decisions on the part of the filmmaker. Keshavarz in this regard said, "In fact, I think we as filmmakers are not separate from the society, and are not separate from the setting that we select for our films."[82] This interconnectedness of documentary and life, private and public, and personal and political resonates throughout *Profession: Documentarist*. The episodes present counter-memories, counter-histories, and counter-narratives providing us with bottom-up perspectives and micronarratives through self-reflexive documentary filmmaking. Ultimately, in the words of Dönmez-Colin, "What emanates from the documentary is the strong love these artists feel for their country whose only wish is to live in peace in an environment respectful of the individual."[83]

The discussion of Iranian women's autobiographical documentaries in this chapter shows that women documentarians, in addition to bringing to the fore their personal female voices and stories, have championed new forms of documentary expression that are unprecedented in Iranian cinema. Their autobiographical works present the filmmakers' perspectives on their own conditions, but they also relate these personal lived experiences to the sociocultural contexts, investigating their interconnectedness and mutual influence. Therefore, instead of offering totalizing points of view, they provide subjective, investigative, and self-reflexive observations and explorations on the individual and the society. In these works, women documentarians have not only revived the female voice and agency in Iranian society, but have also employed and pushed the possibilities of the documentary as a medium for reflection and discovery. They have widened the realms of documentary expression by turning women's personal and daily struggles into the productive sites of female subjectivity and documentary revelations. They show the reconstruction of a female identity through active processes of individual and collective negotiations and contemplations facilitated by the documentary medium, and in doing so, they reject a singular Truth about the Iranian woman, presenting us instead with fragmented and diverse forms of subjectivity and personhood.

CHAPTER 4

Narrating Women's Lives in Biographical Documentaries: Sites of Recognition

Biographical documentaries, similar to autobiographical documentaries, center on subjectivity, individuality, and personhood. They, however, explore these issues in relation to the lives of others rather than the lives of the filmmakers themselves. New forms of female solidarity and female bond are thus created that connect the filmmaking subject behind the camera with the filmed subject in front of the camera. These forms of female connectivity in Iranian women's biographical documentaries featuring Iranian women's lives, as I depict in this chapter, are grounded in a gendered shared experience that turns the biographical documentary practice into a highly subjective and activist mode of representation and discourse. In other words, it is through the connection between these two selves—the documentarian and the female subject—that a strong articulation of female voice and subjectivity is formed that challenges the authoritarian and patriarchal hegemony. I contend that by foregrounding the lives and points of view of ordinary Iranian women, these biographical documentaries accomplish three major tasks: they break the dualities of self/other, private/public, and margin/center by subverting the deeply ingrained gender hierarchies in Iranian society and culture; they highlight female voice and subjectivity within various social, cultural, and familial sites while being attentive to the diversity and multiplicity of Iranian women's experiences and life narratives; and they create productive sites for women's recognition, advocacy, and solidarity through the medium of documentary. In doing so, these biographical works offer groundbreaking insights into the workings of gender relations in contemporary Iran and within social, cultural, familial, and political contexts.

Women's biographical practices, as film scholar Julia Lesage argues, "provide an essential tool for looking in a self-conscious way" at various aspects of women's lives and "their sense of 'embeddedness' in a certain object world."[1] This gendered connectivity creates a form of documentary bond between women as filmmakers and subjects that operates within an artistic and activist ground, offering the possibility to "look at familiar women's elements to define them in a new, uncolonized way."[2] Moreover, women's biographical documentaries foreground narratives of women's lives that are often marginalized or overlooked. And in doing so, they act "as a political intervention and a gesture that gives visibility to other histories that speak back to the grand narratives that dominate official history."[3] These films thus intervene in the overwhelmingly male-dominated biographical representations offering counter-narratives and counter-histories. Of course, some biographical documentaries on women's lives, made by Iranian male filmmakers, may certainly possess such interventionist qualities, but what specifically separates women's biographical documentary practices from their male counterparts is the "intricate links between the personal and political" that bestow upon women's works an activist and political urgency grounded in women's lived experiences.[4]

Discussing the form and structure of feminist biography in a literary context, sociologist Liz Stanley argues for the significance of the recognition that "biography as a genre is by no means separate from the autobiography of those who produce it."[5] Similarly, I believe such a recognition within a documentary context brings new insights into Iranian women's relationships and advocacy efforts, as it is precisely through the connection between the documentarian and the female subject that a strong form of female solidarity and recognition is generated that challenges the authoritarian and patriarchal structures. Susan Mann Trofimenkoff aptly observes that for biography to become feminist biography, a feminist political commitment must be taken into account that serves a particular purpose.[6] As she writes, "The purpose may be as simple as uncovering a past that has been denied women … or it may be as complex as exposing the patterns of patriarchal society in order to be able to change them."[7] As the case studies in this chapter delineate, Iranian women's biographical documentaries strive to serve both of these purposes as they situate their focus on individual lives within a broader sociocultural and gender context to highlight Iranian women's agency and subjectivity and critique patriarchal approaches and dominance. Therefore, as Meryn Stuart argues, "Feminist biography allows us to see women as central *actors*, and from the perspective of their own lived experience. … Secondly, feminist biography allows us to see gender as a historical construct. For, perhaps the most revolutionary aspect of contemporary women's history was the refusal to accept gender-role divisions as natural."[8]

In order to examine these workings of feminist biography through the works of Iranian women documentarians, I first offer a brief review of the development of biographical films in Iranian cinema, with a particular focus on Iranian documentary. Then, I highlight the impact of various sociocultural, gender, and political transformations on biographical documentary practices since the late 1990s, a time frame that has seen a considerable rise in biographical documentaries on Iranian women's lives, many of which are made by Iranian women documentarians. I conclude the discussion by offering a closer look at two documentary films, *Mother of the Earth* (2017), directed by Mahnaz Afzali, and *Braving the Waves* (2016), directed by Mina Keshavarz. It is the goal of this chapter to illuminate the significance of women's biographical documentaries in contemporary Iran, which act as an essential form of documentation and preservation in regard to women's lived experiences within specific sociocultural contexts and historical times. In doing so, these biographical works offer groundbreaking insights into the workings of gender relations in contemporary Iran and in regard to its social, cultural, familial, and political contexts. Furthermore, these documentaries attest to the unique potentiality of the documentary medium to record women's lives and narratives in effective and affective ways. In other words, these works not only offer possibilities for challenging gender norms and sociocultural traditions, but they also serve as a much-needed document of, and advocate for, Iranian women's issues. As film scholars Kristin Lené Hole and Dijana Jelača write, "Documentary film is … an important medium for conveying the complexities and hidden transcripts of women's history, whether the woman in question is a figure already well known but reduced to a simple narrative, or overlooked by dominant historical narratives."[9] Iranian women's biographical documentaries offer nuanced perspectives on women's lives and experiences celebrating their individuality, subjectivity, and activism while highlighting the social, cultural, and political contexts within which they live and operate.

Biography and the Invisibility of Iranian Women: A Brief History

Persian studies scholar Michael Craig Hillmann underlines the scarcity of biographical tradition in Iranian literature and culture, asserting, "In the authoritarian, patriarchal Iranian environment, biographies other than the approved lives of kings, their representatives, and other establishment father figures might not have a place."[10] Hillmann further relates this paucity to reasons such as "Iranian concerns about the reaction of family, friends, neighbors, and society at large," and "self-censorship to avoid governmental censorship or worse."[11] Within this context, biographies in their written forms have not become an established genre and a well-known method for cultural expression in Iran. Therefore, Hillmann contends that "readers cannot be expected to seek out, encourage, or appreciate th[is] literary form."[12] Emphasizing the impact of cultural conventions on the writing of history and (auto)biography, Persian studies scholar William L. Hanaway argues, "The fact that Iranian culture has no tradition of biography and autobiography as we know them in the West does not mean that the would-be biographer has no models at all to look to in writing his or her own life or the life of another."[13] Hanaway considers biographies of Imam Husein, the third Shiite Imam, and Abolqasem Ferdowsi, the quintessential poet of Persian epic poetry, as such cultural examples that for the most part emphasize the "moral and didactic" qualities and values associated with these figures' lives.[14] Yet, according to Hanaway, "Not until the middle of the twentieth century were biographies written, such as that of Shah 'Abbas I, which attempt to be factual and objective in the Western fashion."[15] These arguments thus show that Iranian biographical tradition overwhelmingly centers on the lives of major religious, literary, and political male figures whose portraits range from sacred individuals with holy and eternal values to historical figures with genius and noble characteristics or authoritative commands.

Within a visual context, Iranian studies scholars such as Shahrokh Meskoob and Hamid Dabashi argue that in Iranian visual arts, the attention to ordinary people and their daily lives emerged in the mid-nineteenth century, particularly as the result of the influence of the photographic medium, which according to Meskoob also prompted "the artistic 'imitation' of painters of the time from its possibilities."[16] Still photography thus introduced, in the words of Dabashi, "the first shock," but it was the emergence of cinema that substantially expanded the photographic and visual attention to individuals, in part because it "had a much wider audience," and therefore a broader reach.[17]

One of the early biographical examples in Iranian cinema can be seen in Abdolhossein Sepanta's *Firdausi* (1934), which "was based on the life of the eleventh-century poet Abolqasem Ferdowsi and re-created parts of the mythical and paradigmatic battle of father and son—Rostam and Sohrab—from Ferdowsi's epic poem *Shahnameh*."[18] In its cinematic form, Iranian biographies were in fact embraced by Iranian cinema and society much earlier than autobiographical films. Perhaps the "moral and didactic" values associated with certain lives who had influenced Iranian society and culture made such cinematic depictions not only possible, but also urgent. The crucial point, however, remains that for the most part and even until today, the majority of Iranian biographical films, whether fiction or documentary, have centered on male figures excluding women's lives.

In the documentary field, the recording of diverse individual lives and their daily practices emerged in various documentary forms ranging from ethnographic films to surrealist art films of new wave directors, especially Parviz Kimiavi. The former, according to film and media scholar Hamid Naficy, "emerged strongly in the 1960s," and were an urgent way of "documenting and preserving the country's traditions, cultural expressions, and ways of life," which due to a speedy modernization that Iran was undergoing, were faced with the threat of disappearance.[19] As such, rather than being biographies of specific individuals per se, these films depicted "ways of life" and common routines of some people as presented through tribal traditions, religious customs, and ritual ceremonies.

The latter emerged in the 1970s in the works of filmmakers such as Kimiavi. In his documentaries and fiction films, Kimiavi "employed an authorial, surrealist, and avant-gardist style consisting of real people enacting either their own lives or fictionalized versions thereof; the seamless mixing of fantasy and documentary..."[20] For instance, Kimiavi's short documentary *P Like Pelican* (*Pe mesl-e pelikan*, 1972) depicts the life of an old eccentric figure and recluse, Agha Seyyed Ali Mirza, who lives alone in a remote and ruined building on the outskirts of the city of Tabas. In reality-based fiction film *The Stone Garden* (*Bagh-e sangi*, 1976), Kimiavi again centers on an isolated character, Darvish Khan Esfandiarpour, who is a deaf and mute shepherd and lives with his wife and two sons in a remote desert-like land near Kerman located in the southeast of Iran. In both of these films, Kimiavi portrays the lives of characters who are outcasts living on the margins of the society.[21]

Biographical resonances in documentary film prior to the 1979 Islamic Revolution can also be seen in *Forough Farrokhzad 1313–1345* (1967), made by Naser Taghvai. The documentary pays tribute to the life of contemporary well-known female poet, Farrokhzad, who tragically died in a car accident in 1967.[22] In general, prior to the 1979 Islamic Revolution, biographical films mostly centered on the lives of well-known figures—a trend that continues until today—as well as unknown, yet eccentric, individuals. The surge of depicting ordinary people, especially women, and their daily lives through biographical films had to wait until the late 1990s.

During and after the 1979 Islamic Revolution, a resurgence of biographical documentaries occurred in Iran. In regard to the significance of these films at this particular historical moment, Naficy contends:

> The upheavals of the revolution and its aftermath affected individual lives tremendously, making them more interesting as film subjects. It also brought home an

> important aspect of Iranian modernity: the role of individuals as architects not only of their own lives but also of their society. While historical and compilation documentaries focused primarily on the social and historical forces in shaping history, biographical documentaries emphasized the role of individuals as a force in history.[23]

Featuring pro-Islamic and anti-Western sentiments, the majority of these documentaries were state-sponsored and predominantly portrayed male intellectuals and authors such as Jalal Al-e Ahmad, Samad Behrangi, and Ali Shari'ati, political figures such as Dr. Mohammad Mosaddegh and Mehdi Bazargan, and clerical figures such as Ayatollah Seyyed Hasan Modarres, Ayatollah Seyyed Abolghasem Kashani, and Ayatollah Seyyed Mahmoud Taleghani.[24] As Naficy writes, "In their choice of subject matter, these films underscored the great men theory of history at the same time that they reflected the male-dominated reality of the Iranian politics."[25] By the outbreak of the Iran-Iraq War, these kinds of biographical documentaries continued focusing mostly on the lives of commanders, veterans, and martyrs of the war; subjects that are still common in documentary and fiction films today. In fact, in addition to documentaries, biographical television series and fiction films have also constituted a part of post-revolutionary film and media output. Among television series are: *Imam Ali* (1996), directed by Davood Mir-Bagheri—on the life of the first Shiite Imam; *Guardianship of Love* (*Velayat-e eshgh*, 2000), directed by Mehdi Fakhimzadeh—on the life of the eighth Shiite Imam, Imam Reza; and *Shahriar* (2007), directed by Kamal Tabrizi—on the life of poet Seyyed Mohammad Hossein Behjat Tabrizi, known as Shahriar. Among fiction films are: Ali Hatami's *Kamal ol-Molk* (1984)—on the life of master Iranian painter Mohammad Ghaffari, known as Kamal ol-Molk; Mohammad Hossein Mahdavian's *Standing in the Mist* (*Istadeh dar ghobar*, 2016)—on the life of an Iranian revolutionary commander, Ahmad Motavaselian; and Bahram Tavakoli's *Gholamreza Takhti* (2019)—on the life of athlete Gholamreza Takhti, who was a popular and internationally known wrestling champion. As these examples again show, most of these biographical depictions center on male figures associated with religion, politics, arts, and literature. However, beginning in the 1990s, this male-dominated subject matter in biography gives way to a diverse set of women's lives and perspectives in documentaries.

Biographical Documentaries Since the Late 1990s

Since the late 1990s, biographical documentary in Iran has gone under major transformations, especially in regard to women's presence as both images and image makers, which are in tandem with larger sociocultural, gender, and political alterations in the country. These changes have affected the notions and performances of individuality and subjectivity in Iranian society and their documentary representations in biographical forms. Within this context, documentary filmmaker and critic Omid Balaghati acknowledges a crucial shift in regard to the content of biographical documentaries themselves, asserting, "The portraits of famous figures, marginalized individuals and outcasts, or hot and sensitive subjects, have been substituted by [the portraits of] ordinary individuals and their micro lives."[26] According to Balaghati, "Now, Iranian documentarian aptly knows that featuring such subjects in front of his/her camera and depicting the details of their life do not limit the film to a small world, but they rather posit the power of extensibility of these subjects within newer boundaries of social, political, and historical analysis."[27] In fact, the camera of the Iranian documentarian has now gotten much closer to the lives of various ordinary people in order to offer fresh insights into the fabric of the society through micro narratives. The attention to Iranian individuality thus provides a ground for reflection on larger contexts such as family, society, and politics. This is a shift that also rejects the idea of the individual as a fixed and homogenous entity, and instead represents a dynamic being in a constant state of negotiation, adaptation, and transformation in a society that is entangled with the dualities of modernity and tradition, self and other, public and private, and the spaces in between.

Regardless of various impediments, whether political (forced by conservative factions) or social (imposed by gender traditions and expectations), that procrastinated or blocked the reform efforts during the presidency of Mohammad Khatami (1997–2005), Iranian women strived to push forward for a more equitable and inclusive society. As Iranian journalist and reformist Zahra Nejadbahram writes:

> In this period many more women had access to education and employment and opportunities were created for women to participate in and contribute to the socio-economic and political life of the country. Women played an important role in the burgeoning of NGOs as civil society organisations. But women's participation at the higher levels of employment such as political leadership, managerial and decision-making positions did not increase more than 2.7 per cent.[28]

The Reform Era might have ultimately failed to enact sustained forms of sociopolitical, gender, and economic developments, but for a period of time, it was able to mobilize discourses on civil society, meritocracy, the rule of law, and human rights in Iranian society, which in turn opened up some venues for sociopolitical, cultural, and gender transformations.

Significantly, some of the achievements and failures of the Reform Era, especially regarding women's issues, are presented in a number of biographical documentaries. For instance, Ebrahim Mokhtari's *Zinat, One Special Day* (*Zinat, yek rooz-e behkhosoos*, 2000) introduces us to Zinat Daryaei, who has been a health worker for thirteen years and lives and works in the village of Salakh, on the Qeshm Island. Zinat becomes a candidate in her village's council election. This is the first ever city and village council elections, held in 1999, to offer more executive roles to the local communities. "Some 5,000 women were given a chance to run for 220,000 local council seats in cities, towns, and villages across the country."[29] We see in the film a local man's disagreement with Zinat's decision to run as a candidate mainly because he doubts Zinat's ability and suitability as a "woman" to take on this job. Yet, Zinat remains strong and determined regarding her objectives. She hopes to bring some progressive changes to her village, such as establishing a girls' junior high school and improving conditions of the roads, water pipelines, and telephone. Ultimately, Zinat receives the highest number of votes in her village's council election and thus earns a seat in the council. A male voiceover at the end of the documentary informs us that some of Zinat's plans for the village have begun to materialize. The voiceover says, "Five months after the elections, the pavement of the Salakh road started, and eight months later, Zinat obtained the permit to open Salakh's girls' junior high school." This documentary in fact explicitly highlights a woman's strong perseverance to find her voice and agency in the society regardless of sociocultural and gender limitations, as well as her influential contributions to the society via executive and leadership roles, made possible during the Reform Era.

While *Zinat, One Special Day* provides insights into new possibilities regarding women's social participation that emerged during the presidency of Khatami by focusing on the life of a woman in a southern village, Rakhshan Banietemad's *Our Times* (2002) reflects on the shortcomings of the Reform Era in relation to women's sociopolitical participation by highlighting the life of a woman in the capital Tehran. *Our Times* has a two-part structure. The first section depicts some young people campaigning as supporters of Khatami for the upcoming 2001 presidential election in mostly upper-class parts of the city, located in the north of Tehran. The second and longer part of the film portrays the day-to-day struggles of a single mother from the lower classes, named Arezu, who lives with her daughter and blind mother in a rented home somewhere in the south of Tehran, and nominates herself as a presidential candidate. Banietemad, in an interview for this study, reflected on this film's context:

> Women and youth had an essential role in the second-term presidential election of Seyyed Mohammad Khatami. For the first time even, a lot of presidential candidates were women, who except for a very few, politically and socially did not have the foothold and the capacity for such a post, yet the registration for presidential candidacy was for them a sign of the crystallization of a sort of self-esteem and a possibility for the expression of their demands.[30]

Banietemad met Arezu while filming some of these women, and Arezu's character stood out for the filmmaker. Banietemad described Arezu "as a young woman with various difficulties and responsibilities, who had an extraordinary self-confidence."[31] Ultimately, the candidacy of the women who registered to run as presidential candidates was not approved by the Guardian Council, an entity that supervises and decides the suitability of applicants for each election. More importantly and even ironically, with the many problems that Arezu had to deal with in the days leading to the actual election, including many efforts to find an affordable rented home, she did not even have time and energy to cast her vote! Film scholar Blake Atwood discusses various sociopolitical and economic disparities that this documentary pays attention to in its two-part structure, as well as in its depiction of the overlapping time period in which the events unfold in each part, instead of following a chronological progression from the first to the second segment. In this regard, Atwood observes, "By holding time still, [Banietemad] suggests the lack of progression, and especially the lack of improvement or *reform*."[32]

Nevertheless, the efforts and struggles of Iranian women since the late 1990s have brought about new and urgent demands for portraying Iranian women's lives in documentary films, and therefore have led to a surge in biographical documentaries made by both women and men on Iranian women's lives. Some of these biographical documentaries made by male documentarians include: Ebrahim Mokhtari's *Mokarrameh, Memories and Dreams* (*Mokarrameh, khaterat va roya-ha*, 1999); Mojtaba Mirtahmasb's *Lady of the Roses* (*Banoo-ye gol-e sorkh*, 2009); and Loghman Khaledi's *Nessa* (2012). Some of the biographical documentaries made by women documentarians include: Khatereh Hanachi's *Countdown* (*Shomaresh-e m'akoos*, 2008); Maryam Sepehri's *Thicker than Paint* (*Faratar az rang*, 2014); Rakhshan Banietemad's *All My Trees* (2015); Mina Keshavarz's *Braving the Waves* (2016); Shirin Barghnavard's *Poets of Life* (2017); Mahnaz Afzali's *Mother of the Earth* (2017); and Sahar Mosayebi's *Zero to Podium* (*Sefr ta sakoo*, 2017). Significantly, these women's documentaries tackle various issues related to Iranian women's lives, ranging from pressures to successfully pass Iran's university entrance exam (known as *Konkoor*) to defying gender norms in various professions. In many of these and other examples, the subjects selected are ordinary women who, in one way or another, strive to find and/or perform their agency. Many of these biographical documentaries are also independently produced, which make them distinct from those biographical documentaries produced by the Iranian state television and the Ministry of Culture and Islamic Guidance (MCIG) during and in the early years of the Islamic Revolution, which presented a specific revolutionary and pro-regime ideology through a focus on male figures. The post-1990s biographical documentaries instead present bottom-up narratives and micro perspectives on various ordinary individuals, and expand their underlining themes from the individual to the social, and from the particular to the general. And in doing so, they offer a more nuanced portrait of the Iranian society, and of Iranian women.

In fact, women's biographical documentaries act as an essential form of documentation in regard to both culture and society at specific historical times, and further present women's experiences and their social and artistic interactions within a particular filmic setting. As such, documentary not only provides a ground for defying sociocultural traditions and gender norms, but it also offers possibilities for documenting women's lives and advocating for their issues. In the following, I offer a closer reading of two biographical documentaries, made by Iranian women documentarians on two distinct women's lives, further indicating how these films provide a particular ground for female recognition in which "both sides of the category of 'experience'—the objectivity of circumstance and event and the subjectivity of perception and response—have a role."[33] This feature offers us a form of feminist documentary aesthetics that focuses on the individuality and subjectivity of Iranian women, and relates them to the personal as well as the social, cultural, and political contexts.

Mother of the Earth (2017) by Mahnaz Afzali

Part of the Karestan film series,[34] *Mother of the Earth*, directed by Mahnaz Afzali, portrays the life and contributions of Hayedeh Shirzadi, an ecological expert, who received her Ph.D. in Ecology from Germany. The documentary weaves together various environmental, educational, familial, gender, and political contexts to provide a nuanced portrait of the main character, and to offer insights into the inner workings of the Iranian society, its gender relations, its environmental problems, and some of the ways to deal with these problems.

After completing her study, Shirzadi felt an urgent need for environmental protection and waste recycling in Iran, and thus returned to Iran with her German husband Edmund Lempges. Together, they "established

'Kermanshah Materials Recycling and Organic Fertilizer Production Company' where they blend agriculture and respect for nature to develop clean and healthy agriculture in addition to cleaning the environment."[35] Shirzadi reflects on the establishment of this project in the documentary, saying, "I had the idea of waste separation since 1992. I proposed the project to city officials. Finally, it became operational in 2001." At the moment, "this company carries out consultation, research and executive projects in around 56 towns and 2000 villages, and has provided jobs for 700 people."[36] Yet, many in Iranian society might not have heard of Shirzadi's indispensable efforts and contributions prior to seeing this documentary, and that is why such biographical depictions find a significant role in recognizing and introducing influential women to both Iranian and global audiences.

In an interview for this study, filmmaker Mahnaz Afzali stated that "due to her interest in the environment's condition, she selected this subject" as a Karestan documentary film project.[37] The filmmaker's environmental concerns, in fact, become apparent in the first scene of the documentary, in which various shots depict piles of garbage as rats are feasting among them. Over these images, Afzali's own voiceover says, "Garbage, waste, trash. Waste is my deepest fear these days. … I think of my city, Tehran, a city that produces five tons of waste every minute. That's almost twice the world average. … Knowing Hayedeh Shirzadi and her husband, Edmund Lempges, opened a window of hope for me. I could overcome my anxiety and put an end to my nightmare about garbage …" Such a first-person narration by the documentarian herself explicitly connects the film's topic and its main character to the filmmaker and her personal vision, inviting us on a filmic journey framed by the filmmaker on the life of an influential Iranian woman. The viewer then is introduced to a waste recycling site founded and managed by Hayedeh Shirzadi, in collaboration with her husband, in Kermanshah. Shirzadi gives a tour to some visitors, and along with them, the viewer is delicately exposed to some informative data as well as some aspects of waste recycling process. The documentary therefore performs a two-pronged purpose: it not only introduces the main character and her life and work, but it also informs and educates the viewer regarding environmental matters, especially waste management.

In fact, in these and other moments in the film, one of the major educational themes of the documentary comes to the fore, which is the care and respect for the earth and the environment to which we all belong. In this regard, the film centers on an individual figure, yet the message that both the film and its main character convey is that no human is above and beyond its natural environment, thus importantly breaking away from an anthropocentric perspective. As Shirzadi in the film asserts, "Seasons come and go, but we learn nothing from the nature's cycle. Our behavior is one-way only. We produce, we throw away. … Nature does not need us. But it is us who need the earth for clean air, for clean soil, and [for] clean water." Such a worldview thus creates an urgent mission for Shirzadi and her husband, who through their collaboration and efforts bridge the boundaries of private and public spheres. The personal relationship of Shirzadi and Lempges is indeed entangled with their environmental concerns and commitments. In the documentary, we learn how they met, fell in love, and married, and how their dedication to protecting the natural resources convinced them to come (back) to Iran instead of remaining in Germany. "It was more needed here than in Germany," Lempges explains. The intimate scenes showing the love and respect of the couple for each other abound in the film subverting the idea that a woman's active, professional role in the society negatively affects her performance in the family. Shirzadi's and Lempges's love and support are embedded in their environmental commitments. Lempges accompanies Shirzadi in her visits to governmental and municipal institutions as well as in the management of their own company, and commends Shirzadi for her determination to serve her country. Shirzadi also acknowledges the sacrifices of Lempges for leaving his German life and comfort behind and being willing to live in Iran and to work with all the limitations and difficulties.

The couple's love and care for each other are further extended to their professional setting and the love and care they bring to the work and their interactions with their employees. In a crucial scene, Shirzadi eats her lunch among other female employees and advises them on life matters. Shirzadi tells them, "Today, when we say men and women are equal, we mean women should work as hard as men. It's a privilege to work. … You should build your future and pay for your own needs." Shirzadi therefore encourages women to be financially independent and professionally active, and enhances their confidence to believe in themselves. Such an encouragement is, in fact, instilled in Shirzadi herself by her family, especially by her father, Ali Akbar Khan Shirzadi, who was an elder of the Kalhor tribe. Shirzadi remembers her father in the film saying, "There were no public schools then, and he had private tutors at home. He made sure his daughters get a good education." Reflecting on the status of women's employment in the Islamic Republic of Iran, Zahra Nejadbahram argues:

> [W]omen's experiences since 1979 demonstrate that neither the family nor society as a whole have facilitated the right circumstances for women to fully participate in socio-economic and political spheres. Only in the minority of cases are women encouraged within the family to participate in decision-making positions, managerial

and political leadership positions. As the result, many women believe that the role of women in the family has a great impact on their success and failure in their profession.[38]

With the strong support of her family since her childhood, and her husband since her marriage, Hayedeh Shirzadi might be among the "minority of cases" mentioned by Nejadbahram. However, what is particularly important is the fact that Shirzadi has been relentlessly striving to pass along such a support and encouragement to other women. As such, Shirzadi's efforts have enhanced both the protection of the environment and the lives of many Iranian citizens, who in one way or another have benefited from her visionary leadership and contributions.

The government's response, however, has not been as continuously supportive as it should have been considering the regional and national urgency of such environmental efforts. As we see in the film, Shirzadi and her husband visit governmental and municipal organizations to push for their collaboration and support, at times without any positive results. In a scene, Shirzadi explains about her efforts to expand her waste management project to other Iranian cities. She says, "In 2004, my proposal was placed on the Interior Ministry's agenda, but when the government changed, the plan was scrapped." Here, Shirzadi delicately highlights the role of the government in regard to the enhancement of her project and the governmental transition (here from the reformist government of Khatami to the conservative government of Mahmoud Ahmadinejad), which inevitably affects the government's performance and its political as well as sociocultural and environmental priorities. Considering that the environmental issues affect all individuals regardless of their political affiliations and ideological leanings, the film thus sheds light on the unfortunate obstacles and neglects prompted by political issues. The documentary *Mother of the Earth* offers a multi-faceted perspective on Iranian society attending to various issues within environmental, educational, familial, gender, and political contexts. Instead of following a linear and chronological approach to its character's life narrative, the documentary interweaves the accounts of Shirzadi's past and present. We get to know about Shirzadi's childhood, her family, her education in Germany, her marriage, and her work throughout the course of the film, and in part via the information provided to us by Shirzadi herself as she opens up to the filmmaker's camera and thus to us, the viewers. This brings a form of first-hand knowledge, experience, and testimony that contributes to the viewer's engagement with the character's life. At the end of the film, Afzali's first-person voiceover closes the filmic narrative by saying, "Among us there are only few who dare to step on hard courses. Hayedeh and Edmund's struggle to stop dumping waste is a promise to save the earth, mother earth, generous earth, the source of birth, growth, and renaissance ..." The first-person narration of the opening scene, expressing fear and anxiety over the environmental degradation, now folds into a first-person message of hope with an indirect call for solidarity and action; the same solidarity and shared commitment that connect the filmmaker to her character and prompt her to make the documentary are now relayed to us, the audience.

Braving the Waves (2016) by Mina Keshavarz

Mina Keshavarz's *Braving the Waves* centers on Roghieh Zakeri, a woman from the city of Minab in southern Iran, who is trying to secure jobs for many local women through her Thursday Bazaar. Roghieh has built the bazaar, which was initially located on a dried riverbed without any electricity and water, step by step through dedication and hard work. As the bazaar is receiving more recognition and getting bigger in its size, which in turn is increasing its commercial value, a crisis arrives. Roghieh faces the threat of her bazaar's destruction by the municipality as the mayor wants to make the Thursday Bazaar a property of his organization and sell it to investors. The documentary introduces us to Roghieh's life and her strong character as she fights to keep her bazaar and protect the women vendors whose livelihood depends on it.

Figure 4.1 Women vendors at Roghieh's Thursday Bazaar. *Braving the Waves* (2016), directed by Mina Keshavarz. Courtesy of Mina Keshavarz.

In an interview for this study, Keshavarz mentioned that the initial idea of the documentary came about in 2011 when she received "an offer from Iranian television to make a documentary film in Hormozgan province."[39] At that time, the main story that Keshavarz wanted to narrate "was that of the women vendors of Minab's Thursday Bazaar;" a bazaar that has "hundreds of years of history" and a cultural significance due to "the extensive presence of women as vendors" and their selling of "regional handicrafts."[40] After getting to know Roghieh and her efforts as the manager of the Thursday Bazaar, Keshavarz decided to instead make a documentary on Roghieh's life. By switching her documentary plans to focus more specifically on Roghieh, the television project got cancelled and Keshavarz embarked on an independent production journey to make her film.[41] As Keshavarz recounted, living in Tehran and making a film miles away in another city brought about major economic and logistic challenges. She mentioned, "Sometimes I thought why was I doing this, but when I saw Roghieh, or thought about her a moment, it gave me motivation to finish the film. My purpose was to document her efforts. In a way, Roghieh in front of the camera and I behind the camera were trying together."[42] Such an interconnectivity of struggles and motivations creates a crucial form of women's solidarity and activism through the documentary medium that explicitly shows itself throughout this documentary.

In particular, one night, Roghieh receives a call informing her that the mayor and his agents are destroying the sunshades in the Thursday Bazaar. Roghieh and her husband drive to the scene, and while there, a confrontation breaks out between Roghieh and the mayor's men and shortly afterwards, police arrive to handle the situation. Keshavarz, who has been following Roghieh and filming the incident, also gets caught in the situation. A policeman forcefully asks, "Who is she? Who is filming?" To which Roghieh responds that she is with her. The policeman then commands Keshavarz to turn off the camera. Keshavarz responds that she has a permit to film, but the man approaching the camera insists that she should not film. We see that the camera suddenly gets unleveled with shaky moments capturing the ground, and finally the image freezes. This powerful scene breaks the presumed objectivity of the documentary as well as the third-person, omnipresent exposition of conventional biographical documentaries, by foregrounding the subjective involvement of the camera and the filmmaker in the process of filmmaking. Moreover, the footage captured from this incident provides a valuable document on and a testimony to the harassment of women by the municipality's men. In fact, the next day, the footage is shown to the vendors and people in the bazaar, not only informing them of the municipality's interventional act, but also galvanizing support for Roghieh. A man watching the footage confesses to Roghieh, "Whoever watches this film will be impressed by what you did for us. I feel uneasy that an alone woman has fought with lots of men; I feel guilty …" In his own way, this man thus expresses his recognition of Roghieh's bravery and leadership as well as her commitment to save the bazaar. Roghieh takes the case of the Thursday Bazaar to various governmental organizations, including the Office of Vice President for Women's Affairs in Tehran, and shows them the footage of that night's incident, along with many other documents, to explain the many pressures she is facing from the mayor's office and to advocate for her bazaar. The footage thus here again attests to the role of the documentary medium not only as a tool for documentation, but also as an influential way for advocacy through showcasing bottom-up narratives and discourses. As Keshavarz pointed out: "Many times during the shooting we faced challenges; I was threatened. But I think in some countries such issues have unfortunately become a part of the documentarian's profession. … But what is important is to believe in the work you've done, and that the resulting film should first be pleasant for the film's characters, and then for yourself."[43] The struggles and persistence of women as the filmmaker and the subject are therefore entangled such that they provide a ground for the documentation and representation of the character's life in a self-conscious and subjective way.

As we learn in the film, Roghieh had worked alongside her mother as a vendor, while her father attended to fishing at sea. Roghieh's hard work prompted her father to call her "his little son." Regardless of its admiring intention, such a labeling "reflects gendered divisions of labour which are ingrained in the minds of women and men from childhood."[44] Within this patriarchal context, women's works are considered to belong to the domestic space, while men are considered to be the "breadwinners."[45] As such, "Women's financial contributions to the family are regarded as non-essential and secondary to men's contribution."[46] And if a woman and her contributions are essential and get the acknowledgement, like Roghieh and her works, she might be labeled as a "little son" or someone who is fulfilling a "man's work." However, as soon as Roghieh grew up, her parents pushed her to get married as though she no longer could work and be a "breadwinner." She was now expected to fulfill her womanly duty and be a wife. Roghieh could not find comfort and happiness in that forced marriage. She recalls her feelings at that time in the film, saying, "I found out there is no life for a girl with dreams. It seemed that the dreamful girl was a million miles away." To find solace, Roghieh shares the limitations of her married life with a woman in her neighborhood and gradually their routine discussions on various aspects of women's lives attract other women to their homosocial gatherings. Such a demand for a supportive space, in which women can open up and seek help and solidarity, prompts Roghieh to establish her own NGO, Minab's Beach Women's Association (*Anjoman-e Zanan-e Sahel-e Minab*).

Through her NGO, Roghieh also provides facilities and support to the women vendors in the Thursday Bazaar. Roghieh ultimately gets a divorce and remarries. The husband we see in the documentary is Roghieh's second husband, Akil, who is a farmer and a supportive, loving partner. The leadership of Roghieh regarding the bazaar and her support of the women vendors thus stem from her longer battles and struggles for gender equality and women's rights. This context also raises the stakes for Roghieh to adamantly protect the bazaar with her all means because it is the place that feeds many women, some of whom do not have any other income and/or are widows. In this regard, a woman vendor tells the camera (and the viewers), "Mrs. Zakeri is a supportive woman. Who can be better than her for us? When we don't have money, she does not ask for it. She does not ask anything from widow women like me. … Municipality treats us like objects. If they move us again, we will be in trouble." Roghieh's managerial role, however, is constantly undermined by some governmental and judicial organizations. Even Roghieh's visit and appeal to the Office of Vice President for Women's Affairs cannot change the course of the events on her side. Yet, Roghieh maintains her strong determination and confidence. As she asserts in the documentary, "I will fight for my rights until my last breath." Furthermore, challenging the patriarchal notions of work and the male-dominated network of management, the film emphasizes a mutual form of female support and encouragement from the women vendors to Roghieh and vice versa, as well as from the filmmaker to Roghieh and vice versa. While ultimately the municipality succeeds in confiscating the bazaar's management, the final words of Roghieh to the camera/filmmaker (and to the viewers) at the end of the documentary depict her unwavering belief in hope, resilience, and perseverance. Walking near the sea she says, "Look, the sea goes and comes back again. … The sea wants to say, I'm alive, I'm here. Water is talking to us. Water says: it's my personality. But we, as humans, become hopeless soon. But the sea never gives up. … I think hope is always alive with the sea. … When I'm hopeless, I come to the sea …"

Roghieh's self-determination delineates itself in the ways in which she expresses her voice, strives to get her rights, and performs her agency. Such a self-determination is also reflected through the formal elements employed by the film. In various parts of the film, Roghieh's voiceover conveys the information on her life and work. Some of these voiceovers are accompanied by the images of Roghieh herself in different settings as she

Figure 4.2 Roghieh often visits the sea. *Braving the Waves* (2016), directed by Mina Keshavarz. Courtesy of Mina Keshavarz.

Figure 4.3 Roghieh manages the bazaar's paperwork. *Braving the Waves* (2016), directed by Mina Keshavarz. Courtesy of Mina Keshavarz.

for instance walks on the beach, rides in a taxi, and manages the bazaar's paperwork.

Discussing the communicative elements of biographical discourse in documentary, media scholar John Corner observes that such "availability of subject image and subject voice together" creates a form of "self-accounting" that its strongest example can be seen in the form of "subject's voice over image."[47] In this regard Corner writes:

> Indeed, of all the constituent modes of documentary biography, perhaps the autobiographical device of subject's voice over image is the most powerful. It can attain a register of reflective depth not possible to the synchronised speech of interview sequences, and this can be deepened further when the image includes portrayal of the subject. The combination here of subjectivised, voiced self (self as source) and an objectively rendered self-in-the-world (self as referent) is a potent one. The disjunction between the times and planes of speech and of image, taken together with their convergence, carries a rich semiotics of the personal.[48]

By using this formal technique, Keshavarz underlines the strong position of her documentary subject within both the documentary's narrative and the actual world's conditions within which Roghieh operates. Through this technique the film also offers a subjective and personal view of the events, based on the character's point of view and experiences, that differs from an expository mode of Voice of God used in conventional biographical documentaries. Such a formal technique further contributes to the showcasing of Roghieh's powerful, yet intimate, personality as along with her determined actions and commitments, her personal perspective also frames the documentary narrative.

Both of the biographical documentaries discussed here offer important representations of and perspectives on Iranian women's lives in relation to different sociocultural and familial settings that can enhance our understanding of various women's roles, contributions, and struggles. At the same time, they offer significant forms of women's solidarity and recognition facilitated through the medium of documentary. As such, these works can be considered great examples of feminist biographical documentary, in part for the creative ways that they employ to tackle discourses on gender in Iranian society and to challenge patriarchal notions of female domesticity, passivity, and silence. Writing in regard to a literary context, scholar Lee Chambers-Schiller considers feminist biography,

> as a subgenre, [that] takes as its particular task the examination and analysis of the gender relations of a culture, the ways in which individuals reflect and resist gender roles, internalize and critique conventional gender ideology, push the boundaries of and accommodate to the limitations that society construes as appropriate female experiences while forming relationships, sustaining life, nurturing the spirit, and creating meaning within a specific historical context.[49]

All of these characteristics find their visual manifestations in Afzali's and Keshavarz's biographical documentaries, making these works salient instances of feminist biographical documentary as well as crucial historical documents on Iranian society and its gender issues.

CHAPTER 5

Advocating for Iranian Women through Documentaries: Sites of Negotiation

As documentary filmmaker and scholar Michael Chanan argues, "Independent documentary has always been driven by engagement, either political or social."[1] The significant potential of documentary for activism, grassroots mobilization, consciousness raising, and advocacy has made it a desirable medium for feminist filmmaking. As such, Iranian women filmmakers have used the documentary medium to raise awareness about women's rights and issues in Iran and to advocate for gender equality. In this regard, Lidia Merás writes, "Many post-revolutionary Iranian filmmakers, especially those working in documentary, have rejected flattering representations of their society and have instead sustained the interest in dealing with social issues."[2] While the previous chapters focused on some specific important trends in Iranian women's documentary practices, including autobiographical and biographical approaches, which are, as argued, deeply intertwined with sociopolitical issues, this chapter focuses on diverse social-issue, activist documentaries that aim to bring about social change through awareness raising, community building, and/or social and political impact; documentaries that film scholar Thomas Waugh has called "committed documentary."[3] The committed documentary is an ideologically driven, activist practice that has a "subject-centered" focus.[4] It not only depicts the struggles of disenfranchised and marginalized people involved in "political struggles,"[5] but it also aims to intervene and to motivate change. Waugh traces this form of documentary to the 1920s and the works of Soviet filmmaker Dziga Vertov,[6] which gained momentum in the 1960s and 1970s in parallel with "the growing strength of the women's, peace, and civil rights movements,"[7] and was facilitated by technological transformations, such as lighter and smaller cameras and synchronized sound.

Other scholars have called this form of documentary radical political documentary (Kleinhans 1984), political documentary (Juhasz 1999; Hole and Jelača 2019), social change documentary (Aguayo 2019), and social-issue documentary (Aufderheide 1998; Chattoo 2020),[8] all of which have the main objective of bringing about progressive social change. Emphasizing the significance of documentary "as a medium for feminist politics and interrelated forms of struggle against different forms of systemic discrimination," film scholars Kristin Lené Hole and Dijana Jelača, for example, point to the crucial role of "political documentary" in bringing about social change.[9] As they write, "Rather than presenting an 'objective' account of an issue, [political documentaries] foreground their partisan position and explicitly encourage politicization and position-taking from their audience."[10] Most of the scholarly works that focus on these forms of political and activist documentaries and the intersection of documentary and social change often predominantly position their arguments within a Western context. But what are the particularities of activism and social change in a religious and authoritarian country like Iran, where freedom of expression is often severely constrained and activist work might result in imprisonment, punishment, and even execution? Centering mostly on the United States, media scholar Caty Borum Chattoo, for instance, postulates, "Social change requires open public space for stories and dialogue and critique. Formal activist movements need this freedom to express, but so, too, do smaller acts of communities coming together to uphold values, strengthen solidarity, demand change, and advocate for public good—the underpinnings of democratic practice."[11] By looking at examples of Iranian women's social-issue documentaries in this chapter, however, we can see an astonishing degree of bravery and creativity in the face of censorship and myriad constraints, which, as discussed in Chapter 1 and Chapter 2, inevitably impact the processes of production, distribution, and reception of these works, but cannot diminish their voices and their impact on social change and progressive activism.

This chapter examines a set of documentary examples, made by Iranian women documentarians, to analyze the broader status of women and their rights in Iranian society as investigated in these works. The chapter also discusses the diversity of aesthetic approaches used in these films to present women's voices and concerns in relation to the gender politics of the state and the sociocultural traditions and norms. The chapter's goal is to foreground the significance of the documentary medium for feminist activism, particularly regarding women's issues and social identity explorations. As such, some documentaries that engage with women's rights and situations on a larger societal level—social hierarchies, politics, law, and domestic violence—are closely examined. Case studies include: Mahnaz Afzali's *The Ladies Room* (2003), Rakhshan Banietemad's *We Are Half of Iran's Population* (2009), and Mina Keshavarz's *The Art of Living in Danger* (2020). Crucially, these documentaries do not homogenize the struggles and voices of Iranian women. Rather, they shed light on the nuances of gender discrimination in the country and the nuanced strategies that women have adopted—as both documentarians and documentary subjects—to address and circumvent gender inequalities. Noticeably, these works often rely on elevating the voices of ordinary women and activists as they present bottom-up resistances to patriarchal and authoritarian structures. These documentaries also employ vastly different aesthetic and discursive approaches as part of their activism and in order to present women's activism on the screen. It is thus significant to point out that in these and many other women's documentaries, the spheres of documentary and social change get blurred given various direct and indirect impacts that these documentaries have on the social and political realms through their production and content as well as their reception. Highlighting the unique context within which Iranian filmmakers operate to create social-issue documentaries is crucial for understanding their activist significance. As film scholar Chuck Kleinhans points out:

> Radical documentary needs to get beyond the most immediate level of emotional involvement … and give viewers a way of understanding why this condition exists in the first place, the underlying causes for it, and its relation to other parts of the society. Without such a fuller conception, the immediate emotional response, is easily turned toward a simple solution: change of heart, charity, or legislative reform. And the documentary then leaves the ongoing causes of the problem unexamined.[12]

Given the interconnectedness of documentary practices and sociopolitical conditions in Iran, a brief insight into the historical context within which social-issue documentaries have been made in the country seems necessary.

According to Blake Atwood, the early newsreels and documentaries, showcasing "the country's heritage and development" through a perceived objective representation of reality, were replaced in the 1960s and 1970s with "reflexive documentaries that problematize[d] their relationship to reality as a means of critiquing the social and historical worlds they index[ed]."[13] Documentaries such as Ebrahim Golestan's *Ruinville* (*Kharab-abad*, 1962), Forugh Farrokhzad's *The House Is Black* (1962), Kamran Shirdel's *The Night It Rained* (*An shab keh baran amad*, 1967) and *Tehran Is the Capital of Iran* (*Tehran payetakht-e Iran ast*, 1966), among others, "challenge[d] the presumed indexical relationship to a lived, historical world, and … inspired a trend within Iranian cinema that uses this 'truth form' to reveal, counterintuitively, a series of untruths."[14] Hamid Naficy calls these works "social protest documentaries," that were "critical of things official, although government agencies sponsored most of them and censored the best of them."[15] Through a reflexive and critical style, these documentaries critiqued an authoritative objectivity in regard to Iranian reality; a standpoint that shortly gave way to the revolutionary fervor and protests of the 1979 Islamic Revolution. However, in the 1960s and 1970s and in parallel with these social protest documentaries, there were some major efforts to improve women's legal, familial, and social status. The Women's Organization of Iran (WOI) was established in 1966 to enhance women's rights through a series of legal, social, and cultural efforts. In 1967, "the Parliament passed the first Family Protection Law, followed by its final revised version in 1975."[16] The law brought significant improvements to women's rights, including, among others, prohibiting marriage "before the minimum age of eighteen for women and twenty for men," abolishing men's "unilateral right to divorce," and limiting polygamy "to a second wife, with the consent of the first wife …"[17]

One of the first actions that the new regime implemented after the 1979 Islamic Revolution was "the revocation of the Family Protection Law,"[18] followed by other setbacks, such as "elimination of women from the judiciary, segregation of women in public spaces, … and the campaign to impose the veil."[19] In the documentary realm, as Naficy writes, "Despite the highly visible social presence of women during the revolution and their strong screen presence in the documentaries about it, the initial postrevolution documentary cinema was entirely dominated by male directors."[20] This male-dominated documentary perspective on social and political issues continued during the Iran-Iraq War years (1980–88). Yet, the necessities of the war mobilized Iranian women to serve the country and the war front through various public roles, as cooks, nurses, and office workers. The wartime thus provided opportunities for involvement of women in the social life, which came to resonate once the war was over. In this regard Tahereh Hadian explains, "In the late 1980s, as people's attention moved from integral sovereignty and national unity to domestic policy and civil society, women became conscious of their inferior position in the legal codes and the social discrimination imposed on them."[21] These social conditions fostered the support of Iranian women and youth from the presidency of reformist cleric Mohammad Khatami, who swept to victory in 1997. According to Atwood:

> During [Khatami's] presidency, what appeared to be women's reform marked the streets of Tehran, and the enforcement of dress codes was relaxed considerably … Press restrictions were also relaxed, and in 1998 the secular feminist journal *Jens-e dovom* (Second Sex) received a permit for publication. Khatami also established the Center for Women's Participation … and encouraged the formation of women-based nongovernmental organizations.[22]

As discussed in previous chapters, it is thus in tandem with the presidency of Khatami and the initiation of the so-called Reform Era (1997–2005) that the social-issue documentary gains momentum. What distinguishes this period and its aftermath in Iranian documentary history is the strong presence of women in the documentary field making social-issue and committed documentaries. The possibility of political debates and discussions on women's rights as human rights during the Reform Era to some extent facilitated their expressions within women's documentaries, which can be seen in works such as Rakhshan Banietemad's *Our Times* (2002), Nahid Rezaei's *Dream of Silk* (2003), and Mahvash Sheikholeslami's *Article 61* (2005).

However, the efforts to enhance women's rights at the legislative level often faced an impasse. As Rebecca Barlow and Shahram Akbarzadeh argue, "The reform movement's choice of strategies failed adequately to take into account the contextual constraints they would face. While Iran's constitution exhibits republican aspects, it very clearly bestows ultimate authority upon the most learned Islamic jurist (the Supreme Leader, or *Vali Faqih*) over elected politicians."[23] The more the top-down reform proved inefficient, the more women activists channeled their efforts through grassroots activism by making documentaries, blogging, and initiating such campaigns as "One Million Signatures Campaign for Reform of Discriminatory Laws, also known as the One Million Signatures Campaign for Equality (2006); Stop Stoning Forever Campaign (2006); ... and Banning Domestic Violence Campaign (2016)."[24] Like water through stones, Iranian women have shown their resiliency, bravery, and determination for social progress in different historical times and within various contexts. Regardless of patriarchal and authoritative restrictions, they have not remained silent. Rather, they have adamantly voiced their concerns and engaged in social reform and progressive activism. The following section discusses three different documentaries made by women documentarians to foreground women's creative resistances and the diversity of their activist practices in different political times.

The Ladies Room (2003) by Mahnaz Afzali

The Ladies Room (2003), directed by Mahnaz Afzali, was made during the second-term presidency of reformist cleric Mohammad Khatami (2001–2005). The 55-minute documentary is set entirely inside a women's restroom in one of Tehran's major public parks, Laleh Park. Using a cinema verité style, the film features drug addicts, prostitutes, and runaway women who come to use the ladies' room, catch up with a friend, or just share a comfortable and free space for conversation with other women. The unprecedented glimpses into these women's lives and perspectives reflect an activist stance on the part of the filmmaker. In an interview for this study, Afzali asserted, "*The Ladies Room* had a simple idea. I wanted to create a space for conversation. A space for women who have had less opportunities to be directly seen, without judgment."[25] The need for a "space" to highlight women's lives and issues during a period in which top-down reformist attempts at gender equality proved rather unsuccessful is a considerable activist work. Highlighting the failures of Khatami's administration to bring about substantial progressive changes regarding women's rights, Atwood writes, "Despite, or perhaps because of, these failures, Khatami's presidency brought discussions about women's rights in Iranian society to the forefront in unprecedented ways."[26] It is within this political context that Afzali's focus on women's experiences, particularly those who are struggling to overcome economic, familial, and social hardships within a patriarchal setting, finds significance.

The women of Afzali's documentary open up to her camera and share some of the most intimate, and at times painful, aspects of their lives. The verité-style approach through which Afzali records these accounts—the filmmaker/interviewer is not seen throughout the film—contributes to maintaining the focus on these women and their stories. In response to my question regarding what challenges she faced during the production of this documentary, Afzali mentioned:

> Working in a public ladies' room where a specific social type—women of lower economic and cultural class, street women and prostitutes—frequents, is in and of itself a challenge. To become one with these women was an interesting process; making connections [with them] and creating a feeling of security in them [were] valuable experience[s] for me. ... They believed that I don't judge them and only want to [create] a platform for their accounts, and I did my best to make this happen. I think this might be the first one-person documentary [in terms of production] in Iran, which was also a strange and challenging experience.[27]

The female friendship and trust thus create a crucial ground for elevating marginalized voices. The production of the film, in which Afzali performs as both the director and the cinematographer, might have also contributed to creating an intimate setting for conversations with the women. The use of talking heads is an important aesthetic choice in the film that serves a feminist function. As Julia Lesage argues:

> The visual portrayal of the women in "realist" feminist documentaries is often criticized for its transparency (film's capturing reality) or for the visual dullness of talking heads. Yet the stories that the filmed women tell are not just "slices of

> experience." These stories serve a function aesthetically in reorganizing women viewers' expectations derived from patriarchal narratives and in initiating a critique of those narratives.[28]

Discussing the feminist documentaries of the 1970s, 1980s, and 1990s in the US, Alexandra Juhasz similarly considers the use of talking heads a feminist, political device. Juhasz writes, "Realist codes and talking-head conventions are most typically used to do the political work of entering new opinions, new subjectivities, or newly understood identities into public discourse."[29] This "political work" through the use of talking heads can also be seen in Afzali's documentary, which centers on the realities of marginalized women and their stories. The talking-head style creates a collective formulation of various forms of patriarchy and discrimination that are shared within the intimate, yet public, spaces of a restroom and a documentary setting.

The film opens with the everyday activities in a ladies' room: the female janitor, Mehri, is sweeping the floor and a young woman is washing her hair in one of the bathroom's sinks. The first woman whose story is shared is Rana, a middle-aged prostitute. An off-screen voice asks Rana whether she is afraid of going with men, to which Rana responds, "Why should I? I'm not young. So, if I go to someone's house in broad daylight, people think I'm his grandmother or aunt." As the interview continues, the camera depicts a young girl putting on makeup while listening to Rana's exchanges with the filmmaker. The image then cuts back to Rana as she shares some of her challenges with younger men who might force her into "harmful" tasks or steal from her instead of paying her. Another woman is Maryam, who is washing her face when Mehri, the janitor, tries to attract her attention towards the camera by whistling so that she comes for an interview. Reluctant at first, Maryam, an epileptic young woman who is in the middle of quitting her drug addiction, shares her story with the filmmaker. She is twenty-three years old and has lost her parents during her childhood—her father was executed on drug-related charges. To cope with the pain of life, Maryam became a drug addict herself. As she says, "Opium is the cure of all pains, but it has no cure!" But she is now trying to quit. Maryam shares other hardships she faced growing up, including a forced marriage at twelve and living at a Rehabilitation Center (*Behzisti*), from which she ultimately escaped. Maryam wants to end the interview, but the camera is fixed on her, and Afzali continues asking why the center does not keep her anymore. Maryam responds, "Because I have problems. Addiction, self-mutilation, mental health." Afzali's voice, shocked upon hearing self-harm, asks Maryam to let her see it. Maryam rolls up her sleeves and the camera in a close-up shot depicts the scars on her arms.

Every woman's story is unique, and regardless of their predicaments, they all show their agency to find ways to survive. Rana mostly goes out with middle-aged men to avoid the harms of the younger ones, and Maryam has decided to quit her addiction and change the course of her life. Throughout the film, each woman's account is separated by a black screen and a white text introducing the name of the woman whose life story we are about to hear. Another young woman is Sepideh, whose turbulent relationship with her mother has pushed her to the verge of despair and to a point where she is thinking about suicide. She rushes to the ladies' room crying and her friend tries to calm her down. Other women in the room join in to help her out. An older woman tells Sepideh, "You're young, and the future belongs to you. Get up dear!" After some conversations, it becomes clear that one of the things that has been bothering Sepideh is the double standards of her mother, and by extension the society, in trying to control her sexual and social life. In response to the filmmaker, who asks how she defines modesty (*haya*), she responds while smoking, "I don't know. You tell me what it means. My mother's definition … is that I don't smoke in front of her. That she can have a boyfriend, but I mustn't…" Sepideh's friend from off screen asks, "Do you want to kill yourself [then]?" To which Sepideh positively responds. The camera captures Mehri, whose face looks extremely worried. Her place has offered these women a safe space to share their issues and concerns. Her shoulders have been a place for crying and comfort. But to what extent can she help them? Mehri herself was a runaway woman who ultimately managed to marry, find a job, and build a life for herself. She understands these women, and that's why her restroom, as one of the women emphasizes, is very different from other public restrooms. After recounting one of her previous relationships with a young man, Sepideh is asked by her friend to sing. Sepideh, with a beautiful and confident voice, begins singing. The camera pans on the faces of the women, who are quietly listening and enjoying the moment. In a country where female solo singing in public is banned, recording this scene is a defiant act.

Among the women who are featured is Leila, who has just arrived in Tehran from another province in search of a better life. She is in her second marriage with a newly born girl. She negatively recalls her first marriage, mentioning that her ex-husband abused her physically and mentally. Two Armenian Christian women are also featured. One is an older woman, named Madam Hakopian, who claims she is a clairvoyant and frets over her son's marriage to a Muslim woman. The other is a young woman, named Janet, who believes runaway women need to communicate with their families to solve their issues instead of running away; an argument that receives some pushbacks from other women given that some runaway women have no other means to save themselves. Mehri, for instance, refers to herself, who had to run away when she was eleven years old, but has now made a life for herself.

Taken together, the diversity of women in *The Ladies Room*—old, young, married, single, Muslim, Christian, from Tehran, from other provinces—refutes the homogenization of Iranian women's struggles and experiences, while offering collective acts of solidarity and support. Presenting these voices and lives on the screen to global audiences thus serves as an activist practice expanding the understanding of Iranian women and the diversity of their lived experiences. Distribution and exhibition of such activist independent documentaries, however, have always been a challenging issue. Ezra Winton and Jason Garrison note, "Important films—political and activist films that explore under-represented narratives—often fail to find an audience because of the indifference of exclusive commercial distribution channels."[30] In the case of *The Ladies Room*, the film has been presented and shown at various international film festivals, thanks to an independent Iranian distributor. As Afzali shared in her interview, it was at one of these festivals—most likely the International Documentary Film Festival Amsterdam (IDFA)— that the film was purchased by Women Make Movies,[31] the quintessential US-based and transnationally focused distributor of independent documentaries by and about women. The film thus continues to reach audiences around the world and have an impact by offering new perspectives on Iranian women's lives and experiences, and by showcasing new subjectivities that were previously overlooked.

We Are Half of Iran's Population (2009) by Rakhshan Banietemad

Rakhshan Banietemad's films, both documentary and fiction, have been always driven by social issues. As she pointed out in her interview for this study, "[E]ither in fiction or documentary, women [filmmakers'] approach is mostly toward social domains, and in a society like Iran which has many political, social, and cultural complexities, this approach finds a special significance."[32] Among Banietemad's documentaries, two films directly engage with the sociopolitical discourses of reform in Iranian society, providing nuanced assessments of possibilities and shortcomings of reform movement in contemporary Iran as related to women's rights and status. *Our Times* (2002) focuses on the 2001 presidential election, in which the reformist cleric Mohammad Khatami was the leading candidate and was eventually elected for a second term, serving until 2005. Using the election context, Banietemad highlights women's political engagement and activism as some women register to run for presidency, even though Iranian women are not officially and legally granted such an opportunity.[33] Banietemad focuses on the story of a lower-class single mother, Arezu, who regardless of economic and cultural pressures, decides to register as a presidential candidate, a defiant act that symbolically critiques discriminatory laws and patriarchal structures in Iran. Of course, her candidacy is officially rejected, and at the end, Arezu is so overwhelmed to find a place for her family to live that she even forgets to cast her vote. Banietemad thus subtly presents women's aspirations for reform and the structural shortcomings and failures that prevent improvement of women's rights.

Banietemad continues her political inquiry into social and gendered reform in Iran in her 2009 documentary *We Are Half of Iran's Population*. The film focuses on the 2009 presidential election, in which conservative Mahmoud Ahmadinejad is seeking re-election for a second term. During his first term (2005–09), Ahmadinejad's government tried to undo many of the previous reformist government's works, and tightened the sociocultural sphere by, for instance, supervising women's dress codes in public spaces and monitoring online and social media activities. Asef Bayat notes that during Ahmadinejad's first term, "much of the space for collective campaign had disappeared. The leading feminist magazine *Zanan* was banned, many NGOs were closed down, and women's presence in official institutions declined."[34] It is thus within this restricted sociopolitical context that Banietemad's documentary finds an activist significance.

In fact, from its opening scenes, the film self-reflexively assesses the impact of documentary medium, and film in general, on bringing about transformative social change. The documentary starts with the images of Banietemad's previous films and the voiceover of Banietemad saying, "Who do you show these films to? For almost thirty years behind the camera, I have been hearing this question over and over again, and I have had no answer..." Banietemad thus questions the outreach of social-issue films and ponders if officials and those who have power to enact changes ever come in contact with these filmic contents, and thus to what extent the impact of these films, if any, could be felt and seen. That is why the filmmaker is determined to bridge the gap between the officials and the people through her documentary, and the upcoming 2009 presidential election seems to be a useful ground for such an objective. As Banietemad mentioned in her interview:

> Usually during elections, the political and social conditions become a little more open, and various groups and unions use this opportunity to voice their demands. A few months before this election, all the women activists with various perspectives formed an inclusive coalition for the first time, and presented women's demands in specific chapters. This unprecedented event, which never happened again, became a unique occasion to document women's issues in a documentary film, regardless of all the limitations and sensitivities that exist regarding these issues…[35]

Since the 1979 Islamic Revolution, and until that point in time in 2009, different positions on women's rights and status had led to various official and unofficial women's groups, some of which advocated for an Islamic feminism within the political and religious framework of the Islamic Republic, while others preferred a secular feminist standpoint advocating for women's rights as human rights based on international conventions. The coalition of diverse women activists, called Convergence of Women (*Hamgerai-ye Zanan*), consisted of "forty-two women's groups and 700 individual activists, [and] came into existence on 25 April 2009, less than two months before the presidential elections…"[36] Perhaps four years of conservative presidency of Ahmadinejad convinced many of these women to work together in order to prevent further setbacks.[37]

The documentary presents some of these women activists in front of the camera or within their meetings as they share their demands for the enhancement of women's rights and ask four final presidential candidates about their agendas in this regard. Among the pressing demands are for Iran to join the Convention on the Elimination of All Forms of Discrimination Against Women (CEDAW), which the reformist government of Khatami failed to enact, and the elimination of discriminatory laws against women, including revisions in some specific articles of the Constitution, to include gender equality. The camera of Banietemad also captures the voices and demands of ordinary women in public parks and women's shelters, on the streets, and at universities. All the candidates—except for Mahmoud Ahmadinejad, who refused to participate in the film—along with their wives and/or advisors then separately sit in a room with a screen and see the film to provide some reflections and responses regarding women's issues. The-documentary-within-the-documentary style works as a reflexive device emphasizing the potential of the documentary medium for activism and social change. The style is also reflective of the complexities of tackling women's issues in post-revolution Iran that cannot be captured in one linear narrative.

Throughout the documentary, women present an array of issues: lack of insurance for house workers, restrictions on accessing welfare and social services for divorcees and single mothers, women's addiction, domestic violence and honor-killing, child custody, et cetera. For instance, in one scene a young woman, whose face is covered to protect her anonymity, shares that her mother was executed in Evin prison in Tehran on a murder charge. She had killed her temporary husband in defense to prevent him from raping her daughter. The young woman criticizes her mother's execution based on discriminatory laws, further emphasizing that a man who kills his wife, or his daughter, or his sister, with the excuse of defending his honor, does not get executed, and many also commend him for his act. With a shaky voice on the verge of crying the young woman continues, "But because my mother was a woman … she was unable to prove her point…" The image then cuts back to one of the presidential candidates, Mohsen Rezaei, his wife, and his advisor, all of whom are emotionally moved by the young woman's account. The image then cuts to a woman activist, an attorney and legal consultant, who asks what the (future) president plans to do to address all the gaps in many sections of the law, especially in areas related to family law, so that further damages can be stopped.

The most notable problem that clearly shows itself in candidates' responses, or lack of responses, is the fact that a president in Iran has specific, and at times limited, executive power, and while he can propose bills to the parliament, whether they are passed or blocked depends on many political factors. This was one of the main reasons why the reformist government of Khatami failed to enact many of its promises and to bring about substantial reforms. Moreover, "while the president is the country's second most senior official, it is the Supreme Leader who is constitutionally and ideologically empowered to both determine 'the overall politics of the Islamic Republic' and supervise 'the proper implementation of the general policies of the system' that ultimately decides whether a president will be successful."[38] Iran's judiciary is also a separate entity that works under the supervision of the Supreme Leader and outside of a president's government, albeit at times in coordination and collaboration with it. As Zahra Rahnavard—the wife of Mir-Hussein Mousavi, a leading reformist candidate in the 2009 presidential election with large support from women and youth—emphasizes in the film, "This is discrimination by the law. Currently, 90 per cent of legal decisions are against women. … women's civil law is truly paternalistic. A government should work toward economic progress, and this will solve many of the problems for women, but it won't solve the problem of discrimination." Rahnavard later in the film mentions, "The executive branch alone cannot solve women's problems. This needs the judiciary, the legislative branch as well. Women's NGOs have to agree. The media … I mean a whole collective has to be mobilized."

A mobilization that has proved highly difficult within the authoritarian and patriarchal context of Iran.

The documentary, however, proves successful in its objective: to transfer the voices and demands of women to the officials and prompt them to think about women's rights and issues. Even though one of the candidates did not participate in this project, this film asserts that women are half of Iran's population, and therefore, they cannot be silenced and ignored. Banietemad decided to widen the access to the documentary for ordinary audiences in order to impact social change and encourage people's participation in the election based on candidates' responses to women's issues and their agendas for enhancing gender equality. As Winton and Garrison argue, "Dissent may be the engine of change, but without distribution it doesn't get very far at all."[39] Aware of this significant issue regarding distribution and access, Banietemad ends her documentary with a white note written on a black screen:

> I very much wanted this film to be shown before June 12th, the day of election. But the permit was not granted. Still, I copied and distributed it amongst people. Eighty percent of the Iranian people took part in the voting process. A silent majority went to the ballots for the first time. The next day, the results were announced. None of the candidates who had been in the film obtained the winning votes, and the absent candidate was declared president with twenty-four million votes. People's questions and doubts about these results were left unanswered...

The filmmaker's independent distribution of the film without any official permit is an explicit activist act, using documentary to bring about social change. The high participation of women and youth in the election in support of the reformist candidate, Mir-Hussein Mousavi, was the result of such grassroots activist works. But the outcome of the election—the victory of conservative Mahmoud Ahmadinejad—prompted massive protests that came to be known as the Green Movement. The Green Movement mobilized women and youth, especially in urban areas, to reclaim their votes and voice their demands for a free life without discrimination and oppression. It was, however, met with a heavy and brutal crackdown. Aside from the state's oppressive efforts to contain the protests, Kevan Harris writes, "Organizational disarray within oppositional forces was an even greater impediment."[40] While this "protest mobilization did not last long,"[41] women's activism found new ways to continue via online platforms, grassroots campaigns, and documentary films. The final case study in this chapter focuses on a recent campaign to examine how documentary activism and grassroots activism can merge to motivate and impact social change.

The Art of Living in Danger (2020) by Mina Keshavarz

Co-produced transnationally with Germany and released in 2020, Mina Keshavarz's *The Art of Living in Danger* is a powerful activist documentary on domestic violence in Iran, made during Hasan Rouhani's presidency (2013–21). The film weaves together the personal narrative of the filmmaker about her grandmother with the account of the efforts of a feminist activist group, who in 2016 initiated the "Banning Domestic Violence Against Women Campaign" in order to end gender-based violence against women in Iran through both grassroots activism and pushing for new laws. The political contexts within which the film and the campaign are situated are important for understanding the sociopolitical complexities and difficulties of such activist practices in Iran. After eight years of oppression and crackdown on activists, journalists, artists, and ordinary dissident citizens, the government of Mahmoud Ahmadinejad came to an end in 2013, when Hasan Rouhani, a cleric considered an insider within the political structure of the Islamic Republic, was elected as the president. Rouhani positioned himself as a moderate candidate who is open and willing to follow the course of reform, even though the top-down reform movement in Iran during Khatami's presidency (1997–2005) had already proved untenable within the authoritarian and patriarchal political system of the country. Yet, as anthropologist William O. Beeman notes, "The social agenda presented by Rouhani had been taken up by the voters who were hungry for change. He vowed to increase freedom of expression, free political prisoners, establish greater roles for women, and encourage support of the arts, as well as to deal with the most important issue for Iranians, the economy, which was (and remains) decimated by US and European sanctions."[42] While during his first term (2013–17), Rouhani was able to "move swiftly towards achieving his goal of resolving the nuclear issue and rebuilding the Iranian economy,"[43] the prospect of human and women's rights remained much unclear. As part of the new cabinet, Rouhani appointed Shahindokht Molaverdi as Vice President for Women and Family Affairs, "a woman who belongs to the religious segment of the women's rights movement."[44] As Mehrangiz Kar and Azadeh Pourzand write, "Her office [had] tried to push for improvements in the legal and social aspects of women's rights within the principles of the Islamic Republic. However, the security forces, with their influential elements in the judiciary and the hardliner press, ha[d] stopped this office from realizing its mission."[45] The blockage of top-down reforms as a repetitive scenario was not surprising for the activists who decided to push for change from below, with the hope that such a grassroots act can ultimately impact the official political and legal structures.

It is within this context that the activists of Keshavarz's documentary initiate their grassroots campaign against domestic violence, while simultaneously working with lawyers to draft laws against violence against women. As Heather McIntosh aptly asserts, "Gender-based violence often occurs out of the public eye, reinforcing perpetrators' actions with tacit impunity. Yet its presentation in documentary forms presents a potential means of bringing hidden or private issues to a broad-based audience."[46] At the same time, dealing with such a sensitive topic requires a considerable amount of aesthetic creativity and artistic attentiveness on the part of the documentarian "in order to represent these sometimes unrepresentable truths and to avoid re-victimizing or re-traumatizing the survivors involved in the original violence or subsequent production."[47]

The Art of Living in Danger opens with some white titles written on a black screen. The titles mention: "The Islamic Republic of Iran is one of twelve countries that have no law about domestic violence against women." The texts further highlight that the Family Protection Law (1967; revised 1975), passed during the Pahlavi regime, was deemed invalid after the 1979 Islamic Revolution. The titles then mention: "Women's rights activists in Iran have been struggling for forty-one years to pass laws to give men and women equal rights. In 2016, a group of activists began a campaign aim at creating a law outlawing domestic violence against women. Five women lawyers began drawing up the legal documents for this proposition." These introductory texts give way to a black screen accompanied by the filmmaker's voiceover, who says, "By Iranian law, I am my father's property, to be transferred to my husband after marriage." Then, from a white grainy screen an old family photo emerges. The sharp focus of the camera concentrates on a young girl in the photo and the photo then morphs into other black-and-white family photos.

The voiceover of Keshavarz continues, "My name is Mina. You have never seen me … Nurijan, the grandmother I never saw! Fifty years have passed since you died. Your death was our family's biggest secret … With this film, I am trying to bring you to life for me, and perhaps me for you … You were invisible, like me and millions of other women in this land." This opening monologue powerfully accomplishes some crucial tasks: it connects the personal story of the filmmaker's grandmother and her death due to domestic violence to the main topic of the film introduced earlier in the opening texts; it offers an intergenerational reading of women's rights and status (before and after the Islamic Revolution), thus positioning the struggle for gender equality within a broader historical context; and it aims to provide an against-the-grain understanding of women's struggles and resistances through uncovering marginalized voices of ordinary women

Figure 5.1 Family photos morph into each other. *The Art of Living in Danger* (2020), directed by Mina Keshavarz. Courtesy of Mina Keshavarz.

and activists from past and present. Throughout the film, Keshavarz's voiceover, as she speaks to her grandmother over family photos and archival images, mingles with the account of the activists' campaign and their actions as they work to end violence against women. The film is thus itself an activist reckoning and practice regarding gender equality, and that's why the self-reflexivity both in the form of the filmmaker's addresses and in the explicit acknowledgment of the process of filmmaking becomes an effective stylistic choice for the film.

This opening sequence is followed by the archival images of Iranian women taking part in the 1979 Revolution, but soon realizing that their rights are the first target of the new regime. Keshavarz's voiceover laments, "Gradually, like a film in reverse, we went back in time. One by one, laws in our favor were changed back…" The archival images of newspapers report turbulent times, such as "women stage protests in the courtroom" and "women's protests turn violent." These historical reflections are then connected to the present time of the film in 2018 when a small group of activists are protesting violence against women in front of the parliament. They carry testimonies of women, who were subjected to violence, on placards. The filmmaker's voiceover says, "Nurijan, these papers are filled with screams of women, which have been silenced for years. Women like you and me. I wish you were here to tell us your story. Nurijan, I see traces of you in all these stories. Traces of violence, silence, and fear." According to Kar and Pourzand, "To understand VAW [violence against women] in Iran, one should not solely focus on the physical form of violence, but on sexual, psychological, financial, and political violence as well."[48] They thus argue that in this multi-faceted climate of violence and oppression, many women have become "accustomed to concealing the violence in their lives from others. In particular, they often resist seeking help from courts and public service organizations."[49] The collection of women's stories on various forms of violence is thus a crucial activist effort to shed light on gender-based violence and discriminatory laws affecting it. The film also brings an additional layer of visibility to these stories and to the activists' works in this regard.

There is a scene in which a sonic montage of various women's voices attesting to the violence they have faced is played on the images of apartment buildings at night, presenting the violence, horror, and fear behind some of these walls. One woman's voice says, "When my husband gets angry, his inner monster comes out. He tells me not to push him to his limit." Another voice says, "I was mentally abused for years." Another says, "My mother was killed by her father twenty-four years ago to save his honor…" Ultimately these voices overlap, creating an intangible mumbling effect that points to the sheer magnitude of the instances of gender-based violence; there are so many stories and incidents that it is at times hard to have a clear comprehension of the situation. Here, "Traumatic memories manifest as pieces of an incomplete mosaic, fragmented and incoherent."[50] The overlapping voices in this scene give way to grainy and ambiguous, and at times overlapping, images in the next scene. The images, while

Figure 5.2 Grainy image of women on a street. *The Art of Living in Danger* (2020), directed by Mina Keshavarz. Courtesy of Mina Keshavarz.

avoiding clear recognition, depict women and other people walking on a street's sidewalk.

These individuals who we do not know and cannot clearly see might have stories of gender-based violence like the ones we just heard; the stories and experiences that often remain invisible and unknown to the public. Reflecting on documentary aesthetics in relation to the representations of gender-based violence and trauma, McIntosh writes:

> The connections between trauma and documentary might seem counterintuitive … in that documentary focuses on the representation of reality, while the foundations of trauma lie in the unrepresentability of events in either the highly problematic nature of the visuals, of the unavailability of those visuals, or the accessibility of these events through the lenses of emotion and fantasy. Overall, they become a way of understanding, but they require understanding on new terms and in new ways.[51]

Ambiguous, grainy, and/or overlapping black-and-white images are used throughout the film, often accompanied by the voiceover of Keshavarz, who is trying to understand the violence, repression, and trauma that her grandmother endured, ultimately leading to her death; experiences that many other women have also gone through. Presenting such acts of historical imagination and traumatic experiences thus requires novel aesthetic approaches, which Keshavarz creatively employs in her documentary.

Given the diverse forms of gender-based violence in Iran, activists deploy a diverse set of programs and actions via their campaign, such as

Figure 5.3 Activists hold signs with written stories of women about domestic violence. *The Art of Living in Danger* (2020), directed by Mina Keshavarz. Courtesy of Mina Keshavarz.

staging street protests and rallies, holding workshops for ordinary women and university students in various provinces, distributing educational brochures on the streets, working with lawyers who have volunteered to draft laws addressing violence against women, and meeting with female representatives of the parliament and other officials.

Throughout these activities and the process of filming them, the activists and the filmmaker face various restrictions. After a march on International Women's Day in 2018, some of the activists get arrested, including Banafsheh Jamali, who is an active member of the campaign. Keshavarz manages to escape. Over the shaky camera images her voiceover says, "My heart was beating fast. I felt I was being chased ... I feel my fear is ancient. It's much older than I am. It follows me everywhere. At times, I believe I share it with many other women..." Intersectional feminist solidarity and emphasis on the interconnectedness of various forms of discrimination and violence against women inform awareness-raising activities of the campaign and the filmmaker's documentary practice. These parallel forms of activism—campaigning and filmmaking—thus contribute to bringing visibility to women's voices and lived experiences. That is why the patriarchal system feels threatened and arrests the activists. As we see in a scene filmed in the province of Gilan, a man tries to prevent Keshavarz from filming. In another scene, the establishing shots of the city and images of men and women in their daily activities introduce Marivan, a Kurdish Sunni-majority city in the west of Iran which, as Keshavarz's voiceover explains, is a place with male-dominated traditions and patriarchal values. "These women know you well Nurijan," Keshavarz says, continuing, "Women whose only solution to violence is often suicide;" the same solution that Keshavarz's grandmother came up with in order to put an end to the violence she had faced. In this regard, Kar and Pourzand write:

> According to the laws of Iran, after divorce women may be left in poverty, which often leads them to decide to stay with violent husbands. They may also make such decisions due to Iran's unfavorable child custody rules, fearing that after a divorce, they will lose custody. Moreover, women, contemplating divorce face a situation where society looks down on divorced women. In these circumstances, a woman suffering from violence may choose suicide rather than a divorce.[52]

These circumstances are often worse for ethnic women and minorities in Iran given that these women "experience a complex web of violence; for them, local and legal patterns of patriarchy are often combined with the Islamic Republic's discriminatory policies against ethnic and religious minority groups."[53] That is why through conducting a workshop for

Kurdish women, the activists hope to bring some awareness about domestic violence and ways to build supportive systems to address this issue.

The ending scene of the documentary reflexively provides an overview of the film itself. Over a montage of images from the film in fast and slow motions, Keshavarz's voiceover narrates:

> I have many frames to tell the story of this film. Frames of hopelessness [on the images of a female representative of the parliament]; frames of hope [on the images of the activists getting ready for a rally]; frames of liberty [on the images of activist Banafsheh Jamali's release from prison] ... Frames that could not be described in hundreds of hours of shooting [on the family photos depicting Keshavarz's grandparents]. Nurijan, there is just one frame left of you ... By killing yourself, you told us what you went through. That you killed yourself not because of fear, but out of courage ... You took revenge on all injustices. I must always remember how far back my fear and wrath go, and connect with you, and the women before you, and other women like you. I must remember your story every day ... and the stories of thousands of other women of this land.

These powerful reflections and aesthetic choices situate the activist approach of the documentary within an intersectional, cross-generational, and historical context, offering solidarity and advocacy by bringing some visibility to the issue of gender-based violence. The documentary medium thus becomes an important activist tool in this process; one that has its own specific limitations and shortcomings given that not everything can be captured by and made visible to the documentary camera. As Keshavarz's voiceover in the final scene mentions, some women had something to say but preferred to remain quiet. Others were afraid to be in the film. And there were also scenes that "could not be described in hundreds of hours of shooting." Yet, the documentary manages to capture the complexities of gender-based violence in Iran, and to offer a significant glimpse into the efforts of women's rights activists in the country who bravely and tirelessly work to enhance gender equality.

Moreover, while due to censorship and restrictions, the documentary has not had official public screenings in Iran yet, through private screenings as well as international festival exhibitions, the film has managed to reach its audience. Notably, the arrest of the filmmaker, along with another female documentarian, Firouzeh Khosrovani,[54] on May 10, 2022, attests to the impact of the documentary filmmaking as a form of activism, which is often seen by the Iranian authorities as a political threat that can destabilize the authoritarian structure. One week later, "On May 17, [the documentarians] were released on bail and banned from leaving the country. Almost a year later with no official charges brought against them, Keshavarz and Khosrovani have had their passports returned to them," and their cases have been officially closed.[55] This incident is an indication of the significance of women's documentary practices in Iran as they risk their lives to present women's issues and to bring about social change.

Taken together, the three case studies in this chapter provide important insights into the diversity of Iranian women's activist practices and the documentary approaches representing them. From everyday performances of subjectivity to political engagement to grassroots activism, Iranian women resist various forms of patriarchy and oppression. As Barlow and Akbarzadeh explain:

> The women's movement in Iran is an amorphous and nebulous entity. It includes activists in the classical sense (women who have devoted their lives, and livelihoods, to protest and push back); NGOs (focusing on issue-based areas such as violence against women); and a whole range of individuals working to promote and protect women's rights in their respective spheres of influence (lawyers, publishers, journalists, artists and others).[56]

These women's groups and individuals have shown an incredible amount of tenacity, resilience, and creativity to present Iranian women's voices and experiences and to advocate for gender equality. In this regard, the documentary medium has provided not only an indispensable tool for documentation and preservation of these activisms, but also an effective way for informing, and at times mobilizing, audiences through advocacy efforts, thus broadening the impact on social change.

Coda

Throughout this study, I have examined the state of contemporary Iranian documentary from a gender perspective and in tandem with various sociocultural, political, and technological transformations that Iranian society has undergone since 1997—the beginning of a political period known as the Reform Era (1997–2005)—and the ways in which these alterations along with new aspirations for democracy and social change have affected the state of documentary filmmaking in the country, especially for women. As media scholar Angela J. Aguayo mentions, "Studying documentary's position at the intersection of other social formations, such as civic engagement and social protest, contributes to understanding the shifts of democratic practice."[1] As such, my goal has been to offer a re-reading of documentary cinema in contemporary Iran in terms of its close relation to and interaction with "other social formations" since the Reform Era, and the ways in which these exchanges have affected the practices of Iranian women documentarians within both domestic and transnational settings as well as their films' aesthetic approaches and themes. Moreover, I have discussed the ways in which women's presence in contemporary Iranian documentary, as both the image-makers and the subjects of the films, have contributed to the re-articulations of democratic aspirations and representations as well as progressive gender and sociocultural changes, regardless of various challenges and limitations that have engulfed this presence.

The advancement and proliferation of video and digital technologies in recent decades have facilitated independent and more inclusive modes of filmmaking, allowing many women documentarians to bypass or more effectively negotiate the top-down structures of filmmaking in Iran. Film and media scholar Hamid Naficy highlights the emergence of a "democratized" documentary field as the result of this technological change, further contending, "Technology not only made the recording of unrehearsed and on-the-run footage easier and more intimate but also made the relationship of the subject and the camera more personal."[2] Thus, the technological transformation has also had a direct impact on the aesthetics and the contents of contemporary documentaries made by women who have turned their cameras to women's lives to foreground female voices and subjectivities. As I have argued in Chapters 3, 4, and 5, the attention to women's daily struggles and lives, including the lives of the filmmakers themselves, which particularly shows itself in autobiographical, biographical, and social-issue documentaries, is also part of a larger shift in documentary's formal and thematic experimentations in contemporary Iran that breaks away from an omniscient, hegemonic narrator to instead foreground a highly subjective and personal mode of representation that showcases ordinary women's lived experiences and their day-to-day resistances and activism. Naficy also underlines such a shift, observing:

> Postrevolutionary documentaries became dialogic, vernacular, and accented as ordinary people were allowed to speak in their own regional and ethnic dialects and personal voices and dictions. Likewise, filmmakers moved from treating issues generally, rhetorically, and politically to dealing with them personally and deeply by focusing on a few individuals with subjectivities, who became the film's protagonists. This strengthened documentaries' storytelling power, increased identification with characters, enhanced the comprehension of larger issues, and obviated the necessity of a narrator.[3]

Firouzeh Khosrovani's award-winning documentary *Radiograph of a Family* (2020), a co-production between Iran, Norway, and Switzerland, for instance, depicts such a personal voice and perspective within a larger social and political setting. By focusing on her parents' marriage and their differing points of view—a secular, progressive father and a devout Muslim mother—Khosrovani delicately explores the Iranian history and politics before and after the 1979 Islamic Revolution by connecting the intimate spaces of the home and the family to broader public and national spaces connected through, and impacted by, political and religious upheavals. In the documentary, the personal thus becomes political, and the private public. Through innovative use of archival images and voiceover narration, Khosrovani elegantly connects personal memory and family history to public memory and national history delineating, like an X-ray, the political and religious ruptures and turbulence in Iranian society before and after the revolution.

Another example is Nahid Rezaei's intimate documentary, *Dream of Silk* (2003), which here as a way of conclusion, I closely examine in order to emphasize some of the major issues raised and argued throughout the book. My selection of this documentary for this conclusion is driven by the fact that this film, in both its context and text, can offer us a multi-layered and comprehensive perspective on the state of contemporary women's documentary in Iran in terms of documentary practice, aesthetics, and themes, and as such can work as a useful closing ground for various arguments discussed in this study. *Dream of Silk* is an independent documentary that centers on the return of its director, Nahid Rezaei, to her high school, twenty years after she graduated from there. The director aims to engage with a new generation of young women and learn about their hopes and aspirations, while also putting this encounter within a historical perspective. As such, the overall framework of the documentary is derived from a personal sense of curiosity and nostalgia on the part of the filmmaker, but is inevitably connected to the larger sociocultural, political, and gender contexts. The filmmaker's self and vision and various women's lives and perspectives come into contact in the high school setting, but they also resonate themselves at the core of the documentary's point of view reflecting Iranian women's voices. Nahid Rezaei, in an interview for this study, considered the self-reflexivity presented in the film a "natural" way of approaching the topic. She said:

> Twenty years ago, I had lived in that place [the high school] during a time that was politically and socially special; a time [full of] very big dreams and aspirations. The encounter with some adolescents in that place after twenty years persistently brought back some notions for me. I felt I am facing another self. Moreover, on the eve of turning forty, even without being in such a situation, self-reflexivity is a very natural act.[4]

The documentary thus reflexively connects the aspirations of young Iranian women in contemporary Iran to the reflection of an older generation of women, presented through the figure of the filmmaker, as they ruminate on life and their youth in relation to various sociocultural, political, and gender issues. Reflecting on this cross-generational female exploration that leads to a refreshing female bond, Rezaei mentioned:

> Unlike many, I loved school. When the revolution occurred, I was 17 years old and was still going to the high school. After the revolution, due to the closure of universities, I taught some years at an elementary school and subsequently at a middle school. And then my connection to this space was cut until *Dream of Silk*. At that time, there was a girls' high school next to our house, and every day, I used to see young girls, who passed by the house [full of] freshness, mischief, and noise. And I had an assumption [about them] that these youngsters are more superficial than our generation. ... When I finally got the possibility to enter the school and work [on a film there], I was truly amazed by witnessing so much sense, contemplation, and discussion among this generation, and their issues really shook me up. I decided to be completely flexible in [my approach towards] them and to forget my previously-held assumptions in favor of the actual space and its realities, and the result became *Dream of Silk*.[5]

This fascinating and detailed reflection not only connects the personal to the social and political, the female self to a larger group of women, and the past to the present, but it also attests to the unique potential of the documentary medium to facilitate such kinds of cross-generational female connection and understanding within an intimate and revelatory setting.

Dream of Silk begins with three white titles on a black screen that announce: "January 2002/A school in a middle-class area in Tehran/ Years ago, I studied here." These titles are then followed by some images of the high school depicting empty hallways, corridors, stairways, and classrooms accompanied by a solemn music. Then comes the title of the film and we enter the busy high school yard full of lively female students, who upon hearing the school bell, head to their classrooms. In a classroom, we see the director in front of a class talking to the girls while standing near her camera, which is placed on a tripod. Rezaei asks them: "Just think a few moments; twenty years ago, this was my school! I never thought then that I'd be in this class twenty years later. How do you see yourself? Having four kids, a husband, I don't know, going abroad. How do you picture yourself? What's your status in twenty years?" We then see some girls in the school yard gathering around the director and her camera to respond to these questions or generally share their perspectives. These images are followed by a diverse set of shots depicting the girls in the classrooms and at the yard as they discuss their opinions. We hear a range of responses regarding what some of these girls hope to achieve in the next twenty years from publishing poetry to going abroad to becoming a journalist. One girl sitting in a classroom tells the filmmaker/camera: "Maybe in the past, you didn't worry about the future. But when I look at my future, I believe I have no place here." At the yard, the filmmaker asks the students how many of them think they will achieve what they really want, to which only four out of twenty positively respond, which surprises the filmmaker.

Throughout the documentary we learn about these young women's frustrations, dissatisfactions, concerns, hopes, and aspirations as they reflect on the state of their lives and their country. The range of topics and issues that they tackle is vast and deep, which shocks and moves both the filmmaker, as she reflected in her interview, and the viewer. For some of these young women the prospect of going to a university looms large in their minds, as aside from gaining knowledge and professional skills, attending the university for many of them is a way to find their desired partner and get married, find jobs and become financially and socially independent, and overall improve their social identity and esteem. As one of the girls confesses, "It's not important for me to go to university. What's important is that my future and my identity depend on my university attendance." Some students point to the tight school control over their daily practices and behaviors and further delicately connect such control to the overall state of social governance in the country. One student laments, "They regulate everything for us. For instance, here we have to wear this form of veil and this uniform. They should let us be ourselves, what we believe we are. In a society where everyone's grown up with different beliefs, they are forcing us to accept one idea."

Many of the students are worried about an uncertain future and are also frustrated by various sociocultural norms and rules governing every aspect of their daily lives. Nevertheless, their sociocultural, political, and personal awareness and subjectivity remain strong and unwavering reminding us to acknowledge and respect the new generation's crucial perspectives and see and give space to their agencies. Importantly, at some point in the middle of the documentary, these young women subvert the mostly one-way inquiries presented to them by the filmmaker by asking Nahid Rezaei to reflect on the course of her past life until present. A student asks Rezaei, "Did you think about being a filmmaker twenty years ago?" To which Rezaei negatively responds, mentioning that she actually wanted to become a midwife! The girl also asks, "What do you think? You've returned after twenty years. Any regrets? Or are you satisfied with yourself and your work?" To which Rezaei with surprise responds, "Me? I don't know!" The student insists, asking, "Haven't you thought about it? Or haven't you made up your mind?" Ultimately, the filmmaker opens up mentioning to the students, "I still have some questions. … The first days I came to the school, I thought nothing had changed. The buildings, walls, corridors. … But over the last couple of days, I understand many things have changed."

Indeed, such is also the state of contemporary independent documentary in Iran: many things have changed in this field in the past decades! As I have explained throughout this book, a dynamic new range of modes in regard to production and dissemination, and various experimentations and innovations regarding forms and themes have emerged, making the Iranian documentary a vibrant and vital venue for artistic expression and cultural exploration. As Naficy points out, "Experimentation with the documentary form had already begun with the works of Kimiavi and Shirdel before the revolution, but it deepened and widened after the revolution. … documentaries became truly modern, both embodying the modern subjectivity of their characters and engendering the modern subjectivity of their viewers."[6] In this regard, the formal, thematic, and practical aspects of independent documentary filmmaking have significantly evolved, giving way to diverse and bold documentary works that tackle various sociocultural, gender, and political issues. Among these works, women's documentaries have offered creative ways of presenting women's lives in autobiographical, biographical, and social-issue documentaries. Nahid Rezaei's *Dream of Silk* incorporates parts of these approaches, offering a fertile ground for discussions on Iranian women's social issues and their personal lives and perspectives.

In terms of its production, *Dream of Silk* exemplifies a form of independent documentary filmmaking in which personal resources and efforts take center stage. In regard to the process of this documentary's production Rezaei told me: "In the beginning, a filmmaking center agreed to help out, but when they saw the first rough cut, they said they cannot support this film, and therefore I had to change the film's name, which was *Twenty Years Later*, and I myself took the responsibility of producing the film."[7] Rezaei further pointed to the predicaments of filming in a gender-segregated, all-female high school. She said:

> I was not allowed to take a male cinematographer to the school, and in that time … there were no more than one or two female cinematographers who [worked for] the television, and they did not share my point of view. I decided to work with a friend of mine who was a photographer, and I liked her frames … Naghmeh Ghasemloo hesitantly agreed and joined me. Two other friends of mine who were filmmakers and editors also helped me as assistants. Due to the limited time that the school had granted us [for shooting], some days I also shot [some footage], and in fact, we had two cameras.[8]

As I discussed in previous chapters, independent women documentarians often face various financial and logistic challenges during their filmmaking process, and subsequently during the circulation of their documentaries. Yet, in one way or another, they manage to find a way to overcome these challenges and to materialize their ideas and projects, an example of which can be seen in Rezaei's efforts to make her documentary *Dream of Silk*. In fact, what these visionary women documentarians produce and represent, and the ways through which they do it, reflect what filmmaker and film scholar Trinh T. Minh-ha calls "[a] responsible work."[9] This is a work that according to Minh-ha,

> shows, on the one hand, a political commitment and an ideological lucidity, and is, on the other hand interrogative by nature, instead of being merely prescriptive. In other words, a work that involves her story in history; a work that acknowledges the difference between lived experience and representation; a work that is careful not to turn a struggle into an object of consumption, and requires that responsibility be assumed by the maker as well as by the audience, without whose participation no solution emerges, for no solution exists as a given.[10]

These "responsible" documentaries thus present us with crucial and indispensable perspectives on Iranian women's lives at the same time that they creatively interrogate sociocultural, political, and gendered hegemonies. Through their nuanced representations, they also invite us, the audience, to participate in their makers' creative and activist journeys, and to remain engaged and responsible supporters of their progressive commitments and ideologies.

Notes

Introduction

1 For an overview of the history of Iranian women's activism in light of the Woman, Life, Freedom movement, see: Nazanin Shahrokni, "Women, Life, Freedom," *History Today* 72, no. 11 (2022): https://www.historytoday.com/archive/history-matters/women-life-freedom, accessed July 23, 2023. For more information on Iranian artists' activism in the Islamic Republic of Iran, especially regarding the Woman, Life, Freedom movement, see: Pamela Karimi, "The Many Shades of Iran's Protest Art," *Hyperallergic*, October 11, 2022, https://hyperallergic.com/768539/the-many-shades-of-iran-protest-art/, accessed June 3, 2024.

2 Kristin Lené Hole and Dijana Jelača, *Film Feminisms: A Global Introduction* (New York: Routledge, 2019), 214.

3 Homa Hoodfar and Shadi Sadr, "Islamic Politics and Women's Quest for Gender Equality in Iran," *Third World Quarterly* 31, no. 6 (2010): 893 (original emphasis).

4 While cinema in Iran has a persistent history of state control and censorship, after the 1979 Islamic Revolution, the emphasis in this regard shifted to particularly form an Islamized film culture, at the center of which resided the control of women's bodies both on- and off-screen. As Naficy explains, "The Regulations Governing the Exhibition of Movies, Videos, and Slides of 1982 codified and instituted veiling and modesty for the first time." Hamid Naficy, *A Social History of Iranian Cinema, Volume 4: The Globalizing Era, 1984–2010* (Durham: Duke University Press, 2012), 111. According to Agnès Devictor, "Then, almost every year between 1984 and 1997, a booklet of regulations concerning the production, distribution and screening of films was published." It was in 1997, and "[f]ollowing Khatami's election as [P]resident … [that] censorship became less stringent." Agnès Devictor, "Classic Tools, Original Goals: Cinema and Public Policy in the Islamic Republic of Iran (1979–97)," in *The New Iranian Cinema: Politics, Representation and Identity*, ed. Richard Tapper (London: I.B. Tauris, 2002), 70. Pointing to the adoption of a more open policy towards cinema by Khatami's government, Blake Atwood writes that "[d]uring this time, a number of films that had been previously banned … were reissued exhibition permits. This period also witnessed new thematic possibilities within film, including explicitly political subject

matter, critiques of the Iran-Iraq War, and love stories." Blake Atwood, *Reform Cinema in Iran: Film and Political Change in the Islamic Republic* (New York: Columbia University Press, 2016), 20.

5 Naficy, *A Social History of Iranian Cinema, Volume 4*, 3.

6 Started in 1989, "when members of the board of directors appointed by the Ministry of Culture and Islamic Guidance of the time were put in charge of the establishment of this guild body," the House of Cinema was officially registered as a "non-commercial institute and company" in 1993 and works as an umbrella organization for various motion picture guilds. "Among the principle [sic] objectives of the establishment of House of Cinema is to protect and maintain the financial and non-financial rights of the decent and dedicated individuals and bodies of cinema art-industry that are involved in production, distribution and screening of films, to provide social and job security for all members and to upgrade the professional and educational knowledge level of all those working within the cinema of the Islamic Republic of Iran." *Khaneh Cinema*, https://www.khanehcinema.ir/en/about, accessed October 27, 2018.

7 Ebrahim Mokhtari writes that the IRDFA founders first started the discussions on the establishment of the guild with Seyfollah Dad at a House of Cinema Board meeting where he was the head of the Board of Directors. Dad initially rejected the idea, yet after his new appointment as the Deputy Minister for Cinematic Affairs, Mokhtari and other documentary filmmakers met with him again at his new office and after further discussions, he finally recognized the importance of a guild for Iranian documentary cinema. Ebrahim Mokhtari, *Seifollah Dad va Mostanadsazan* (*Seifollah Dad and Documentarians*). https://irandocfilm.org/clink/founder-group/, accessed June 6, 2020.

8 Naficy, *A Social History of Iranian Cinema, Volume 4*, 3.

9 In regard to the Iranian women's movement, the Constitutional Revolution (1905–1911) marked a significant development in women's sociopolitical participation as, according to Arzoo Osanloo, they "participated in nationalist struggles against imperialist encroachment as well as on the side of constitutionalists hoping to abolish the monarchy." In regard to the significance of this period, Osanloo further points to the increasing "formation of women's political councils (*anjoman*)" asserting, "Although such councils were not particularly new, the public acknowledgment of such groups and their improved organization led to more structured agendas for women's activism. … The councils began publications, magazines, and newspapers focused solely on women's concerns, with special emphasis on their education and literacy." Arzoo Osanloo, *The Politics of Women's Rights in Iran* (Princeton: Princeton University Press, 2009), 25.

10 Lindsey Moore, "Women in a Widening Frame: (Cross-)Cultural Projection, Spectatorship, and Iranian Cinema," *Camera Obscura* 20, no. 2 (59) (2005): 15.

11 Moore, "Women in a Widening Frame," 2.

12 Belinda Smaill, "The Documentary: Female Subjectivity and Problem of Realism," in *The Routledge Companion to Cinema and Gender*, eds. Kristin Lené Hole, Dijana Jelača, E. Ann Kaplan, and Patrice Petro (New York: Routledge, 2017), 174.

13 For documentary studies in a broad historical context see: Mohammad Tahaminejad's "Documentary Tradition," in *Directory of World Cinema: Iran 2*, ed. Parviz Jahed (Bristol, UK: Intellect, 2017): 87–101; Hamid Naficy's four volumes of *A Social History of Iranian Cinema* (Durham: Duke University Press, 2011 and 2012); Hamid Naficy's "Iranian Documentary," *Jump Cut* 26 (1981): 41–46. For comparative or case studies of documentary films see: Lidia Merás's "*Profession: Documentarist*: Underground Documentary Making in Iran," in *Female Agency and Documentary Strategies: Subjectivities, Identity and Activism*, eds. Boel Ulfsdotter and Anna Backman Rogers (Edinburgh: Edinburgh University Press, 2018): 170–183; Niki Akhavan's "Nonfiction Form and the 'Truth' about Muslim Women in Iranian Documentary," *Feminist Media Histories* 1, no. 1 (2015): 89–111; Nasrin Rahimieh's "Divorce Seen through Women's Cinematic Lens," *Iranian Studies* 42, no. 1 (2009): 97–112.

14 See for example, Hadi Gharabaghi's doctoral dissertation, "'American Mice Grow Big!': The Syracuse Audiovisual Mission in Iran and the Rise of Documentary Diplomacy" (New York: New York University, 2018); Blake Atwood's *Reform Cinema in Iran* (2016); Persheng Sadegh-Vaziri's doctoral dissertation, "Iranian Documentary Film Culture: Cinema, Society, and Power 1997–2014" (Philadelphia: Temple University, 2015).

15 For Persian-language texts on Iranian documentary cinema see: Mohammad Tahaminejad's *Sinema-ye mostanad-e Iran: Arse-ye tafavot-ha*, 2nd edition [*Iranian Documentary Cinema: A Field of Differences*] (Tehran: Soroush Press, 2011); Homayoun Emami's *Sinema-ye mardom-shenakhti-ye Iran* [*Iranian Anthropological Cinema*] (Tehran: Afkar Press, 2006); Hamid Dehghanpour's *Sinema-ye mostanad-e Iran va jahan* [*Iranian and World Documentary Cinema*] (Tehran: SAMT-The Organization for Researching and Composing University Textbooks in the Humanities, 2003).

16 I also discuss, like Sadegh-Vaziri, the conditions of production, distribution, and exhibition of documentary films as well as the formal and textual aspects of these films; yet in my readings, I focus on mid-length (forty to seventy minutes) and feature-length documentaries (longer than seventy minutes) made by Iranian women on Iranian women. I agree with film and media scholar Janet Staiger's observation that "[i]n purely practical terms, a scholar of cinema cannot study every film ever made. Selection becomes a necessity and with selection usually comes a politics of inclusion and exclusion." Janet Staiger, "The Politics of Film Canons," *Cinema Journal* 24, no. 3 (1985): 8. My choice of the documentary lengths is thus driven by the practicality of the scope of study and the fact that mid-length and feature-length documentaries have wider distribution possibilities and thus provide easier access for a researcher.

17 See for example: Negar Mottahedeh's *Displaced Allegories: Post-Revolutionary Iranian Cinema* (Durham: Duke University Press, 2008); Kamran Talattof's *Modernity, Sexuality, and Ideology in Iran: The Life and Legacy of a Popular Female Artist* (Syracuse: Syracuse University Press, 2011); Hamid Naficy's "Veiled Voice and Vision in Iranian Cinema: The Evolution of Rakhshan Banietemad's Films," *Social Research* 67, no. 2 (2000): 559–576; Hamid Naficy's "Veiled Vision/Powerful Presences: Women in Post-revolutionary Iranian Cinema," in *In the Eye of the Storm: Women in Post-revolutionary Iran*, eds. Mahnaz Afkhami and Erika Friedl (Syracuse: Syracuse University Press, 1994): 131–150; Roshanak Kheshti's "Cross-Dressing and Gender (Tres)Passing: The Transgender Move as a Site of Agential Potential in the New Iranian Cinema," *Hypatia* 24, no. 3 (2009): 158–177.

18 Pointing to the success of the post-revolutionary Iranian films in international film festivals in the 1990s, Sara Saljoughi emphasizes that "the term 'New Iranian Cinema' seems to have been coined largely as a way of naming the 'discovery' of art cinema existing in Iran, a discovery on the part of programmers, critics, and audiences outside of the country. Thus in many respects the 'newness' of the New Iranian Cinema connotes its newness to/for foreign audiences." Sara Saljoughi, *Burning Visions: The Iranian New Wave and the Politics of the Image, 1962–1979*, Ph.D. dissertation (Minneapolis: University of Minnesota, 2015), 33.

19 Naficy, *A Social History of Iranian Cinema, Volume 4*, 1.

20 Pirooz Kalantari, "Chera in bist sal?" ("Why These Twenty Years?"). *Film Monthly* 516 (1395/2016): 7.

21 Kalantari, "Chera in bist sal?," 7.

22 Teresa De Lauretis, *Technologies of Gender* (Bloomington: Indiana University Press, 1987), 38.

23 Margaret A. McLaren, *Feminism, Foucault, and Embodied Subjectivity* (Albany: State University of New York Press, 2002), 13.

24 De Lauretis, *Technologies of Gender*, 5.

25 Patricia White, *Women's Cinema, World Cinema: Projecting Contemporary Feminisms* (Durham, NC: Duke University Press, 2015), 2–3.

26 Boel Ulfsdotter and Anna Backman Rogers, "Introduction," in *Female Authorship and the Documentary Image: Theory, Practice and Aesthetics*, eds. Boel Ulfsdotter and Anna Backman Rogers (Edinburgh: Edinburgh University Press, 2018), 2.

27 White, *Women's Cinema, World Cinema*, 43.

28 For studies focused on male *auteurs*, see for example: Hamid Dabashi's *Makhmalbaf at Large: The Making of a Rebel Filmmaker* (London: I.B. Tauris, 2008); Alberto Elena's *The Cinema of Abbas Kiarostami* (London: Saqi, 2005); Mehrnaz Saeed-Vafa and Jonathan Rosenbaum's *Abbas Kiarostami* (Urbana: University of Illinois Press, 2003); Tina Hassannia's *Asghar Farhadi: Life and Cinema* (Raleigh, NC: The Critical Press, 2014).

29 Hole and Jelača, *Film Feminisms*, 184.
30 Moore, "Women in a Widening Frame," 15.

Chapter 1

1 "The first wave" of Iranian documentary filmmaking according to Tahaminejad occurred in "the 1950s to the 1970s" and "the second wave from the [1979] Revolution … to the end of 1990s." Mohammad Tahaminejad, "Barresi-ye film-haye nasl-e sevvom-e sinema-ye mostanad-e Iran" ("Analysis of the Third-Generation Films of Iranian Documentary Cinema"), in *Haghighat-e Sinema va Sinema Haghighat: Jostojooei dar Arse-ye Sinema-ye Mostanad*, ed. Zaven Ghookasian (Tehran: Documentary and Experimental Film Center, 1386/2007), 139–140.
2 Shweta Kishore, *Indian Documentary Film and Filmmakers: Independence in Practice* (Edinburgh: Edinburgh University Press, 2018), 14.
3 Kishore, *Indian Documentary Film and Filmmakers*, 14.
4 As this chapter shows, the inequalities that Iranian women documentarians face are unique given the specificities of their sociocultural and religious contexts. For a discussion on the gendered context of documentary production, women's negative experiences of gender inequality, and their resistances within a neoliberal, Western context, see: Anne O'Brien, "(Not) Getting the Credit: Women, Liminal Subjectivity and Resisting Neoliberalism in Documentary Production," *Media, Culture & Society* 40, no. 5 (2018): 673–688.
5 Mina Keshavarz, email interview with the author, November 25, 2018.
6 Keshavarz, email interview with the author, November 25, 2018.
7 Kishore, *Indian Documentary Film and Filmmakers*, 103.
8 Kishore, *Indian Documentary Film and Filmmakers*, 103.
9 Persheng Sadegh-Vaziri writes, "According to the [Iranian] Documentary [Filmmakers] Association, IRDFA, their members are independent filmmakers, who are not employed by state television system or other governmental entities. Most of these filmmakers have more autonomy and explore styles and topics that do not always fall within the dominant discourses." Persheng Sadegh-Vaziri, "Iranian Documentary Film Culture: Cinema, Society, and Power 1997–2014," PhD Dissertation (Philadelphia: Temple University, 2015), 1.
10 Hamid Naficy, *A Social History of Iranian Cinema, Volume 2: The Industrializing Years, 1941–1978* (Durham: Duke University Press, 2011), 81.
11 M. Ali Issari, *Cinema in Iran, 1900–1979* (Metuchen: The Scarecrow Press, 1989), 190.
12 Issari, *Cinema in Iran*, 190.
13 Naficy, *A Social History of Iranian Cinema, Volume 2*, 76.
14 Nasrin Rahimieh, "Capturing the Abject of the Nation in *The House Is Black*," in *Forugh Farrokhzad, Poet of Modern Iran: Iconic Woman and*

Feminine Pioneer of New Persian Poetry, eds. Dominic Parviz Brookshaw and Nasrin Rahimieh (London: I.B. Tauris, 2010), 126.

15 Rahimieh, "Capturing the Abject of the Nation in *The House Is Black*," 127.

16 Niki Akhavan, "Nonfiction Form and the "Truth" about Muslim Women in Iranian Documentary," *Feminist Media Histories* 1, no. 1 (2015): 92. Regarding *Fortress*, Hamid Naficy writes that "in 1980, after the revolution, the negatives and soundtracks were rediscovered in the MCA's film lab; apparently, a sympathetic lab employee had buried them years ago for safekeeping." Naficy, *A Social History of Iranian Cinema, Volume 2*, 121.

17 Hamid Naficy, *A Social History of Iranian Cinema, Volume 3: The Islamicate Period, 1978–1984* (Durham: Duke University Press, 2012), 55.

18 Mohammad Tahaminejad, *Sinema-ye Mostanad-e Iran: Arse-ye Tafavot-ha* [*Iranian Documentary Cinema: A Field of Differences*], 2nd ed. (Tehran: Soroush Press, 1390/2011), 131.

19 Tahaminejad, *Sinema-ye Mostanad-e Iran*, 132.

20 Tahaminejad, *Sinema-ye Mostanad-e Iran*, 133.

21 These TV documentaries include: *The Culture of Consumption* (*Farhang-e masrafi*, 1979), *The Occupation of Migrant Peasants in the City* (*Eshteghal-e mohajerin-e roustai dar shahr*, 1980), *The War Economic Planning* (*Tadabir-e eghtesadi-ye jang*, 1981), and *Centralization* (*Tamarkoz*, 1986).

22 Hamid Naficy, *A Social History of Iranian Cinema, Volume 4: The Globalizing Era, 1984–2010* (Durham: Duke University Press, 2012), 165.

23 Saeed Rashtian, "Anam arezoost…: Tahiyeh-konandegi dar sinema-ye mostanad-e ma" ("I Wish That…: Producer['s Role] in Our Documentary Cinema"), *Film Monthly* 516 (1395/2016): 75.

24 Rashtian, "Anam arezoost…," 75.

25 Sadegh-Vaziri, "Iranian Documentary Film Culture," 129.

26 Blake Atwood, *Reform Cinema in Iran: Film and Political Change in the Islamic Republic* (New York: Columbia University Press, 2016), 100.

27 Rashtian, "Anam arezoost…," 75.

28 Rashtian, "Anam arezoost…," 75.

29 *Cinema Vérité: Iran International Documentary Film Festival*, "86 mostanad-saz-e zan motaghazi-ye sherkat dar Sinema Haghighat shodand" ("86 Women Documentarians Applied for Participation in Cinema Vérité"), September 22, 2017, https://irandocfest.ir/News/6447/86_مستندساز_زن_متقاضی_شرکت_در_سینماحقیقت_شدند_, accessed July 12, 2023.

30 Mahvash Sheikholeslami, email interview with the author, March 16, 2019.

31 Sadegh-Vaziri, "Iranian Documentary Film Culture," 142.

32 For a discussion on the Islamic codes of modesty in post-revolutionary Iranian cinema see: Najmeh Moradiyan Rizi, "Iranian Women, Iranian Cinema: Negotiating with Ideology and Tradition," *Journal of Religion & Film* 19, no.1 (2015), Article 35: 6–7.

33 Rakhshan Banietemad, email interview with the author, October 30, 2018.

34 Banietemad, email interview with the author, October 30, 2018.

35 Nahid Rezaei, email interview with the author, February 7, 2019.
36 It is also known as *Sazman tose'e-ye sinema-iye Soureh*. Hozeh Honari is the cultural and artistic section of *Sazman tablighat-e eslami* (Islamic Propagation Organization), and its (unofficial) cinematic activities date back to 1981.
37 Orod Atarpour, "Nemishod edameh dad: Goftegoo ba Orod Atarpour darbari-ye tajrobe-ye tahiyeh-ye do majmoe'-ye mostand-e *Ganjine-haye Penhan* va Bist Shab" ("It Was Impossible to Continue: A Conversation with Orod Atarpour on His Experience of Producing Two Documentary Series *Hidden Treasures* and *Twenty Nights*"), interview by Pirooz Kalantari, *Film Monthly* 516 (1395/2016): 83.
38 Mohammadmahdi Tabatabaeinejad, "Sarmayeh-gozar-e kafi nadarim: Goftegoo ba Mohammadmahdi Tabatabaeinejad, modir-e Markaz Gostaresh-e Sinema-ye Mostanad va Tajrobi" ("We Do Not Have Enough Financiers: A Conversation with Mohammadmahdi Tabatabaeinejad, the President of the Documentary and Experimental Film Center"), interview by Nasim Najafi, *Film Monthly* 516 (1395/2016): 84.
39 Rezaei, email interview with the author, February 7, 2019.
40 Azadeh Bizargiti, email interview with the author, April 19, 2019.
41 Bizargiti, email interview with the author, April 19, 2019.
42 Azadeh Bizargiti, email interview with the author, April 26, 2019.
43 Bizargiti, email interview with the author, April 19, 2019.
44 Bizargiti, email interview with the author, April 19, 2019.
45 Sadegh-Vaziri, "Iranian Documentary Film Culture," 121.
46 Tabatabaeinejad, "Sarmayeh-gozar-e kafi nadarim," 85.
47 Mohammad Afarideh, "Goftegoo ba Mohammad Afarideh, modir-amel-e Markaz Gostaresh-e Sinema-ye Mostanad va Tajrobi va dabir-e jashnvare-ye Sinema Haghighat" ("A Conversation with Mohammad Afarideh, the Managing Director of the Documentary and Experimental Film Center and the Secretary of the Cinema Vérité Festival"), interview by Esmail Mihandoost, in *Haghighat dar Ghab-e Mostanad: Majmoe' Maghalat Darbare-ye Sinema-ye Mostanad*, ed. Esmail Mihandoost (Tehran: Documentary and Experimental Film Center, 1387/2008), 24. See also: Masoud Bakhshi, "Tamhid dar Sinema Haghighat, honar-e Sinemast" ("Planning in Cinema Vérité is the Art of Cinema"), interview by Zaven Ghookasian, in *Haghighat-e Sinema va Sinema Haghighat 2: Jostojooei dar Arse-ye Sinema-ye Mostanad*, ed. Zaven Ghookasian (Tehran: Documentary and Experimental Film Center, 1387/2008), 202–203.
48 Bakhshi, "Tamhid dar Sinema Haghighat, honar-e Sinemast," 202.
49 Bakhshi, "Tamhid dar Sinema Haghighat, honar-e Sinemast," 202.
50 *Documentary and Experimental Film Center*, "Entekhab-e behtarin film az negah-e tamashagaran dastavard-e mohem-e jashnvare-ye davazdahom" ("The Selection of the Best Film from Audiences' Perspective as the Important Achievement of the 12th Festival"), December 15, 2018, https://www.defc.ir/Post/2834/, accessed July 18, 2023.

51 Bizargiti, email interview with the author, April 19, 2019.
52 Rezaei, email interview with the author, February 7, 2019.
53 Moradiyan Rizi, "Iranian Women, Iranian Cinema," 20. I further argue that because of this gender consciousness, "the notions and practices of gender and sexuality are no longer stigmatized among the Iranian young generation. They might be covered or controlled by the Islamic regime, but Iranian youth steadily continue to explore sexual practices and challenge the fixed gender boundaries." Moradiyan Rizi, "Iranian Women, Iranian Cinema," 20.
54 Norma Claire Moruzzi, "Trying to Look Different: *Hijab* as the Self-Presentation of Social Distinctions," *Comparative Studies of South Asia, Africa and the Middle East* 28, no. 2 (2008): 225–226.
55 Moruzzi, "Trying to Look Different," 226 (original emphasis).
56 Keshavarz, email interview with the author, November 25, 2018.
57 Sadegh-Vaziri, "Iranian Documentary Film Culture," 3.
58 Homa Hoodfar and Shadi Sadr, "Islamic Politics and Women's Quest for Gender Equality in Iran," *Third World Quarterly* 31, no. 6 (2010): 895.
59 Hoodfar and Sadr, "Islamic Politics and Women's Quest for Gender Equality in Iran," 899. For a discussion on Iranian women's online activism see: K. Soraya Batmanghelichi and Leila Mouri, "Cyberfeminism, Iranian Style: Online Feminism in Post-2009 Iran," *Feminist Media Histories* 3, no. 1 (2017): 50–80.
60 *Kara Film Studio*, "About Karestan," https://www.karafilm.ir/en/karestan/about-karestan, accessed July 13, 2023.
61 Banietemad, email interview with the author, October 30, 2018.
62 Banietemad, email interview with the author, October 30, 2018.
63 *Kara Film Studio*, "About Karestan."
64 Shirin Barghnavard, email interview with the author, August 7, 2018.
65 Mahnaz Afzali, email interview with the author, September 4, 2018.
66 Barghnavard, email interview with the author, August 7, 2018.
67 Banietemad, email interview with the author, October 30, 2018.
68 *TorinoFilmLab*, "Katayoon Shahabi (Iran)," https://www.torinofilmlab.it/people/810723/Katayoon-Shahabi, accessed July 13, 2023.
69 Naficy, *A Social History of Iranian Cinema, Volume 4*, 333.
70 Naficy, *A Social History of Iranian Cinema, Volume 4*, 334.
71 Katayoon Shahabi, email interview with the author, June 17, 2019.
72 Shahabi, email interview with the author, June 17, 2019.
73 Shahabi, email interview with the author, June 17, 2019.
74 Shahabi, email interview with the author, June 17, 2019.
75 Keshavarz, email interview with the author, November 25, 2018.
76 *Braving the Waves* portrays a woman named Roghieh in the southern city of Minab who works hard to organize and secure jobs for saleswomen in her community through a self-made bazaar. But the Mayor obstructs Roghieh's work and plans to destroy the bazaar to build a shopping mall instead.

77 According to 2015 money exchange rates, $1 equals 34,680 Iranian rial. For more information see: *Naghdineh*, http://naghdineh.com/page/14700/139 آخرین+نرخ+انواع+ارز+در+سال+4.html, accessed December 24, 2019.

78 *Hamijoo*, "Aya ou dar in mobarezeh pirooz mishavad?—Mina Keshavarz," August 5, 2015, https://hamijoo.com/projects/آیا-او-در-این-مبارزه-پیروز-می- شود؟-مین/, accessed August 17, 2019.

79 Inge Ejbye Sørensen, "Crowdsourcing and Outsourcing: The Impact of Online Funding and Distribution on the Documentary Film Industry in the UK," *Media, Culture & Society* 34, no. 6 (2012): 739.

80 Keshavarz, email interview with the author, November 25, 2018.

81 Keshavarz, email interview with the author, November 25, 2018.

82 Keshavarz, email interview with the author, November 25, 2018.

83 Sheikholeslami, email interview with the author, March 16, 2019.

84 Rezaei, email interview with the author, February 7, 2019.

85 Kishore, *Indian Documentary Film and Filmmakers*, 79.

86 Kishore, *Indian Documentary Film and Filmmakers*, 78.

87 Kishore, *Indian Documentary Film and Filmmakers*, 78.

88 Keshavarz, email interview with the author, November 25, 2018.

89 Barghnavard, email interview with the author, August 7, 2018.

90 Barghnavard, email interview with the author, August 7, 2018.

91 Kishore, *Indian Documentary Film and Filmmakers*, 78.

92 Barghnavard, email interview with the author, August 7, 2018.

93 Afzali, email interview with the author, September 4, 2018.

94 Kishore, *Indian Documentary Film and Filmmakers*, 103.

95 Chris Berry, "Independently Chinese: Duan Jinchuan, Jiang Yue, and Chinese Documentary," in *From Underground to Independent: Alternative Film Culture in Contemporary China*, eds. Paul G. Pickowicz and Yingjin Zhang (Lanham: Roman & Littlefield Publishers, 2006), 120.

Chapter 2

1 Persheng Sadegh-Vaziri, "Iranian Documentary Film Culture: Cinema, Society, and Power 1997–2014," Ph.D. Dissertation (Philadelphia: Temple University, 2015), 154.

2 Ramon Lobato, *Shadow Economies of Cinema: Mapping Informal Film Distribution* (London: BFI/ Palgrave Macmillan, 2012), 2.

3 Lobato, *Shadow Economies of Cinema*, 10.

4 Virginia Crisp, *Film Distribution in the Digital Age: Pirates and Professionals* (Basingstoke: Palgrave Macmillan, 2015), 4.

5 Crisp, *Film Distribution in the Digital Age*, 4.

6 Ramon Lobato, "Subcinema: Theorizing Marginal Film Distribution," *Limina: A Journal of Historical and Cultural Studies* 13 (2007): 114.

7 Lobato, *Shadow Economies of Cinema*, 4. Lobato further articulates, "Formal distribution is characterised by revenue-sharing business models, complex

systems of statistical enumeration and a 'windowing' releasing pattern driven by theatrical premiers. Informal distribution is mostly nontheatrical and is characterised by handshake deals, flat-fee sales and piracy." Lobato, *Shadow Economies of Cinema*, 4.

8 Lobato, *Shadow Economies of Cinema*, 4.
9 Mahnaz Afzali, email interview with the author, September 4, 2018.
10 Lobato, *Shadow Economies of Cinema*, 2.
11 Rakhshan Banietemad, email interview with the author, October 30, 2018.
12 Quoted in *Documentary and Experimental Film Center*, "Olaviyat-haye jadid-e Markaz Gostaresh elam shod: A'rze-ye mostanad va hozoor dar bazar-ha" ("The Priorities of the DEFC Were Announced: Documentary Distribution and Presence in the Markets"), September 1, 2017, https://defc.ir/Post/2480/اولویت_های_جدید_مرکز_گسترش_اعلام_شد/_عرضه_مستند_و_حضور_در_بازارها, accessed July 19, 2023.
13 Mohammad Afarideh, "Goftegoo ba Mohammad Afarideh, modir-amel-e Markaz Gostaresh-e Sinema-ye Mostanad va Tajrobi va dabir-e jashnvare-ye Sinema Haghighat" ("A Conversation with Mohammad Afarideh, the Managing Director of the Documentary and Experimental Film Center and the Secretary of the Cinema Vérité Festival"), interview by Esmail Mihandoost, in *Haghighat dar Ghab-e Mostanad: Majmoe' Maghalat Darbare-ye Sinema-ye Mostanad*, ed. Esmail Mihandoost (Tehran: Documentary and Experimental Film Center, 1387/2008), 16.
14 Banietemad, email interview with the author, October 30, 2018.
15 Mohammad Attebai, "Bazar-e sinema-ye mostanad dar Oroopa" ("Documentary Cinema's Market in Europe"), in *Haghighat-e Sinema va Sinema Haghighat: Jostojooei dar Arse-ye Sinema-ye Mostanad*, ed. Zaven Ghookasian (Tehran: Documentary and Experimental Film Center, 1386/2007), 234.
16 Gholam Khiabany, *Iranian Media: The Paradox of Modernity* (New York: Routledge, 2010), 164.
17 *Documentary Channel*, https://www.doctv.ir/AboutUs, accessed July 20, 2023.
18 *Documentary Channel*, https://www.doctv.ir/AboutUs
19 *Documentary Channel*, https://www.doctv.ir/AboutUs
20 Shahram Derakhshan, "Nehzat-e arzan-sazi!: Kanal-e mostanad-e television" ("The Cheapening Movement!: The Television's Documentary Channel"), *Film Monthly* 516 (1395/2016): 94.
21 Mohammadmahdi Tabatabaeinejad, "Sarmayeh-gozar-e kafi nadarim: Goftegoo ba Mohammadmahdi Tabatabaeinejad, modir-e Markaz Gostaresh-e Sinema-ye Mostanad va Tajrobi" ('We Do Not Have Enough Financiers: A Conversation with Mohammadmahdi Tabatabaeinejad, the President of the Documentary and Experimental Film Center"), interview by Nasim Najafi, *Film Monthly* 516 (1395/2016): 85.

22 Mohammadmahdi Tabatabaeinejad, “Tabatabaeinejad az dahomin jashnvare-ye beinolmelali-e Sinema Haghighat migooyad” (“Tabatabaeinejad Discusses the 10th International Cinema Vérité Festival”), interview by Mahmoud Sadeghlou-Givi, *Documentary and Experimental Film Center*, December 5, 2016, https://www.defc.ir/Post/2259/, accessed July 20, 2023.

23 According to the DEFC’s 2018 production report, the Center supported a total of 81 documentary projects of which 28 were short documentaries (4 directed by women), 28 were mid-length documentaries (3 directed by women), 20 were “distinguished” (*Fakher*) documentaries (2 directed by women), and 5 were international co-productions (2 directed by women). *Documentary and Experimental Film Center*, “Gozaresh-e amalkard-e mali-ye Markaz Gostaresh-e Sinema-ye Mostanad va Tajrobi dar sal-e 97 elam shod” (“The Report on the Financial Performance of the Documentary and Experimental Film Center in 2018 Is Announced”), May 26, 2019, https://defc.ir/Post/2890/گزارش_عملکرد_مالی_مرکز_گسترش_سینمای_مستند_و_تجربی_در_سال97_اعلام_شد, accessed July 22, 2023.

24 Mina Keshavarz, email interview with the author, November 25, 2018.

25 Sadegh-Vaziri, “Iranian Documentary Film Culture,” 64.

26 Niki Akhavan, “Nonfiction Form and the ‘Truth’ about Muslim Women in Iranian Documentary,” *Feminist Media Histories* 1, no. 1 (2015): 95.

27 Akhavan, “Nonfiction Form and the ‘Truth’ about Muslim Women in Iranian Documentary,” 95.

28 *Bridge to Iran*, http://www.cemproductions.org/bridgetoiran/, accessed July 20, 2023. Pointing to her collaboration with the network for launching the series, Sadegh-Vaziri writes, “In 2006 I began to work with Link TV producers in New York to launch their *Bridge to Iran* documentary series, acquiring Iranian documentary films and contextualizing the films with interviews with filmmakers.” Sadegh-Vaziri, “Iranian Documentary Film Culture,” 29.

29 *Bridge to Iran*, http://www.cemproductions.org/bridgetoiran/. According to Persheng Vaziri, “the series ended in 2012.” Persheng Vaziri, “Watching Docs in Tehran: A Festival Thrives in Iran.” *International Documentary Association*, March 5, 2019. https://www.documentary.org/online-feature/watching-docs-tehran-festival-thrives-iran, accessed July 23, 2023.

30 *Bridge to Iran*. http://www.cemproductions.org/bridgetoiran/.

31 *Isna*, “Mojtaba Mirtahmasb azad shod” (“Mojtaba Mirtahmasb Is Released”), December 11, 2011, https://www.isna.ir/news/9009-11658/مجتبی-میرطهماسب-آزاد-شد, accessed August 25, 2019.

32 Attebai, “Bazar-e sinema-ye mostanad dar Oroopa,” 235–236.

33 *Documentary and Experimental Film Center*, “Arze-ye mostanad-ha va animation-haye markaz gostaresh dar ‘ketabkhaneh-ye videoei’” (“Exhibition of the Center’s Documentaries and Animations in a ‘Video Library’”), July 1, 2023, https://defc.ir/Post/6255/«عرضه_مستندها_و_انیمیشن_های_مرکز_گسترش_در»_کتابخانه_ویدیویی, accessed July 23, 2023.

34 Sadegh-Vaziri, "Iranian Documentary Film Culture," 136.
35 Keshavarz, email interview with the author, November 25, 2018.
36 Mohammad Tahaminejad, *Sinema-ye Mostanad-e Iran: Arse-ye Tafavot-ha* [*Iranian Documentary Cinema: A Field of Differences*], 2nd ed. (Tehran: Soroush Press, 1390/2011), 167.
37 Pamela Cohn, "Cinema Vérité Iran International Documentary Film Festival," *Filmmaker* 17, no. 2 (Winter 2009): 26.
38 Cohn, "Cinema Vérité Iran International Documentary Film Festival," 26.
39 *Financial Tribune*, "Identity, Reality and Creativity," December 2, 2017, https://financialtribune.com/articles/art-and-culture/77179/identity-reality-and-creativity, accessed July 23, 2023.
40 *Documentary and Experimental Film Center*, "Amar-e mosharekat-e zanan dar sinema-ye mostanad-e Iran 10 darsad ast: 86 mostandsaz-e zan motaghazi-ye sherkat dar Sinema Haghighat shodand" ("Women's Participation Statistics in Iran's Documentary Cinema is 10 Per Cent: 86 Women Documentarians Applied for Participation in Cinema Vérité"), 17 October 2017, https://defc.ir/Post/2521/_10_آمار_مشارکت_زنان_در_سینمای_مستند_ایران_درصد_است_86_مستندساز_زن_متقاضی_شرکت_در_سینماحقیقت_شدند, accessed July 23, 2023.
41 Vaziri, "Watching Docs in Tehran."
42 Hamid Naficy, *A Social History of Iranian Cinema, Volume 4: The Globalizing Era, 1984–2010* (Durham: Duke University Press, 2012), 89.
43 For more information see: Nazanin Shahrokni, "Women, Life, Freedom," *History Today* 72, no. 11 (2022): https://www.historytoday.com/archive/history-matters/women-life-freedom, accessed July 23, 2023.
44 *IranWire*, "Tahrim-e jashnvare-ye Sinema Haghighat tavasote jame'i az mostanadsazan va faalan-e farhangi" (The Boycott of Cinema Vérité Festival by a Group of Documentarians and Cultural Activists"), December 2, 2022, https://iranwire.com/fa/news-1/110729-تحریم-جشنواره-سینما-حقیقت-توسط-جمعی-از-مستندسازان-و-فعالان-فرهنگی-/, accessed July 23, 2023.
45 Vaziri, "Watching Docs in Tehran."
46 *Sheffield DocFest*, "Rakhshan Banietemad's Retrospective," https://sheffdocfest.com/festival/2023/special-programmes-presentations/rakhshan-banietemads-retrospective, accessed July 23, 2023.
47 *Sheffield DocFest*, "Perspectives on Iran," https://sheffdocfest.com/festival/2023/special-programmes-presentations/perspectives-iran, accessed July 23, 2023.
48 Svetla Turnin, "Beyond the Female Gaze and Towards a Documentary Gender Equality," *Point Of View (POV) Magazine*, November 2, 2015, https://povmagazine.com/beyond-the-female-gaze-and-towards-a-documentary-gender-equality/, accessed July 23, 2023.
49 Turnin, "Beyond the Female Gaze and Towards a Documentary Gender Equality."

50 Dina Iordanova and Stefanie Van de Peer, "Introduction," in *Film Festival Yearbook 6: Film Festivals and the Middle East*, eds. Dina Iordanova and Stefanie Van de Peer (St Andrews: St Andrews Film Studies, 2014), xxii.

51 Amirhosein Sanaei, "In film-ha ro koja neshoon midin?" ("Where Do You Show These Films?"), *Film Monthly* 516 (1395/2016): 89.

52 Art and Experience Cinema provides rather general and vague definitions for these categories. It considers, "an art film, a cinematic work—either short or feature-length fiction, documentary, or animation film—that in its form and content can prompt audiences' aesthetic sensibilities and curiosities and enhance their visual taste. Experimental film is a film that experiments with new approaches to expression and cinematic storytelling which the mainstream cinema in the country does not employ." *Art and Experience Cinema*, "Aeinnameh-ye namayesh-e film dar gorooh sinemai-ye honar va tojrobeh" ("Film Screening Regulations in Art and Experience Cinema"), August 9, 2022, https://honartajrobeh.ir/Explain/5/آیین_نامه_, accessed July 27, 2023.

53 *Cinematic Organization*, "Roykard-ha, rahbord-ha, va siyasat-haye sazman-e sinema-iye dolat-e tadbir va omid" ("Approaches, Strategies, and Policies of the Cinematic Organization of the Government of Tact and Hope"), Tehran: Ministry of Culture and Islamic Guidance (Spring 2014): 20.

54 Payam Ghanipour and Sayyed Ali Rohani, "Tahlil-e jaygah-e gorooh-e honar va tajrobeh dar sinema-ye Iran be onvan-e meydani mostaghel, az manzar-e araye Pierre Bourdieu" ("An Analysis on the Standpoint of Art & Experience Cinema in Iran's Cinema as an Independent Field (From Pierre Bourdieu Perspective)"), *Quarterly Journal of Interdisciplinary Studies in Communication and Media* 4, no. 11 (2021): 90.

55 *Art and Experience Cinema*, "Aeinnameh-ye namayesh-e film dar gorooh sinemai-ye honar va tojrobeh."

56 *Cinematic Organization*, "Roykard-ha, rahbord-ha, va siyasat-haye sazman-e sinema-iye dolat-e tadbir va omid," 62.

57 Ghanipour and Rohani, "Tahlil-e jaygah-e gorooh-e honar va tajrobeh dar sinema-ye Iran be onvan-e meydani mostaghel, az manzar-e araye Pierre Bourdieu," 96.

58 Tabatabaeinejad, "Sarmayeh-gozar-e kafi nadarim," 85.

59 For further details see: https://honartajrobeh.ir/Explain/5/آیین_نامه_

60 Nahid Rezaei, email interview with the author, February 7, 2019.

61 Mahvash Sheikholeslami, Email interview with the author. March 16, 2019. *Article 61* features "candid stories by women in the Evin Prison in Tehran who killed their husbands in self-defence and are sentenced to death for it." The film thus explicitly challenges the existent law in this regard as well as the women's legal and social status in Iran. *Mubi*, "Article 61," https://mubi.com/films/article-61, accessed July 27, 2023.

62 Katayoon Shahabi, email interview with the author, June 17, 2019.

63 Azadeh Bizargiti, email interview with the author, May 10, 2019.
64 Bizargiti, email interview with the author, May 10, 2019.
65 *Art and Experience Cinema*, "Aeinnameh-ye namayesh-e film dar gorooh sinemai-ye honar va tojrobeh."
66 *Mehr News Agency*, "Mostanad-ha bedoun-e tabligh mokhatab peida nemikonand/ Film-e rayegan namayesh nadahim" ("Documentaries Do Not Find Audiences without Advertisement/ Do Not Exhibit Free Films"), May 15, 2016, https://www.mehrnews.com/news/3617682/مستندها-بدون-تبلیغ-مخاطب-پیدا-نمی-کنند-فیلم-رایگان-نمایش-ندهیم, accessed July 27, 2023.
67 In regard to instances of restrictions on promoting some documentary films, Saffarian in his interview with the *Mehr News Agency* points to Mojtaba Mirtahmasb's *Six Centuries, Six Years* (2014). Due to "sensitivities on the name of [Mohammadreza] Shajarian," a veteran musician and singer featured in the documentary whose voice and image have been banned by the Iranian authorities, the advertisement for this film was restricted. *Mehr News Agency*, "Mostanad-ha bedoun-e tabligh mokhatab peida nemikonand/ Film-e rayegan namayesh nadahim."
68 Keshavarz, email interview with the author, November 25, 2018.
69 Keshavarz, email interview with the author, November 25, 2018.
70 Afzali, email interview with the author, September 4, 2018
71 Afzali, email interview with the author, September 4, 2018.
72 The AIDP includes "producers of documentary films and programs (televisual, cinematic, and other media)," and consists of five committees: education and research, assistance and welfare, public relations, member recruitment, and exhibition. *Association of Iranian Documentary Producers*, "Asasnameh" ("Statute"). https://aoidp.com/اساسنامه/, accessed July 28, 2023.
73 Sanaei, "In film-ha ro koja neshoon midin?," 88.
74 Fakhroddin Seyedi, "E'ish-e modam: Chahardah sal namayesh-e film-e mostanad dar Khaneh Honarmandan" ("Continuous Pleasure: Fourteen Years of Documentary Film Exhibition in the House of Artists"), *Film Monthly* 516 (1395/2016): 90.
75 Keshavarz, email interview with the author, November 25, 2018.
76 *Filmba*, "Gorooh-e Rokhdad-e Tazeh-ye Mostanad" ("Rokhdad-e Tazeh-ye Mostanad Group"), http://www.filmba.ir/index.php/list-film-center/1126-rokhdade-taze-mostanad, accessed July 28, 2023.
77 *Filmba*, "Gorooh-e Rokhdad-e Tazeh-ye Mostanad."
78 *Filmba*, "Gorooh-e Rokhdad-e Tazeh-ye Mostanad."
79 Sanaei, "In film-ha ro koja neshoon midin?," 88.
80 Sanaei, "In film-ha ro koja neshoon midin?," 88.
81 Zahra Molouki, "Doshanbe-haye mostanad: Revayat-e mehmani-haye mostanad-bini" ("Documentary Mondays: The Account of Documentary-Watching Gatherings"), *Film Monthly* 516 (1395/2016): 10.
82 Molouki, "Doshanbe-haye mostanad," 10–11.

83 Rezaei, email interview with the author, February 7, 2019.

84 Newsha Roozban, "Mostanadsazan campaign-e 'film-e mostanad rayegan nist' rahandazi kardand" ("Documentarians Initiated the Campaign 'Exhibiting Documentary Film Is Not Free'"), *Mehr News Agency*. April 9, 2016. https://www.mehrnews.com/news/3593190/مستندسازان-کمپین-نمایش-فیلم-مستند-رایگان-نیست-راه-اندازی-کردند, accessed July 28, 2023.

85 Roozban, "Mostanadsazan campaign-e 'film-e mostanad rayegan nist' rahandazi kardand."

86 Azadeh Bizargiti, email interview with the author, April 19, 2019.

87 *TorinoFilmLab*, "Katayoon Shahabi (Iran)," https://www.torinofilmlab.it/people/810723/Katayoon-Shahabi, accessed July 13, 2023.

88 Shahabi, email interview with the author, June 17, 2019.

89 Shahabi, email interview with the author, June 17, 2019.

90 Shahabi, email interview with the author, June 17, 2019.

91 For a discussion on this contestation see: Dina Iordanova, "The Film Festival Circuit," in *Film Festival Yearbook 1: The Festival Circuit*, eds. Dina Iordanova and Ragan Rhyne (St Andrews: St Andrews Film Studies, 2009), 27.

92 The so-called A festivals are a designated group of accredited film festivals overseen and regulated by the International Federation of Film Producers Associations (FIAPF), an organization that "decides the status of major festivals, keeping the number of so-called A-level festivals limited to assure the hierarchy on the circuit." Marijke de Valck and Skadi Loist, "Film Festival Studies: An Overview of a Burgeoning Field," in *Film Festival Yearbook 1: The Festival Circuit*, eds. Dina Iordanova and Ragan Rhyne (St Andrews: St Andrews Film Studies, 2009), 183.

93 Skadi Loist, "The Film Festival Circuit: Networks, Hierarchies, and Circulation," in *Film Festivals: History, Theory, Method, Practice*, eds. Marijke de Valck, Brendan Kredell and Skadi Loist (New York: Routledge, 2016), 56.

94 Iordanova, "The Film Festival Circuit," 24.

95 Iordanova, "The Film Festival Circuit," 25.

96 Shahabi, email interview with the author, June 17, 2019.

97 Shahabi, email interview with the author, June 17, 2019.

98 Nick Vivarelli, "Escalating U.S. Pressure, Sanctions on Iran Take Toll on Its Film Industry," *Variety*, May 19, 2019, https://variety.com/2019/film/news/trump-pressure-iran-toll-film-industry-1203220112/, accessed July 30, 2023.

99 Vivarelli, "Escalating U.S. Pressure, Sanctions on Iran Take Toll on Its Film Industry."

100 *Kara Film Studio*, https://www.karafilm.ir/en/, accessed July 30, 2023.

101 *Kara Film Studio*, https://www.karafilm.ir/en/.

102 *Kara Film Studio*, "Touran Khanom," https://www.karafilm.ir/en/films/released/124-touran-khanum, accessed July 30, 2023.

103 *Kara Film Studio*, "Maryam Bagheri Reports From 'Kara Film Studio' Appearance at IDFA," December 4, 2017, https://www.karafilm.ir/en/news/newslist/139-maryam-bagheri-reports-from-%E2%80%98kara-film-studio%E2%80%99-appearance-at-idfa, accessed July 30, 2023.
104 Sanaei, "In film-ha ro koja neshoon midin?," 89.
105 Sanaei, "In film-ha ro koja neshoon midin?," 89.
106 Sanaei, "In film-ha ro koja neshoon midin?," 89.
107 Naser Saffarian, "Man ke dashtam zendegi-am ra mikardam!: Pakhsh-e video-iye chand film-e mostanad" (I Was Living My Own Life!: Video Distribution of Some Documentary Films"), *Film Monthly* 516 (1395/2016): 86.
108 Saffarian, "Man ke dashtam zendegi-am ra mikardam!, 87.
109 See: Shahr-e Ketab, https://shahreketabonline.com/.
110 Brian Winston, Gail Vanstone, and Wang Chi, *The Act of Documenting: Documentary in the 21st Century* (London: Bloomsbury, 2017): 8. In regard to these three aspects, the authors explain that Western documentary's hegemony "has depended on the scientism of objectivity and evidential integrity of the photographic image; the eurocentricism of its production modes and exhibition infrastructure; and the patriarchal cast of its dominant tone and narrative voice." Winston, Vanstone, and Chi, *The Act of Documenting*, 8–9.
111 Winston, Vanstone, and Chi, *The Act of Documenting*, 9 (original emphasis).
112 Khiabany, *Iranian Media*, 149.
113 Paul Bischoff, "Internet Censorship 2023: A Global Map of Internet Restrictions," *Comparitech*, January 26, 2023, https://www.comparitech.com/blog/vpn-privacy/internet-censorship-map/, accessed August 1, 2023.
114 The use of VPNs (Virtual Private Networks) and anti-filter software is one of the ways that has, to some extent, provided access to blocked and/or restricted online platforms and social media sites.
115 Khiabany, *Iranian Media*, 155.
116 Naficy, *A Social History of Iranian Cinema, Volume 4*, 4.
117 Film Net, Filimo, and Hashure are some examples of VOD platforms in Iran.
118 According to Mahsa Salamti, "In April 2018, the conservative members of the Cultural Commission of the Iranian Parliament agreed to grant the rights for the regulation of online audiovisual content to IRIB. The parliament never voted on the bill;" nevertheless since then, in addition to the MCIG, "IRIB's nascent Organisation for Regulating Online Audio and Video (referred to as SATRA) became the hegemonic authority, which seeks to set rules not only regarding VODs but also domestic social media and user-generated content." Mahsa Salamati, "The Politics of Video on Demand Platforms in Iran: In Between Formal and Informal Distribution," *Studies in World Cinema* 2, no. 1–2 (2022): 178–179.

119 For more information see: https://hashure.com/en and *Financial Tribune*, "VOD Site Offers Documentaries," June 11, 2018, https://financialtribune.com/articles/art-and-culture/87856/vod-site-offers-documentaries, accessed July 31, 2023.

120 Keshavarz, email interview with the author, November 25, 2018.

121 Keshavarz, email interview with the author, November 25, 2018.

122 Narges Ashuri, "Touran Khanom parastar-e farhang-e koodakan-e Iran zamin" ("Touran Khanom, the Caregiver of the Culture of Iran's Children"), *Iran Newspaper*, June 11, 2018, https://www.magiran.com/article/3755422, accessed July 31, 2023.

123 Ashuri, "Touran Khanom parastar-e farhang-e koodakan-e Iran zamin."

124 Banietemad, email interview with the author, October 30, 2018.

125 For more information see: https://www.imvbox.com/en/faq and https://www.imvbox.com/en/about

126 *IMVBox*, "FAQ: What is IMVBox," https://www.imvbox.com/en/faq, accessed July 31, 2023.

127 Ahmad Kiarostami, "Docunight," https://www.ahmadkiarostami.com/docunight, accessed July 31, 2023.

128 Kiarostami, "Docunight."

129 Lobato, "Subcinema," 116.

130 Lobato, "Subcinema," 116.

131 Sreberny and Khiabany write, "In 2009, the realities of the media markets in Iran indicate further polarisation of media consumers between urban and rural areas, between Tehran and smaller cities, and between those with differing levels of disposable income." Annabelle Sreberny and Gholam Khiabany, *Blogistan: The Internet and Politics in Iran* (London: I.B. Tauris, 2010), 21.

132 Keshavarz, email interview with the author, November 25, 2018.

133 Dan Edwards, *Independent Chinese Documentary: Alternative Visions, Alternative Publics* (Edinburgh: Edinburgh University Press, 2015), 39.

134 Sadegh-Vaziri, "Iranian Documentary Film Culture," 161.

135 Lobato, *Shadow Economies of Cinema*, 18 (original emphasis).

136 Keshavarz, email interview with the author, November 25, 2018.

137 Keshavarz, email interview with the author, November 25, 2018.

138 Nasim Najafi, "Neveshtan baray-e mostanad" ("Writing for Documentary"), in *Haghighat dar Ghab-e Mostanad: Majmoe' Maghalat Darbare-ye Sinema-ye Mostanad*, ed. Esmail Mihandoost (Tehran: Documentary and Experimental Film Center, 1387/2008), 396.

139 Shweta Kishore, *Indian Documentary Film and Filmmakers: Independence in Practice*, (Edinburgh: Edinburgh University Press, 2018), 123.

140 Kishore, *Indian Documentary Film and Filmmakers*, 124.

Chapter 3

1 Farzaneh Milani, *Veils and Words: The Emerging Voices of Iranian Women Writers* (Syracuse: Syracuse University Press, 1992), 201.
2 Kristin Lené Hole and Dijana Jelača, *Film Feminisms: A Global Introduction* (New York, Routledge, 2019), 188.
3 Mina Keshavarz, email interview with the author, November 25, 2018.
4 Keshavarz, email interview with the author, November 25, 2018.
5 Shirin Barghnavard, email interview with the author, August 7, 2018.
6 Bill Nichols, *Introduction to Documentary* (Bloomington: Indiana University Press, 2001), 14.
7 Alisa Lebow, "Introduction," in *The Cinema of Me: The Self and Subjectivity in First Person Documentary*, ed. Alisa Lebow (New York: Wallflower Press, 2012), 1.
8 Lebow, "Introduction," 1.
9 Alisa Lebow, "First Person Political," in *The Documentary Film Book*, ed. Brian Winston (London: Palgrave Macmillan/ BFI, 2013), 258.
10 Michelle Langford, "Iranian Cinema and Social Media," in *Social Media in Iran: Politics and Society after 2009*, eds. David M. Faris and Babak Rahimi (Albany: State University of New York Press, 2015), 252. It is also noteworthy to mention that Langford believes "In the decade since 2009, Iranian [fiction] cinema has taken a considerable turn away from allegorical modes of expression …" This significant shift, according to Lanford, "suggests that Iranian film-makers are becoming more direct, emboldened to confront social issues head on, rather than relying on allegory and poetry." Michelle Langford, *Allegory in Iranian Cinema: The Aesthetics of Poetry and Resistance*. London: Bloomsbury, 2019, 10.
11 Hamid Naficy, *A Social History of Iranian Cinema, Volume 4: The Globalizing Era, 1984-2010* (Durham: Duke University Press, 2012), 111–135.
12 Milani, *Veils and Words*, 201.
13 Farzaneh Milani, "Veiled Voices: Women's Autobiographies in Iran," in *Women's Autobiographies in Contemporary Iran*, ed. Afsaneh Najmabadi (Cambridge: Harvard University Press, 1990), 2.
14 Hamid Dabashi, *Close Up: Iranian Cinema, Past, Present and Future* (London: Verso, 2001), 16.
15 Milani, *Veils and Words*, 215.
16 Milani, *Veils and Words*, 215.
17 Milani, *Veils and Words*, 201.
18 For more discussion on this issue see: Najmeh Moradiyan Rizi, "Iranian Women, Iranian Cinema: Negotiating with Ideology and Tradition," *Journal of Religion & Film* 19, no.1 (2015), Article 35: 6–9. Cultural and film studies scholar Negar Mottahedeh also observes that "the veil confronts the voyeurism inscribed in cinematic spectatorship," and protects the female body "from the spectators' voyeuristic gaze …" Negar Mottahedeh, *Displaced*

Allegories: Post-Revolutionary Iranian Cinema (Durham: Duke University Press, 2008), 10.

19 Karl J. Weintraub, "Autobiography and Historical Consciousness," *Critical Inquiry* 1, no. 4 (1975): 822 (original emphasis).

20 Weintraub, "Autobiography and Historical Consciousness," 824.

21 Weintraub, "Autobiography and Historical Consciousness," 824.

22 Dabashi, *Close Up*, 216.

23 Milani, "Veiled Voices," 8.

24 Milani, "Veiled Voices," 8.

25 Shireen Mahdavi, "Reflections in the Mirror—How Each Saw the Other: Women in the Nineteenth Century," in *Women in Iran: From 1800 to the Islamic Republic*, eds. Lois Beck and Guity Nashat (Urbana: University of Illinois Press, 2004), 76 (original emphasis).

26 Afsaneh Najmabadi, "A Different Voice: Taj os-Saltaneh," in *Women's Autobiographies in Contemporary Iran*, ed. Afsaneh Najmabadi (Cambridge: Harvard University Press, 1990), 20.

27 For more information see: Bibi Khanum Astarabadi, "The Vices of Men," in *The Education of Women and The Vices of Men: Two Qajar Tracts*, trans. Hasan Javadi and Willem Floor (Syracuse: Syracuse University Press, 2010), 55–126.

28 Najmabadi, "A Different Voice," 20.

29 Najmabadi, "A Different Voice," 21.

30 Najmabadi, "A Different Voice," 29.

31 Najmabadi, "A Different Voice," 29.

32 As Farzaneh Milani in this regard writes, "Taj os-Saltaneh, holding on to her voice and vision, tried to kill herself thrice; Forugh Farrokhzad and Mahshid Amirshahi each attempted suicide once. Thus, to write autobiographically with the individual and individualized imprint of a female voice … has proved to be a costly enterprise for the Iranian woman." Milani, "Veiled Voices," 16.

33 Milani, "Veiled Voices," 12.

34 Dabashi, *Close Up*, 28.

35 Milani, "Veiled Voices," 10.

36 Margaret A. McLaren, *Feminism, Foucault, and Embodied Subjectivity* (Albany: State University of New York Press, 2002), 152.

37 In the interviews that I conducted with Iranian women documentarians for this study, Forugh Farrokhzad was mentioned as a filmmaker whose documentary film and practices were among the most influential ones for these documentarians.

38 Azra Ghandeharion and Maryam Sadat Mousavi Tekiyeh, "Ideology Behind the Covers of the Bestselling Books in Iran: Female Narrators in War Literature," *Frontiers: A Journal of Women Studies* 40, no. 1 (2019): 149.

39 Farzaneh Milani, "Iranian Women's Life Narratives," *Journal of Women's History* 25, no. 2 (2013): 145.

40 Asef Bayat, *Life as Politics: How Ordinary People Change the Middle East*, 2nd ed. (Stanford: Stanford University Press, 2013), 15.
41 Bayat, *Life as Politics*, 17.
42 Bayat, *Life as Politics*, 18.
43 Bayat, *Life as Politics*, 119.
44 Bayat, *Life as Politics*, 119.
45 Kevan Harris, *A Social Revolution: Politics and the Welfare State in Iran* (Oakland: University of California Press, 2017), 176.
46 Harris, *A Social Revolution*, 176.
47 Bayat, *Life as Politics*, 174.
48 Orkideh Behrouzan, *Prozak Diaries: Psychiatry and Generational Memory in Iran* (Stanford: Stanford University Press, 2016), 21.
49 Behrouzan, *Prozak Diaries*, 30.
50 Miriam Berkley, "Boll`s Stories Mark German Culture Reborn," *Chicago Tribune*, March 23, 1986, https://www.chicagotribune.com/news/ct-xpm-1986-03-23-8601220077-story.html, accessed February 29, 2020.
51 Blake Atwood, *Reform Cinema in Iran: Film and Political Change in the Islamic Republic* (New York: Columbia University Press, 2016), 97.
52 Atwood, *Reform Cinema in Iran*, 97.
53 Masserat Amir-Ebrahimi, "Transgression in Narration: The Lives of Iranian Women in Cyberspace," *Journal of Middle East Women's Studies* 4, no. 3 (2008): 93.
54 Behrouzan, *Prozak Diaries*, 9 (original emphasis).
55 Sara Tafakori, "Iran's #MeToo Movement Challenges Patriarchy and Western Stereotypes," *Open Democracy*, September 1, 2020, https://www.opendemocracy.net/en/north-africa-west-asia/irans-metoo-movement-challenges-patriarchy-and-western-stereotypes/, accessed 10 September, 2022.
56 Langford, "Iranian Cinema and Social Media," 254.
57 Naficy, *A Social History of Iranian Cinema, Volume 4*, 86.
58 Persheng Sadegh-Vaziri, "Iranian Documentary Film Culture: Cinema, Society, and Power 1997–2014," PhD Dissertation (Philadelphia: Temple University, 2015), 75.
59 The portrayal of self-dissolution, derived from Islamic mysticism, mostly emerged in documentaries and fiction films made during and after the Iran-Iraq War. Naficy mentions that the best instances of such cinema can be seen in "the work of Avini, Hatamikia, Rasul Mollaqolipur, and Kamal Tabrizi, [who] attempted both to depict and to embody an immersive 'sacred' subjectivity." Naficy, *A Social History of Iranian Cinema, Volume 4*, 13.
60 Sadegh-Vaziri, "Iranian Documentary Film Culture," 75.
61 Omid Balaghati, "Dar Khiaban-haye bi-saranjam: Iran-e napeida dar sinema-ye mostanad-e in sal-ha" ("In Endless Streets: Invisible Iran in These Years' Documentary Cinema"), *Film Monthly* 516 (1395/2016): 67.

62 Mehdi Bagheri, "Dar jostojoo-ye hamzad: Mostanad-haye khod-bayangar" ("In Search of a Companion: Self-Reflexive Documentaries"), *Film Monthly* 516 (1395/2016): 50.
63 Lebow, "Introduction," 1.
64 Lebow, "Introduction," 3.
65 Milani, *Veils and Words*, 226.
66 Catherine Russell, *Experimental Ethnography: The Work of Film in the Age of Video* (Durham: Duke University Press, 1999), 276.
67 Gönül Dönmez-Colin, *Women in the Cinemas of Iran and Turkey: As Images and As Image-Makers* (New York: Routledge, 2020), 194.
68 Mina Keshavarz, email interview with the author, November 25, 2018.
69 Russell, *Experimental Ethnography*, 276.
70 Keshavarz, email interview with the author, November 25, 2018.
71 Gabrielle McNally, "The Feminist Voice: Improvisation in Women's Autobiographical Filmmaking," in *Female Authorship and the Documentary Image: Theory, Practice, and Aesthetics*, eds. Boel Ulfsdotter and Anna Backman Rogers (Edinburgh: Edinburgh University Press, 2018), 76.
72 Lebow, "Introduction," 1.
73 Shirin Barghnavard, email interview with the author, August 7, 2018.
74 Dönmez-Colin, *Women in the Cinemas of Iran and Turkey*, 193.
75 Laura Rascaroli, *The Personal Camera: Subjective Cinema and the Essay Film* (London: Wallflower Press, 2009), 14.
76 Rascaroli, *The Personal Camera*, 14.
77 Barghnavard, email interview with the author, August 7, 2018.
78 Barghnavard, email interview with the author, August 7, 2018.
79 Russell, *Experimental Ethnography*, 313.
80 Dönmez-Colin, *Women in the Cinemas of Iran and Turkey*, 194.
81 Keshavarz, email interview with the author, November 25, 2018.
82 Keshavarz, email interview with the author, November 25, 2018.
83 Dönmez-Colin, *Women in the Cinemas of Iran and Turkey*, 194.

Chapter 4

1 Julia Lesage, "Feminist Documentary: Aesthetics and Politics," in *"Show Us Life": Toward a History and Aesthetics of the Committed Documentary*, ed. Thomas Waugh (Metuchen, N.J.: The Scarecrow Press, 1984), 235.
2 Lesage, "Feminist Documentary," 235.
3 Kristin Lené Hole and Dijana Jelača, *Film Feminisms: A Global Introduction* (New York: Routledge, 2019), 184.
4 Hole and Jelača, *Film Feminisms*, 184.
5 Liz Stanley, "Moments of Writing: Is There a Feminist Auto/biography?," *Gender & History* 2, no. 1 (1990): 59.
6 Susan Mann Trofimenkoff, "Feminist Biography," *Atlantis* 10, no. 2 (1985): 3.
7 Trofimenkoff, "Feminist Biography," 4.

8 Meryn Stuart, "Making the Choices: Writing about Marguerite Carr-Harris," in *All Sides of the Subject: Women and Biography*, ed. Teresa Iles (New York: Teachers College Press, 1992), 62 (original emphasis).
9 Hole and Jelača, *Film Feminisms*, 187.
10 Michael Craig Hillmann, "An Autobiographical Voice: Forugh Farrokhzad," in *Women's Autobiographies in Contemporary Iran*, ed. Afsaneh Najmabadi (Cambridge, MA: Harvard University Press, 1990), 34–35.
11 Hillmann, "An Autobiographical Voice," 34.
12 Hillmann, "An Autobiographical Voice," 35.
13 William L. Hanaway, "Half-Voices: Persian Women's Lives and Letters," in *Women's Autobiographies in Contemporary Iran*, ed. Afsaneh Najmabadi (Cambridge, MA: Harvard University Press, 1990), 59–60.
14 Hanaway, "Half-Voices," 60.
15 Hanaway, "Half-Voices," 60.
16 Shahrokh Meskoob, "Naghashi-ye Qajar: Tamayoz, esalat amma door az vagheiyat" ("Qajar Painting: Distinction, Originality but Far from Reality"), *Tavoos Quarterly* 5 & 6 (2000). http://www.tavoosonline.com/Articles/ArticleDetailFa.aspx?src=51&Page=1, accessed February 7, 2020. Hamid Dabashi also traces the main origin of attention to individuals in Iranian visual arts to the emergence of photography. Dabashi writes, "In the entire spectrum of Persian visual arts that commenced and predicted itself on the Qur'anic conception of man, mankind was kept outside history, safely sinful in the Garden of Eden. With the introduction of newer forms of visual representation, the picture began to change. Still photography was the first shock." Hamid Dabashi, *Close Up: Iranian Cinema, Past, Present and Future* (London: Verso, 2001), 15.
17 Dabashi, *Close Up*, 15.
18 Hamid Naficy, *A Social History of Iranian Cinema, Volume 2: The Industrializing Years, 1941–1978* (Durham: Duke University Press, 2011), 222.
19 Naficy, *A Social History of Iranian Cinema, Volume 2*, 99–100.
20 Naficy, *A Social History of Iranian Cinema, Volume 2*, 387.
21 In 2004, Kimiavi made a documentary short as an update on the life of Darvish Khan, titled *The Old Man and His Stone Garden* (*Pirmard va bagh-e sang-iyash*), in which in addition to pointing to Kimiavi's earlier film, the film offers an insight into the recent state of the main character's life and his family.
22 According to Naficy, the film contained "shots of her [Farrokhzad's] grave and her burial, as well as eulogies offered by her friends and an interview with her." Naficy, *A Social History of Iranian Cinema, Volume 2*, 444. After the revolution, Naser Saffarian made an in-depth biographical documentary of Farrokhzad's life, titled *The Green Cold* (*Sard-e sabz*, 2002).
23 Hamid Naficy, *A Social History of Iranian Cinema, Volume 3: The Islamicate Period, 1978–1984* (Durham: Duke University Press, 2012), 109.

24 Naficy, *A Social History of Iranian Cinema, Volume 3*, 110–112.
25 Naficy, *A Social History of Iranian Cinema, Volume 3*, 109.
26 Omid Balaghati, "Dar Khiaban-haye bi-saranjam: Iran-e napeida dar sinema-ye mostanad-e in sal-ha" ("In Endless Streets: Invisible Iran in These Years' Documentary Cinema"), *Film Monthly* 516 (1395/2016), 67.
27 Balaghati, "Dar Khiaban-haye bi-saranjam," 67.
28 Zahra Nejadbahram, "Women and Employment," in *Women, Power and Politics in 21st Century Iran*, eds. Tara Povey and Elaheh Rostami-Povey (Farnham, Surrey: Ashgate, 2012), 83–84.
29 Mahmood Monshipouri, "Introduction: Social Change in Post-Khomeini Iran," in *Inside the Islamic Republic: Social Change in Post-Khomeini Iran*, ed. Mahmood Monshipouri (Oxford: Oxford University Press, 2016), 7.
30 Rakhshan Banietemad, email interview with the author, October 30, 2018.
31 Banietemad, email interview with the author, October 30, 2018.
32 Blake Atwood, *Reform Cinema in Iran: Film and Political Change in the Islamic Republic* (New York: Columbia University Press, 2016), 93 (original emphasis).
33 John Corner, "Biography Within the Documentary Frame: A Note," *Framework: The Journal of Cinema and Media* 43, no.1 (2002): 95.
34 The Karestan documentary film series showcases less-publicly-known but eminent Iranian entrepreneurs. This series was formed as a collaboration between the Kara Film Studio—an independent documentary collective consisting of a group of documentarians involved in production and distribution of documentary films—and the Entrepreneurship Development Foundation for Women and Youth (*Bonyad-e tosea'-ye kar-afarini-e zanan va javanan*), an NGO "whose primary goal is the promotion and development of the culture of creativity, innovation and entrepreneurship at national level." Kara Film Studio, "About Karestan," https://www.karafilm.ir/en/karestan/about-karestan, accessed July 13, 2023.
35 *Kara Film Studio*, "Hayedeh Shirzadi," https://www.karafilm.ir/en/karestan/entrepreneurs/207-hayedeh-shirzadi, accessed March 19, 2020.
36 *Kara Film Studio*, "Hayedeh Shirzadi."
37 Mahnaz Afzali, email interview with the author, September 4, 2018.
38 Nejadbahram, "Women and Employment," 77.
39 Mina Keshavarz, email interview with the author, November 25, 2018.
40 Keshavarz, email interview with the author, November 25, 2018.
41 Keshavarz, email interview with the author, November 25, 2018.
42 Keshavarz, email interview with the author, November 25, 2018.
43 Keshavarz, email interview with the author, November 25, 2018.
44 Nejadbahram, "Women and Employment," 80.
45 Nejadbahram, "Women and Employment," 80.
46 Nejadbahram, "Women and Employment," 80.
47 Corner, "Biography Within the Documentary Frame: A Note," 99.
48 Corner, "Biography Within the Documentary Frame: A Note," 99–100.

49 Lee Chambers-Schiller, "The Value of Female Public Rituals for Feminist Biography: Maria Weston Chapman and the Boston Anti-Slavery Anniversary," *a/b: Auto/Biography Studies* 8, no. 2 (1993): 217.

Chapter 5

1 Michael Chanan, *The Politics of Documentary* (London: British Film Institute, 2007), 23.
2 Lidia Merás, "*Profession: Documentarist*: Underground Documentary Making in Iran," in *Female Agency and Documentary Strategies: Subjectivities, Identity and Activism*, eds. Boel Ulfsdotter and Anna Backman Rogers (Edinburgh: Edinburgh University Press, 2018), 173.
3 Thomas Waugh, "Introduction: Why Documentary Filmmakers Keep Trying to Change the World, or Why People Changing the World Keep Making Documentaries," in *"Show Us Life": Toward a History and Aesthetics of the Committed Documentary*, ed. Thomas Waugh (Metuchen, NJ: The Scarecrow Press, 1984), xiv.
4 Waugh, "Introduction," xiv.
5 Waugh, "Introduction," xiv.
6 Waugh, "Introduction," xii.
7 Heather McIntosh, "Introduction: The Intersections of Documentary and Gendered Violence," in *Documenting Gendered Violence: Representations, Collaborations, and Movements*, eds. Lisa M. Cuklanz and Heather McIntosh (London: Bloomsbury, 2015), 5.
8 Chuck Kleinhans, "Forms, Politics, Makers and Contexts: Basic Issues for a Theory of Radical Political Documentary," in *"Show Us Life": Toward a History and Aesthetics of the Committed Documentary*, ed. Thomas Waugh (Metuchen, NJ: The Scarecrow Press, 1984), 318–342; Alexandra Juhasz, "They Said We Were Trying to Show Reality—All I Want to Show Is My Video: The Politics of the Realist Feminist Documentary," in *Collecting Visible Evidence*, eds. Jane M. Gaines and Michael Renov (Minneapolis: University of Minnesota Press, 1999), 190–215; Kristin Lené Hole and Dijana Jelača, *Film Feminisms: A Global Introduction* (New York, Routledge, 2019); Angela J. Aguayo, *Documentary Resistance: Social Change and Participatory Media* (New York: Oxford University Press, 2019); Patricia Aufderheide, "The Camera as Conscience: How Social Issues Inspire Moving Documentaries," *The Chronicle of Higher Education*, October 23, 1998, https://www.chronicle.com/article/the-camera-as-conscience-how-social-issues-inspire-moving-documentaries/, accessed July 12, 2023; Caty Borum Chattoo, *Story Movements: How Documentaries Empower People and Inspire Social Change* (New York: Oxford University Press, 2020).
9 Hole and Jelača, *Film Feminisms*, 177.
10 Hole and Jelača, *Film Feminisms*, 177.
11 Chattoo, *Story Movements*, 59.

12 Kleinhans, "Forms, Politics, Makers and Contexts," 326.
13 Blake Atwood, *Reform Cinema in Iran: Film and Political Change in the Islamic Republic* (New York: Columbia University Press, 2016), 66.
14 Atwood, *Reform Cinema in Iran*, 67.
15 Hamid Naficy, *A Social History of Iranian Cinema, Volume 2: The Industrializing Years, 1941–1978* (Durham: Duke University Press, 2011), 118.
16 Mehrangiz Kar and Azadeh Pourzand, "IRAN," in *Feminist Advocacy, Family Law and Violence Against Women: International Perspectives*, eds. Mahnaz Akhami, Yakın Ertürk, and Ann Elizabeth Mayer (New York: Routledge, 2019), 72.
17 Kar and Pourzand, "IRAN," 73.
18 Kar and Pourzand, "IRAN," 74.
19 Afsaneh Najmabadi, "Hazards of Modernity and Morality: Women, State and Ideology in Contemporary Iran," in *Women, Islam and the State*, ed. Deniz Kandiyoti (Philadelphia: Temple University Press, 1991), 69.
20 Hamid Naficy, *A Social History of Iranian Cinema, Volume 3: The Islamicate Period, 1978–1984* (Durham: Duke University Press, 2012), 106.
21 Tahereh Hadian, "The Politics of Documentary Films on Iran: A Comparative Analysis," *Iranian Review of Foreign Affairs* 4, no. 3 (2013): 176.
22 Atwood, *Reform Cinema in Iran*, 119.
23 Rebecca Barlow and Shahram Akbarzadeh, "Top-Down or Bottom-Up? Towards a Theory of Change for Human Rights Practice in Iran," in *Human Rights and Agents of Change in Iran: Towards a Theory of Change*, eds. Rebecca Barlow and Shahram Akbarzadeh (Singapore: Palgrave Macmillan, 2018), 10 (original emphasis).
24 Kar and Pourzand, "IRAN," 86.
25 Mahnaz Afzali, email interview with the author, September 4, 2018.
26 Atwood, *Reform Cinema in Iran*, 119.
27 Afzali, email interview with the author, September 4, 2018.
28 Julia Lesage, "Feminist Documentary: Aesthetics and Politics," in "*Show Us Life": Toward a History and Aesthetics of the Committed Documentary*, ed. Thomas Waugh (Metuchen, NJ: The Scarecrow Press, 1984), 236.
29 Juhasz, "They Said We Were Trying to Show Reality—All I Want to Show Is My Video," 203.
30 Ezra Winton and Jason Garrison, "'If a Revolution Is Screened and No One Is There to See It, Does It Make a Sound?' The Politics of Distribution and Counterpublics," in *Challenge for Change: Activist Documentary at the National Film Board of Canada*, eds. Thomas Waugh, Michael Brendan Baker, and Ezra Winton (Montreal: McGill-Queen's University Press, 2010), 404.
31 Afzali, email interview with the author, September 4, 2018.
32 Rakhshan Banietemad, email interview with the author, October 30, 2018.
33 According to Article 115 of the Islamic Republic of Iran's Constitution, only men (*rejal*) can run for presidency. In this regard, Samira Ghoreishi explains

that "in the 1997 Presidential Election, for the first time, Azam Taleghani, the daughter of Ayatollah Taleghani who was usually identified as a religious/ Islamic women's rights activist, announced that she herself would stand as a candidate. Her candidacy was a severe challenge to the Guardian Council, which is responsible for confirming the qualifications of the candidates for the presidency. … Although this resistance to Article 115 was initiated by the individual action of an Islamic women's rights activist and somehow a female elite, it gave rise to a form of collective action against the discriminatory laws that aim to eliminate women from the public sphere, particularly from the public political sphere." Samira Ghoreishi, *Women's Activism in the Islamic Republic of Iran: Political Alliance and the Formation of Deliberative Civil Society* (Cham: Palgrave Macmillan, 2021), 150.

34 Asef Bayat, *Life as Politics: How Ordinary People Change the Middle East*, 2nd ed. (Stanford: Stanford University Press, 2013), 104.

35 Banietemad, email interview with the author, October 30, 2018.

36 Leila Alikarami, *Women and Equality in Iran: Law, Society and Activism* (London: I.B. Tauris/Bloomsbury, 2019), 196.

37 According to Samira Ghoreishi, "In the 2013 election, where Rouhani was elected as the president, women again formed a coalition to raise their demands in the election and they had meetings with a representative of Rouhani as a moderate candidate." Ghoreishi, *Women's Activism in the Islamic Republic of Iran*, 149.

38 Dara Conduit and Shahram Akbarzadeh, "The 'Inside-Track' Approach to Change in Iran Under President Rouhani: The Case of Freedom on the Internet," in *Human Rights and Agents of Change in Iran: Towards a Theory of Change*, eds. Rebecca Barlow and Shahram Akbarzadeh (Singapore: Palgrave Macmillan, 2018), 38.

39 Winton and Garrison, "'If a Revolution Is Screened and No One Is There to See It, Does It Make a Sound?' The Politics of Distribution and Counterpublics," 405.

40 Kevan Harris, *A Social Revolution: Politics and the Welfare State in Iran* (Oakland: University of California Press, 2017), 197.

41 Harris, *A Social Revolution*, 197.

42 William O. Beeman, "Post-Revolutionary Iran: Democracy of Theocracy?" in *Inside the Islamic Republic: Social Change in Post-Khomeini Iran*, ed. Mahmood Monshipouri (Oxford: Oxford University Press, 2016), 42.

43 Conduit and Akbarzadeh, "The 'Inside-Track' Approach to Change in Iran Under President Rouhani," 31.

44 Kar and Pourzand, "IRAN," 80.

45 Kar and Pourzand, "IRAN," 80.

46 McIntosh, "Introduction," 1.

47 McIntosh, "Introduction," 2.

48 Kar and Pourzand, "IRAN," 75.

49 Kar and Pourzand, "IRAN," 75.

50 McIntosh, "Introduction," 11.
51 McIntosh, "Introduction," 11.
52 Kar and Pourzand, "IRAN," 75.
53 Kar and Pourzand, "IRAN," 75.
54 Firouzeh Khosrovani's film, *Radiograph of a Family* (2020), was released in 2020, the same year *The Art of Living in Danger* was released. It won best feature-length documentary award at the International Documentary Festival Amsterdam (IDFA) in 2020.
55 Mona Tabbara, "Iranian Authorities Officially Close Cases of Arrested Filmmakers Mina Keshavarz, Firouzeh Khosrovani," *Screen Daily*, April 13, 2023, https://www.screendaily.com/news/iranian-authorities-officially-close-cases-of-arrested-filmmakers-mina-keshavarz-firouzeh-khosrovani/5181034.article, accessed July 12, 2023.
56 Barlow and Akbarzadeh, "Top-Down or Bottom-Up?," 14.

Coda

1 Angela J. Aguayo, *Documentary Resistance: Social Change and Participatory Media* (New York: Oxford University Press, 2019), ix.
2 Hamid Naficy, *A Social History of Iranian Cinema, Volume 4: The Globalizing Era, 1984–2010* (Durham, NC: Duke University Press, 2012), 51.
3 Naficy, *A Social History of Iranian Cinema, Volume 4*, 51.
4 Nahid Rezaei, email interview with the author, February 7, 2019.
5 Rezaei, email interview with the author, February 7, 2019.
6 Naficy, *A Social History of Iranian Cinema, Volume 4*, 51–52.
7 Rezaei, email interview with the author, February 7, 2019.
8 Rezaei, email interview with the author, February 7, 2019.
9 Trinh T. Minh-ha, *When the Moon Waxes Red: Representation, Gender and Cultural Politics* (New York: Routledge, 1991), 149.
10 Minh-ha, *When the Moon Waxes Red*, 149.

Bibliography

Afarideh, Mohammad. "Goftegoo ba Mohammad Afarideh, modir-amel-e Markaz Gostaresh-e Sinema-ye Mostanad va Tajrobi va dabir-e jashnvare-ye Sinema Haghighat" ("A Conversation with Mohammad Afarideh, the Managing Director of the Documentary and Experimental Film Center and the Secretary of the Cinema Vérité Festival"), interview by Esmail Mihandoost. In *Haghighat dar Ghab-e Mostanad: Majmoe' Maghalat Darbare-ye Sinema-ye Mostanad*, edited by Esmail Mihandoost, 11–38. Tehran: Documentary and Experimental Film Center, 1387/2008.

Afzali, Mahnaz. Email interview with the author. September 4, 2018.

Aguayo, Angela J. *Documentary Resistance: Social Change and Participatory Media*. New York: Oxford University Press, 2019.

Akhavan, Niki. "Nonfiction Form and the 'Truth' about Muslim Women in Iranian Documentary." *Feminist Media Histories* 1, no. 1 (2015): 89–111.

Alikarami, Leila. *Women and Equality in Iran: Law, Society and Activism*. London: I.B. Tauris / Bloomsbury, 2019.

Amir-Ebrahimi, Masserat. "Transgression in Narration: The Lives of Iranian Women in Cyberspace." *Journal of Middle East Women's Studies* 4, no. 3 (2008): 89–118.

Art and Experience Cinema. "Aeinnameh-ye namayesh-e film dar gorooh sinemai-ye honar va tojrobeh" ("Film Screening Regulations in Art and Experience Cinema"). August 9, 2022. https://honartajrobeh.ir/Explain/5/آیین_نامه_. Accessed July 27, 2023.

Ashuri, Narges. "Touran Khanom parastar-e farhang-e koodakan-e Iran zamin" ("Touran Khanom, the Caregiver of the Culture of Iran's Children"). *Iran Newspaper*. June 11, 2018. https://www.magiran.com/article/3755422. Accessed July 31, 2023.

Association of Iranian Documentary Producers. "Asasnameh" ("Statute"). https://aoidp.com/اساسنامه/. Accessed July 28, 2023.

Astarabadi, Bibi Khanum. "The Vices of Men." In *The Education of Women and The Vices of Men: Two Qajar Tracts*, translated by Hasan Javadi and Willem Floor, 55–126. Syracuse: Syracuse University Press, 2010.

Atarpour, Orod. "Nemishod edamed dad: Goftegoo ba Orod Atarpour darbari-ye tajrobe-ye tahiyeh-ye do majmoe'-ye mostand-e *Ganjine-haye Penhan* va *Bist Shab*" ("It Was Impossible to Continue: A Conversation with Orod Atarpour on His Experience of Producing Two Documentary Series *Hidden*

Treasures and *Twenty Nights*"), interview by Pirooz Kalantari. *Film Monthly* 516 (1395/2016): 82–83.

Attebai, Mohammad. "Bazar-e sinema-ye mostanad dar Oroopa" ("Documentary Cinema's Market in Europe"). In *Haghighat-e Sinema va Sinema Haghighat: Jostojooei dar Arse-ye Sinema-ye Mostanad*, edited by Zaven Ghookasian, 231–241. Tehran: Documentary and Experimental Film Center, 1386/2007.

Atwood, Blake. *Reform Cinema in Iran: Film and Political Change in the Islamic Republic*. New York: Columbia University Press, 2016.

Aufderheide, Patricia. "The Camera as Conscience: How Social Issues Inspire Moving Documentaries." *The Chronicle of Higher Education*. October 23, 1998. https://www.chronicle.com/article/the-camera-as-conscience-how-social-issues-inspire-moving-documentaries/. Accessed July 12, 2023.

Bagheri, Mehdi. "Dar jostojoo-ye hamzad: Mostanad-haye khod-bayangar" ("In Search of a Companion: Self-Reflexive Documentaries"). *Film Monthly* 516 (1395/2016): 50–51.

Bakhshi, Masoud. "Tamhid dar Sinema Haghighat, honar-e Sinemast" ("Planning in Cinema Vérité is the Art of Cinema"), interview by Zaven Ghookasian. In *Haghighat-e Sinema va Sinema Haghighat 2: Jostojooei dar Arse-ye Sinema-ye Mostanad*, edited by Zaven Ghookasian, 193–206. Tehran: Documentary and Experimental Film Center, 1387/2008.

Balaghati, Omid. "Dar Khiaban-haye bi-saranjam: Iran-e napeida dar sinema-ye mostanad-e in sal-ha" ("In Endless Streets: Invisible Iran in These Years' Documentary Cinema"). *Film Monthly* 516 (1395/2016): 66–68.

Banietemad, Rakhshan. Email interview with the author. October 30, 2018.

Barghnavard, Shirin. Email interview with the author. August 7, 2018.

Barlow, Rebecca, and Shahram Akbarzadeh. "Top-Down or Bottom-Up? Towards a Theory of Change for Human Rights Practice in Iran." In *Human Rights and Agents of Change in Iran: Towards a Theory of Change*, edited by Rebecca Barlow and Shahram Akbarzadeh, 3–24. Singapore: Palgrave Macmillan, 2018.

Batmanghelichi, Soraya K. and Leila Mouri. "Cyberfeminism, Iranian Style: Online Feminism in Post-2009 Iran." *Feminist Media Histories* 3, no. 1 (2017): 50–80.

Bayat, Asef. *Life as Politics: How Ordinary People Change the Middle East*, 2nd edition. Stanford: Stanford University Press, 2013.

Beeman, William O. "Post-Revolutionary Iran: Democracy of Theocracy?" In *Inside the Islamic Republic: Social Change in Post-Khomeini Iran*, edited by Mahmood Monshipouri, 37–62. Oxford: Oxford University Press, 2016.

Behrouzan, Orkideh. *Prozak Diaries: Psychiatry and Generational Memory in Iran*. Stanford: Stanford University Press, 2016.

Berkley, Miriam. "Boll`s Stories Mark German Culture Reborn." *Chicago Tribune*. March 23, 1986. https://www.chicagotribune.com/news/ct-xpm-1986-03-23-8601220077-story.html. Accessed February 29, 2020.

Berry, Chris. "Independently Chinese: Duan Jinchuan, Jiang Yue, and Chinese Documentary." In *From Underground to Independent: Alternative Film Culture in Contemporary China*, edited by Paul G. Pickowicz and Yingjin Zhang, 109–122. Lanham: Roman & Littlefield Publishers, 2006.

Bischoff, Paul. “Internet Censorship 2023: A Global Map of Internet Restrictions.” *Comparitech*. January 26, 2023. https://www.comparitech.com/blog/vpn-privacy/internet-censorship-map/. Accessed August 1, 2023.

Bizargiti, Azadeh. Email interview with the author. April 19, 2019.

Bizargiti, Azadeh. Email interview with the author. April 26, 2019.

Bizargiti, Azadeh. Email interview with the author. May 10, 2019.

Bridge to Iran. http://www.cemproductions.org/bridgetoiran/. Accessed July 20, 2023.

Chambers-Schiller, Lee. “The Value of Female Public Rituals for Feminist Biography: Maria Weston Chapman and the Boston Anti-Slavery Anniversary.” *a/b: Auto/Biography Studies* 8, no. 2 (1993): 217–232.

Chanan, Michael. *The Politics of Documentary*. London: British Film Institute, 2007.

Chattoo, Caty Borum. *Story Movements: How Documentaries Empower People and Inspire Social Change*. New York: Oxford University Press, 2020.

Cinema Organization. “Roykard-ha, rahbord-ha, va siyasat-haye sazman-e sinema-iye dolat-e tadbir va omid” (“Approaches, Strategies, and Policies of the Cinematic Organization of the Government of Tact and Hope”). Tehran: Ministry of Culture and Islamic Guidance (Spring 2014): 4–65.

Cinema Vérité: Iran International Documentary Film Festival. “86 mostanadsaz-e zan motaghazi-ye sherkat dar Sinema Haghighat shodand” (“86 Women Documentarians Applied for Participation in Cinema Vérité”). September 22, 2017. https://irandocfest.ir/News/6447/86_مستندساز_زن_متقاضی_شرکت_در_سینماحقیقت_شدند. Accessed July 12, 2023.

Conduit, Dara, and Shahram Akbarzadeh. “The ‘Inside-Track’ Approach to Change in Iran Under President Rouhani: The Case of Freedom on the Internet.” In *Human Rights and Agents of Change in Iran: Towards a Theory of Change*, edited by Rebecca Barlow and Shahram Akbarzadeh, 27–50. Singapore: Palgrave Macmillan, 2018.

Corner, John. “Biography Within the Documentary Frame: A Note.” *Framework: The Journal of Cinema and Media* 43, no. 1 (2002): 95–101.

Crisp, Virginia. *Film Distribution in the Digital Age: Pirates and Professionals*. Basingstoke: Palgrave Macmillan, 2015.

Cohn, Pamela. “Cinema Vérité Iran International Documentary Film Festival.” *Filmmaker* 17, no. 2 (Winter 2009): 26.

Dabashi, Hamid. *Close Up: Iranian Cinema, Past, Present and Future*. London: Verso, 2001.

Dabashi, Hamid. *Makhmalbaf at Large: The Making of a Rebel Filmmaker*. London: I.B. Tauris, 2008.

Dehghanpour, Hamid. *Sinema-ye Mostanad-e Iran va Jahan* (*Iranian and World Documentary Cinema*). Tehran: SAMT-The Organization for Researching and Composing University Textbooks in the Humanities, 1382/2003.

De Lauretis, Teresa. *Technologies of Gender*. Bloomington: Indiana University Press, 1987.

Derakhshan, Shahram. "Nehzat-e arzan-sazi!: Kanal-e mostanad-e television" ("The Cheapening Movement!: The Television's Documentary Channel"). *Film Monthly* 516 (1395/2016): 94.

de Valck, Marijke and Skadi Loist. "Film Festival Studies: An Overview of a Burgeoning Field." In *Film Festival Yearbook 1: The Festival Circuit*, edited by Dina Iordanova and Ragan Rhyne, 179–215. St. Andrews: St. Andrews Film Studies, 2009.

Devictor, Agnès. "Classic Tools, Original Goals: Cinema and Public Policy in the Islamic Republic of Iran (1979–97)." In *The New Iranian Cinema: Politics, Representation and Identity*, edited by Richard Tapper, 66–76. London: I.B. Tauris, 2002.

Documentary and Experimental Film Center. "Entekhab-e behtarin film az negah-e tamashagaran dastavard-e mohem-e jashnvare-ye davazdahom" ("The Selection of the Best Film from Audiences' Perspective as the Important Achievement of the 12th Festival"). December 15, 2018. https://www.defc.ir/Post/2834/. Accessed July 18, 2023.

Documentary and Experimental Film Center. "Amar-e mosharekat-e zanan dar sinema-ye mostanad-e Iran 10 darsad ast: 86 mostandsaz-e zan motaghazi-ye sherkat dar Sinema Haghighat shodand" ("Women's Participation Statistics in Iran's Documentary Cinema is 10 Per Cent: 86 Women Documentarians Applied for Participation in Cinema Vérité"). 17 October 2017. https://defc.ir/Post/2521/آمار_مشارکت_زنان_در_سینمای_مستند_ایران_10_درصد_است_86_مستندساز_زن_متقاضی_شرکت_در_سینماحقیقت_شدند. Accessed July 23, 2023.

Documentary and Experimental Film Center. "Arze-ye mostanad-ha va animation-haye markaz gostaresh dar 'ketabkhaneh-ye videoei'" ("Exhibition of the Center's Documentaries and Animations in a 'Video Library'"). July 1, 2023. https://defc.ir/Post/6255/عرضه_مستندها_و_انیمیشن_های_مرکز_گسترش_در_«کتابخانه_ویدیویی». Accessed July 23, 2023.

Documentary and Experimental Film Center. "Gozaresh-e amalkard-e mali-ye Markaz Gostaresh-e Sinema-ye Mostanad va Tajrobi dar sal-e 97 elam shod" ("The Report on the Financial Performance of the Documentary and Experimental Film Center in 2018 Is Announced"). May 26, 2019. https://defc.ir/Post/2890/گزارش_عملکرد_مالی_مرکز_گسترش_سینمای_مستند_و_تجربی_در_سال97_اعلام_شد. Accessed July 22, 2023.

Documentary and Experimental Film Center. "Olaviyat-haye jadid-e Markaz Gostaresh elam shod: A'rze-ye mostanad va hozoor dar bazar-ha" ("The Priorities of the DEFC Were Announced: Documentary Distribution and Presence in the Markets"). September 1, 2017. https://defc.ir/Post/2480/اولویت_های_جدید_مرکز_گسترش_اعلام_شد/_عرضه_مستند_و_حضور_در_بازارها. Accessed July 19, 2023.

Documentary Channel. https://www.doctv.ir/AboutUs. Accessed July 20, 2023.

Dönmez-Colin, Gönül. *Women in the Cinemas of Iran and Turkey: As Images and As Image-Makers*. New York: Routledge, 2020.

Edwards, Dan. *Independent Chinese Documentary: Alternative Visions, Alternative Publics*. Edinburgh: Edinburgh University Press, 2015.

Elena, Alberto. *The Cinema of Abbas Kiarostami*. London: Saqi, 2005.

Emami, Homayoun. *Sinema-ye Mardom-Shenakhti-ye Iran* (*Iranian Anthropological Cinema*). Tehran: Afkar Press, 1385/2006.

Filmba. "Gorooh-e Rokhdad-e Tazeh-ye Mostanad" ("Rokhdad-e Tazeh-ye Mostanad Group"). http://www.filmba.ir/index.php/list-film-center/1126-rokhdade-taze-mostanad. Accessed July 28, 2023.

Financial Tribune. "Identity, Reality and Creativity." December 2, 2017. https://financialtribune.com/articles/art-and-culture/77179/identity-reality-and-creativity. Accessed July 23, 2023.

Financial Tribune. "VOD Site Offers Documentaries." June 11, 2018. https://financialtribune.com/articles/art-and-culture/87856/vod-site-offers-documentaries. Accessed July 31, 2023.

Ghandeharion, Azra and Maryam Sadat Mousavi Tekiyeh. "Ideology Behind the Covers of the Bestselling Books in Iran: Female Narrators in War Literature." *Frontiers: A Journal of Women Studies* 40, no. 1 (2019): 146–175.

Ghanipour, Payam and Sayyed Ali Rohani. "Tahlil-e jaygah-e gorooh-e honar va tajrobeh dar sinema-ye Iran be onvan-e meydani mostaghel, az manzar-e araye Pierre Bourdieu" ("An Analysis on the Standpoint of Art & Experience Cinema in Iran's Cinema as an Independent Field (From Pierre Bourdieu Perspective)"). *Quarterly Journal of Interdisciplinary Studies in Communication and Media* 4, no. 11 (2021): 81–102.

Gharabaghi, Hadi. "'American Mice Grow Big!': The Syracuse Audiovisual Mission in Iran and the Rise of Documentary Diplomacy." Ph.D. Dissertation. New York: New York University, 2018.

Ghoreishi, Samira. *Women's Activism in the Islamic Republic of Iran: Political Alliance and the Formation of Deliberative Civil Society*. Cham: Palgrave Macmillan, 2021.

Hadian, Tahereh. "The Politics of Documentary Films on Iran: A Comparative Analysis." *Iranian Review of Foreign Affairs* 4, no. 3 (2013): 173–200.

Hamijoo. "Aya ou dar in mobarezeh pirooz mishavad?—Mina Keshavarz." August 5, 2015, https://hamijoo.com/projects/آیا-او-در-این-مبارزه-پیروز-می-شود؟-مین/. Accessed August 17, 2019.

Hanaway, William L. "Half-Voices: Persian Women's Lives and Letters." In *Women's Autobiographies in Contemporary Iran*, edited by Afsaneh Najmabadi, 55–63. Cambridge, MA: Harvard University Press, 1990.

Harris, Kevan. *A Social Revolution: Politics and the Welfare State in Iran*. Oakland: University of California Press, 2017.

Hashure. https://hashure.com/en. Accessed July 31, 2023.

Hassannia, Tina. *Asghar Farhadi: Life and Cinema*. Raleigh, NC: The Critical Press, 2014.

Hillmann, Michael Craig. "An Autobiographical Voice: Forugh Farrokhzad." In *Women's Autobiographies in Contemporary Iran*, edited by Afsaneh Najmabadi, 33–53. Cambridge, MA: Harvard University Press, 1990.

Hole, Kristin Lené and Dijana Jelača. *Film Feminisms: A Global Introduction*. New York: Routledge, 2019.

Hoodfar, Homa and Shadi Sadr. "Islamic Politics and Women's Quest for Gender Equality in Iran." *Third World Quarterly* 31, no. 6 (2010): 885–903.

IMVBox. "FAQ: What is IMVBox." https://www.imvbox.com/en/faq. Accessed July 31, 2023.

Iordanova, Dina. "The Film Festival Circuit." In *Film Festival Yearbook 1: The Festival Circuit*, edited by Dina Iordanova and Ragan Rhyne, 23–39. St. Andrews: St. Andrews Film Studies, 2009.

Iordanova, Dina and Stefanie Van de Peer. "Introduction." In *Film Festival Yearbook 6: Film Festivals and the Middle East*, edited by Dina Iordanova and Stefanie Van de Peer, xxi–lvi. St. Andrews: St. Andrews Film Studies, 2014.

IranWire. "Tahrim-e jashnvare-ye Sinema Haghighat tavasote jame'i az mostanad-sazan va faalan-e farhangi" (The Boycott of Cinema Vérité Festival by a Group of Documentarians and Cultural Activists"). December 2, 2022. https://iranwire.com/fa/news-1/110729--تحریم-جشنواره-سینما-حقیقت-توسط-جمعی-از-مستندسازان-و-فعالان-فرهنگی/. Accessed July 23, 2023.

Isna. "Mojtaba Mirtahmasb azad shod" ("Mojtaba Mirtahmasb Is Released"). December 11, 2011. https://www.isna.ir/news/9009-11658/مجتبی-میرطهماسب-آزاد-شد. Accessed August 25, 2019.

Issari, M. Ali. *Cinema in Iran, 1900–1979*. Metuchen: The Scarecrow Press, 1989.

Juhasz, Alexandra. "They Said We Were Trying to Show Reality—All I Want to Show Is My Video: The Politics of the Realist Feminist Documentary." In *Collecting Visible Evidence*, edited by Jane M. Gaines and Michael Renov, 190–215. Minneapolis: University of Minnesota Press, 1999.

Kalantari, Pirooz. "Chera in bist sal?" ("Why These Twenty Years?"). *Film Monthly* 516 (1395/2016): 7.

Kar, Mehrangiz, and Azadeh Pourzand. "IRAN." In *Feminist Advocacy, Family Law and Violence Against Women: International Perspectives*, edited by Mahnaz Akhami, Yakın Ertürk, and Ann Elizabeth Mayer, 71–89. New York: Routledge, 2019.

Kara Film Studio. "About Karestan." https://www.karafilm.ir/en/karestan/about-karestan. Accessed July 13, 2023.

Kara Film Studio. https://www.karafilm.ir/en/. Accessed July 30, 2023.

Kara Film Studio. "Touran Khanom." https://www.karafilm.ir/en/films/released/124-touran-khanum. Accessed July 30, 2023.

Kara Film Studio. "Maryam Bagheri Reports From 'Kara Film Studio' Appearance at IDFA." December 4, 2017. https://www.karafilm.ir/en/news/newslist/139-maryam-bagheri-reports-from-%E2%80%98kara-film-studio%E2%80%99-appearance-at-idfa. Accessed July 30, 2023.

Kara Film Studio. "Hayedeh Shirzadi." https://www.karafilm.ir/en/karestan/entrepreneurs/207-hayedeh-shirzadi. Accessed March 19, 2020.

Karimi, Pamela. "The Many Shades of Iran's Protest Art." *Hyperallergic*. October 11, 2022. https://hyperallergic.com/768539/the-many-shades-of-iran-protest-art/. Accessed June 3, 2024.

Keshavarz, Mina. Email interview with the author. November 25, 2018.

Khaneh Cinema. https://www.khanehcinema.ir/en/about. Accessed October 27, 2018.

Kheshti, Roshanak. "Cross-Dressing and Gender (Tres)Passing: The Transgender Move as a Site of Agential Potential in the New Iranian Cinema." *Hypatia* 24, no. 3 (2009): 158–177.

Khiabany, Gholam. *Iranian Media: The Paradox of Modernity*. New York: Routledge, 2010.

Kiarostami, Ahmad. "Docunight." https://www.ahmadkiarostami.com/docunight. Accessed July 31, 2023.

Kishore, Shweta. *Indian Documentary Film and Filmmakers: Independence in Practice*. Edinburgh: Edinburgh University Press, 2018.

Kleinhans, Chuck. "Forms, Politics, Makers and Contexts: Basic Issues for a Theory of Radical Political Documentary." In *"Show Us Life": Toward a History and Aesthetics of the Committed Documentary*, edited by Thomas Waugh, 318–342. Metuchen, NJ: The Scarecrow Press, 1984.

Langford, Michelle. "Iranian Cinema and Social Media." In *Social Media in Iran: Politics and Society after 2009*, edited by David M. Faris and Babak Rahimi, 251–269. Albany: State University of New York Press, 2015.

Langford, Michelle. *Allegory in Iranian Cinema: The Aesthetics of Poetry and Resistance*. London: Bloomsbury, 2019.

Lebow, Alisa. "Introduction." In *The Cinema of Me: The Self and Subjectivity in First Person Documentary*, edited by Alisa Lebow, 1–11. New York: Wallflower Press, 2012.

Lebow, Alisa. "First Person Political." In *The Documentary Film Book*, edited by Brian Winston, 257–265. London: Palgrave Macmillan/BFI, 2013.

Lesage, Julia. "Feminist Documentary: Aesthetics and Politics." In *"Show Us Life": Toward a History and Aesthetics of the Committed Documentary*, edited by Thomas Waugh, 223–251. Metuchen, NJ: The Scarecrow Press, 1984.

Lobato, Ramon. *Shadow Economies of Cinema: Mapping Informal Film Distribution*. London: BFI/Palgrave Macmillan, 2012.

Lobato, Ramon. "Subcinema: Theorizing Marginal Film Distribution." *Limina: A Journal of Historical and Cultural Studies* 13 (2007): 113–120.

Loist, Skadi. "The Film Festival Circuit: Networks, Hierarchies, and Circulation." In *Film Festivals: History, Theory, Method, Practice*, edited by Marijke de Valck, Brendan Kredell and Skadi Loist, 49–64. New York: Routledge, 2016.

Mahdavi, Shireen. "Reflections in the Mirror—How Each Saw the Other: Women in the Nineteenth Century." In *Women in Iran: From 1800 to the Islamic*

Republic, edited by Lois Beck and Guity Nashat, 63–84. Urbana: University of Illinois Press, 2004.

McIntosh, Heather. "Introduction: The Intersections of Documentary and Gendered Violence." In *Documenting Gendered Violence: Representations, Collaborations, and Movements*, edited by Lisa M. Cuklanz and Heather McIntosh, 1–24. London: Bloomsbury, 2015.

McLaren, Margaret A. *Feminism, Foucault, and Embodied Subjectivity*. Albany: State University of New York Press, 2002.

McNally, Gabrielle. "The Feminist Voice: Improvisation in Women's Autobiographical Filmmaking." In *Female Authorship and the Documentary Image: Theory, Practice, and Aesthetics*, edited by Boel Ulfsdotter and Anna Backman Rogers, 75–89. Edinburgh: Edinburgh University Press, 2018.

Mehr News Agency. "Mostanad-ha bedoun-e tabligh mokhatab peida nemikonand/Film-e rayegan namayesh nadahim" ("Documentaries Do Not Find Audiences without Advertisement/Do Not Exhibit Free Films"). May 15, 2016. https://www.mehrnews.com/news/3617682/مستندها-بدون-تبلیغ-مخاطب-پیدا-نمی-کنند-فیلم-رایگان-نمایش-ندهیم. Accessed July 27, 2023.

Merás, Lidia. "Profession: Documentarist: Underground Documentary Making in Iran." In *Female Agency and Documentary Strategies: Subjectivities, Identity and Activism*, edited by Boel Ulfsdotter and Anna Backman Rogers, 170–183. Edinburgh: Edinburgh University Press, 2018.

Meskoob, Shahrokh. "Naghashi-ye Qajar: Tamayoz, esalat amma door az vagheiyat" ("Qajar Painting: Distinction, Originality but Far from Reality"). *Tavoos Quarterly* 5 & 6 (2000). http://www.tavoosonline.com/Articles/ArticleDetailFa.aspx?src=51&Page=1. Accessed February 7, 2020.

Milani, Farzaneh. *Veils and Words: The Emerging Voices of Iranian Women Writers*. Syracuse: Syracuse University Press, 1992.

Milani, Farzaneh. "Veiled Voices: Women's Autobiographies in Iran." In *Women's Autobiographies in Contemporary Iran*, edited by Afsaneh Najmabadi, 1–16. Cambridge: Harvard University Press, 1990.

Milani, Farzaneh. "Iranian Women's Life Narratives." *Journal of Women's History* 25, no. 2 (2013): 130–152.

Minh-ha, Trinh T. *When the Moon Waxes Red: Representation, Gender and Cultural Politics*. New York: Routledge, 1991.

Mokhtari, Ebrahim. *Seifollah Dad va Mostanadsazan* (*Seifollah Dad and Documentarians*). https://irandocfilm.org/clink/founder-group/. Accessed June 6, 2020.

Molouki, Zahra. "Doshanbe-haye mostanad: Revayat-e mehmani-haye mostanadbini" ("Documentary Mondays: The Account of Documentary-Watching Gatherings"). *Film Monthly* 516 (1395/2016): 10–11.

Monshipouri, Mahmood. "Introduction: Social Change in Post-Khomeini Iran." In *Inside the Islamic Republic: Social Change in Post-Khomeini Iran*, edited by Mahmood Monshipouri, 1–20. Oxford: Oxford University Press, 2016.

Moore, Lindsey. "Women in a Widening Frame: (Cross-)Cultural Projection, Spectatorship, and Iranian Cinema." *Camera Obscura* 20, no. 2 (59) (2005): 1–33.

Moradiyan Rizi, Najmeh. "Iranian Women, Iranian Cinema: Negotiating with Ideology and Tradition." *Journal of Religion & Film* 19, no. 1 (2015): Article 35.

Moruzzi, Norma Claire. "Trying to Look Different: Hijab as the Self-Presentation of Social Distinctions." *Comparative Studies of South Asia, Africa and the Middle East* 28, no. 2 (2008): 225–234.

Mottahedeh, Negar. *Displaced Allegories: Post-Revolutionary Iranian Cinema.* Durham: Duke University Press, 2008.

Mubi. "Article 61." https://mubi.com/films/article-61. Accessed July 27, 2023.

Naficy, Hamid. *A Social History of Iranian Cinema, Volume 1: The Artisanal Era, 1897–1941*. Durham: Duke University Press, 2011.

Naficy, Hamid. *A Social History of Iranian Cinema, Volume 2: The Industrializing Years, 1941–1978*. Durham: Duke University Press, 2011.

Naficy, Hamid. *A Social History of Iranian Cinema, Volume 3: The Islamicate Period, 1978–1984*. Durham: Duke University Press, 2012.

Naficy, Hamid. *A Social History of Iranian Cinema, Volume 4: The Globalizing Era, 1984–2010*. Durham: Duke University Press, 2012.

Naficy, Hamid. "Iranian Documentary." *Jump Cut* 26 (1981): 41–46.

Naficy, Hamid. "Veiled Voice and Vision in Iranian Cinema: The Evolution of Rakhshan Banietemad's Films." *Social Research* 67, no. 2 (2000): 559–576.

Naficy, Hamid. "Veiled Vision/Powerful Presences: Women in Post-revolutionary Iranian Cinema." In *In the Eye of the Storm: Women in Post-revolutionary Iran*, edited by Mahnaz Afkhami and Erika Friedl, 131–150. Syracuse: Syracuse University Press, 1994.

Naghdineh. http://naghdineh.com/page/14700/1394+آخرین+نرخ+انواع+ارز+در+سال.html. Accessed December 24, 2019.

Najafi, Nasim. "Neveshtan baray-e mostanad" ("Writing for Documentary"). In *Haghighat dar Ghab-e Mostanad: Majmoe' Maghalat Darbare-ye Sinema-ye Mostanad*, edited by Esmail Mihandoost, 391–401. Tehran: Documentary and Experimental Film Center, 1387/2008.

Najmabadi, Afsaneh. "A Different Voice: Taj os-Saltaneh." In *Women's Autobiographies in Contemporary Iran*, edited by Afsaneh Najmabadi, 17–31. Cambridge: Harvard University Press, 1990.

Najmabadi, Afsaneh. "Hazards of Modernity and Morality: Women, State and Ideology in Contemporary Iran." In *Women, Islam and the State*, edited by Deniz Kandiyoti, 48–76. Philadelphia: Temple University Press, 1991.

Nejadbahram, Zahra. "Women and Employment." In *Women, Power and Politics in 21st Century Iran*, edited by Tara Povey and Elaheh Rostami-Povey, 73–90. Farnham, Surrey: Ashgate, 2012.

Nichols, Bill. *Introduction to Documentary*. Bloomington: Indiana University Press, 2001.

O'Brien, Anne. "(Not) Getting the Credit: Women, Liminal Subjectivity and Resisting Neoliberalism in Documentary Production." *Media, Culture & Society* 40, no. 5 (2018): 673–688.

Osanloo, Arzoo. *The Politics of Women's Rights in Iran*. Princeton: Princeton University Press, 2009.

Rahimieh, Nasrin. "Capturing the Abject of the Nation in The House Is Black." In *Forugh Farrokhzad, Poet of Modern Iran: Iconic Woman and Feminine Pioneer of New Persian Poetry*, edited by Dominic Parviz Brookshaw and Nasrin Rahimieh, 125–136. London: I.B. Tauris, 2010.

Rahimieh, Nasrin. "Divorce Seen through Women's Cinematic Lens." *Iranian Studies* 42, no. 1 (2009): 97–112.

Rascaroli, Laura. *The Personal Camera: Subjective Cinema and the Essay Film*. London: Wallflower Press, 2009.

Rashtian, Saeed. "Anam arezoost…: Tahiyeh-konandegi dar sinema-ye mostanad-e ma" ("I Wish That…: Producer['s Role] in Our Documentary Cinema"). *Film Monthly* 516 (1395/2016): 74–76.

Rezaei, Nahid. Email interview with the author. February 7, 2019.

Roozban, Newsha. "Mostanadsazan campaign-e 'film-e mostanad rayegan nist' rahandazi kardand" ("Documentarians Initiated the Campaign 'Documentary Film Is Not Free'"). *Mehr News Agency*. April 9, 2016. https://www.mehrnews.com/news/3593190/مستندسازان-کمپین-نمایش-فیلم-مستند-رایگان-نیست-راه-اندازی-کردند. Accessed July 28, 2023.

Russell, Catherine. *Experimental Ethnography: The Work of Film in the Age of Video*. Durham: Duke University Press, 1999.

Sadegh-Vaziri, Persheng. "Iranian Documentary Film Culture: Cinema, Society, and Power 1997–2014." Ph.D. Dissertation. Philadelphia: Temple University, 2015.

Saeed-Vafa, Mehrnaz and Jonathan Rosenbaum. *Abbas Kiarostami*. Urbana: University of Illinois Press, 2003.

Saffarian, Naser. "Man ke dashtam zendegi-am ra mikardam!: Pakhsh-e video-iye chand film-e mostanad" ("I Was Living My Own Life!: Video Distribution of Some Documentary Films"). *Film Monthly* 516 (1395/2016): 86–87.

Salamati, Mahsa. "The Politics of Video on Demand Platforms in Iran: In Between Formal and Informal Distribution." *Studies in World Cinema* 2, no. 1–2 (2022): 161–184.

Saljoughi, Sara. "Burning Visions: The Iranian New Wave and the Politics of the Image, 1962–1979." Ph.D. Dissertation. Minneapolis: University of Minnesota, 2015.

Sanaei, Amirhosein. "In film-ha ro koja neshoon midin?" ("Where Do You Show These Films?"). *Film Monthly* 516 (1395/2016): 88–89.

Seyedi, Fakhroddin. "E'ish-e modam: Chahardah sal namayesh-e film-e mostanad dar Khaneh Honarmandan" ("Continuous Pleasure: Fourteen Years of Documentary Film Exhibition in the House of Artists"). *Film Monthly* 516 (1395/2016): 90.

Shahabi, Katayoon. Email interview with the author. June 17, 2019.

Shahr-e Ketab. https://shahreketabonline.com/. Accessed September 7, 2019.

Shahrokni, Nazanin. "Women, Life, Freedom." *History Today* 72, no. 11, 2022. https://www.historytoday.com/archive/history-matters/women-life-freedom. Accessed July 23, 2023.

Sheffield DocFest. "Rakhshan Banietemad's Retrospective." https://sheffdocfest.com/festival/2023/special-programmes-presentations/rakhshan-banietemads-retrospective. Accessed July 23, 2023.

Sheffield DocFest. "Perspectives on Iran." https://sheffdocfest.com/festival/2023/special-programmes-presentations/perspectives-iran. Accessed July 23, 2023.

Sheikholeslami, Mahvash. Email interview with the author. March 16, 2019.

Smaill, Belinda. "The Documentary: Female Subjectivity and Problem of Realism." In *The Routledge Companion to Cinema and Gender*, edited by Kristin Lené Hole, Dijana Jelača, E. Ann Kaplan, and Patrice Petro, 174–183. New York: Routledge, 2017.

Sørensen, Inge Ejbye. "Crowdsourcing and Outsourcing: The Impact of Online Funding and Distribution on the Documentary Film Industry in the UK." *Media, Culture & Society* 34, no. 6 (2012): 726–743.

Sreberny, Annabelle and Gholam Khiabany. *Blogistan: The Internet and Politics in Iran*. London: I.B. Tauris, 2010.

Staiger, Janet. "The Politics of Film Canons." *Cinema Journal* 24, no. 3 (1985): 4–23.

Stanley, Liz. "Moments of Writing: Is There a Feminist Auto/biography?" *Gender & History* 2, no. 1 (1990): 58–67.

Stuart, Meryn. "Making the Choices: Writing about Marguerite Carr-Harris." In *All Sides of the Subject: Women and Biography*, edited by Teresa Iles, 59–67. New York: Teachers College Press, 1992.

Tabatabaeinejad, Mohammadmahdi. "Sarmayeh-gozar-e kafi nadarim: Goftegoo ba Mohammadmahdi Tabatabaeinejad, modir-e Markaz Gostaresh-e Sinema-ye Mostanad va Tajrobi" ("We Do Not Have Enough Financiers: A Conversation with Mohammadmahdi Tabatabaeinejad, the President of the Documentary and Experimental Film Center"), interview by Nasim Najafi. *Film Monthly* 516 (1395/2016): 84–86.

Tabatabaeinejad, Mohammadmahdi. "Tabatabaeinejad az dahomin jashnvare-ye beinolmelali-e Sinema Haghighat migooyad" ("Tabatabaeinejad Discusses the 10th International Cinema Vérité Festival"), interview by Mahmoud Sadeghlou-Givi. *Documentary and Experimental Film Center*. December 5, 2016. https://www.defc.ir/Post/2259/. Accessed July 20, 2023.

Tabbara, Mona. "Iranian Authorities Officially Close Cases of Arrested Filmmakers Mina Keshavarz, Firouzeh Khosrovani." *Screen Daily*. April 13, 2023. https://www.screendaily.com/news/iranian-authorities-officially-close-cases-of-arrested-filmmakers-mina-keshavarz-firouzeh-khosrovani/5181034.article. Accessed July 12, 2023.

Tafakori, Sara. "Iran's #MeToo Movement Challenges Patriarchy and Western Stereotypes." *Open Democracy*. September 1, 2020. https://www.opendemocracy.net/en/north-africa-west-asia/irans-metoo-movement-challenges-patriarchy-and-western-stereotypes/. Accessed 10 September, 2022.

Tahaminejad, Mohammad. "Barresi-ye film-haye nasl-e sevvom-e sinema-ye mostanad-e Iran" ("Analysis of the Third-Generation Films of Iranian Documentary Cinema"). In *Haghighat-e Sinema va Sinema Haghighat: Jostojooei dar Arse-ye Sinema-ye Mostanad*, edited by Zaven Ghookasian, 139–179. Tehran: Documentary and Experimental Film Center, 1386/2007.

Tahaminejad, Mohammad. *Sinema-ye Mostanad-e Iran: Arse-ye Tafavot-ha* (*Iranian Documentary Cinema: A Field of Differences*), 2nd edition. Tehran: Soroush Press, 1390/2011.

Tahaminejad, Mohammad. "Documentary Tradition." In *Directory of World Cinema: Iran 2*, edited by Parviz Jahed, 87–101. Bristol, UK: Intellect, 2017.

Talattof, Kamran. *Modernity, Sexuality, and Ideology in Iran: The Life and Legacy of a Popular Female Artist*. Syracuse: Syracuse University Press, 2011.

TorinoFilmLab. "Katayoon Shahabi (Iran)." https://www.torinofilmlab.it/people/810723/Katayoon-Shahabi. Accessed July 13, 2023.

Trofimenkoff, Susan Mann. "Feminist Biography." *Atlantis* 10, no. 2 (1985): 1–10.

Turnin, Svetla. "Beyond the Female Gaze and Towards a Documentary Gender Equality." *Point Of View (POV) Magazine*. November 2, 2015. https://povmagazine.com/beyond-the-female-gaze-and-towards-a-documentary-gender-equality/. Accessed July 23, 2023.

Ulfsdotter, Boel and Anna Backman Rogers. "Introduction." In *Female Authorship and the Documentary Image: Theory, Practice and Aesthetics*, edited by Boel Ulfsdotter and Anna Backman Rogers, 1–6. Edinburgh: Edinburgh University Press, 2018.

Vaziri, Persheng. "Watching Docs in Tehran: A Festival Thrives in Iran." *International Documentary Association*. March 5, 2019. https://www.documentary.org/online-feature/watching-docs-tehran-festival-thrives-iran. Accessed July 23, 2023.

Vivarelli, Nick. "Escalating U.S. Pressure, Sanctions on Iran Take Toll on Its Film Industry." *Variety*. May 19, 2019. https://variety.com/2019/film/news/trump-pressure-iran-toll-film-industry-1203220112/. Accessed July 30, 2023.

Waugh, Thomas. "Introduction: Why Documentary Filmmakers Keep Trying to Change the World, or Why People Changing the World Keep Making Documentaries." In *"Show Us Life": Toward a History and Aesthetics of the Committed Documentary*, edited by Thomas Waugh, xi–xxvii. Metuchen, NJ: The Scarecrow Press, 1984.

Weintraub, Karl J. "Autobiography and Historical Consciousness." *Critical Inquiry* 1, no. 4 (1975): 821–848.

White, Patricia. *Women's Cinema, World Cinema: Projecting Contemporary Feminisms*. Durham, NC: Duke University Press, 2015.

Winton, Ezra, and Jason Garrison. "'If a Revolution Is Screened and No One Is There to See It, Does It Make a Sound?' The Politics of Distribution and Counterpublics." In *Challenge for Change: Activist Documentary at the National Film Board of Canada*, edited by Thomas Waugh, Michael Brendan Baker, and Ezra Winton, 404–424, Montreal: McGill-Queen's University Press, 2010.

Winston, Brian, Gail Vanstone, and Wang Chi. *The Act of Documenting: Documentary in the 21st Century*. London: Bloomsbury, 2017.

Index

Note: Page numbers followed by n refer to notes,
and those in *italics* are illustrations.

EU Authorised Representative:
Easy Access System Europe Mustamäe tee 50, 10621 Tallinn, Estonia
gpsr.requests@easproject.com

Printed and bound by CPI Group (UK) Ltd, Croydon, CR0 4YY
29/09/2026
02224981-0002